In this book, Lisl Klein and Ken Eason look at the various issues involved when attempts are made to make use of the theories, methods and findings of the social sciences in practical affairs. They consider how human and social considerations may be successfully integrated with technical and economic ones in the design and development of organisations and work.

Their study is both empirical and theoretical. Its core is the examination of fourteen case studies from manufacturing and service organisations in Britain and Germany. The various projects were carried out by units within the organisations themselves, by university departments, commercial consultants and an independent research institute. Outside the field of organisations the authors consider the background and strategies of a number of individual practitioners, and also an attempt at national level (in Germany) to make systematic use of research. Their study is informed by their own extensive experience as researchers and practitioners of social science.

The book concludes with a discussion of what contributes to successful practice. Its findings will be invaluable to all social scientists interested in the application of their disciplines as well as to potential clients in the world of business and industry.

Putting social science to work

Putting social science to work

The ground between theory and use explored through case studies in organisations

LISL KLEIN and KEN EASON

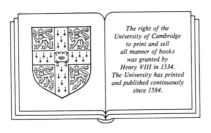

The right of the
University of Cambridge
to print and sell
all manner of books
was granted by
Henry VIII in 1534.
The University has printed
and published continuously
since 1584.

CAMBRIDGE UNIVERSITY PRESS

Cambridge
New York *Port Chester*
Melbourne *Sydney*

Published by the Press Syndicate of the University of Cambridge
The Pitt Building, Trumpington Street, Cambridge CB2 1RP
40 West 20th Street, New York, NY 10011–4211 USA
10 Stamford Road, Oakleigh, Melbourne 3166, Australia

First published 1991

Printed in Great Britain at the University Press, Cambridge

British Library cataloguing in publication data

Klein, Lisl
    Putting social science to work.
    1. Management. Applications of behavioural sciences
    I. Title II. Eason, Ken
    658.4

Library of Congress cataloguing in publication data applied for

ISBN 0 521 372429

CE

Contents

List of figures   *page ix*
Preface: why bother?   *xi*
Acknowledgements   *xiv*
List of abbreviations   *xvii*

1. Introduction   1

Part I Issues in social science utilisation

2. Issues of content: the use of knowledge and the dynamics of
    action   7

3. A framework for diagnosis   21

4. A practice profession   33

Part II An empirical study of social science utilisation

5. The research programme   45

6. Cases in organisational structure and policy   61

7. Cases in technical systems development   90

8. Cases in behavioural change/problem-solving for specific
    groups   117

9. Cases in behavioural change/development for management   141

10. The content and process of social science utilisation   157

11. What supports and hinders social science utilisation   173

12. Five practitioners   190

13. The work of the Commission for Economic and Social Change
    in Germany   205

Part III Discussion

14.   A collaborative venture   219

15.   Elements of practice   228

       References   256
       Index   259

Figures

1. Layout of operating theatre complex (a)   *page*   31
2. Layout of operating theatre complex (b)   32
3. Classification of case studies   56
4. Comparative analysis of work methods   104
5. Methods and strategies supporting OD team seminars   153
6. Approaches to utilisation in the case studies   169
7. Factors contributing to successful outcomes   182
8. Contextual variables supporting and hindering success   187
9. System study on technical, social and economic change   208
10. Movement of resources: basic model   226
11. Action and resource: content and context   226

Preface: why bother?

This book begins where *A Social Scientist in Industry* (Klein, 1976) left off. The research it includes is self-contained. However, the impetus behind that research was the need to follow the detailed description and analysis of a single, five-year-long experience in making use of the social sciences in an industrial organisation (Esso Petroleum), contained in the earlier book, with a comparative study of a number of such cases.

The question at the head of this preface is therefore being posed in two senses: why is it important to bring the social sciences to bear on organisations? And why is it important to investigate this process?

To deal with the second question first: experience, including the Esso experience, has shown that relating the social sciences to practical affairs, which to some of us seems such a self-evidently necessary and good thing to do, turns out to be extremely difficult. Different kinds of social science make different contributions and are hard to relate to each other, 'expertness' in matters concerning human relations can be experienced as threatening and is resented, sponsors do not stay in post long enough to see work through, consultants compete with each other or are played off against each other, no-one is sure how to handle the boundary between science and ideology – the list of problems seems endless, with the result that experience does not match expectation and there is much disappointment.

Moreover, these problems have been experienced for a long time. At a discussion of a Task Force on the Practice of Psychology in Industry, published in 1971 by the American Psychological Association, the comment was recorded 'You know, I have a tremendous feeling of déjà vu. I have been having the same discussions with you same guys for twenty-five years' (Task Force on the Practice of Psychology in Industry, 1971).

The work in Esso exemplified many of these issues and problems. It began to put them in a research framework, so that the present enquiry does not start from first principles. Three findings from the earlier work may be recalled in particular, as they form the starting assumptions of the present one.

Firstly, models of the use of social science which assume that it is a matter of transferring help or knowledge from a 'resource' system to a 'client' system are inadequate. These are the models underlying much of the work on the utilisation and diffusion of knowledge. They leave out of account, on the one hand, the fact that social science has needs as well as resources, both as regards its institutions and as regards its individual professionals; and that some of these needs are fulfilled, overtly or covertly, by the client or the field site. On the other hand, they also leave out of account the fact that clients – both institutions and individuals at the receiving end – have resources as well as needs. It is therefore a matter of relating the new input to the resources – personal or institutional – which already exist as well as relating it to a problem directly. This leads to the second starting assumption, which is that making use of social science depends on successfully relating the content of the work done to its context, in both the client system and the resource system. This is frequently called 'politics', and our third starting assumption is that the politics are part of the data.

One way of looking at and summarising the situation is to say that in the social sciences the 'Development' part of the 'Research and Development' continuum has been substantially neglected and there is a serious gap between the world of research and the world of practice. By tracing in detail the stories of a number of attempts at utilisation, and by making explicit the dynamics involved, the aim of the research was to make a contribution towards filling this gap.

There is, however, the other question to be answered. Why? If it is all so difficult, why does it matter? Why did one of us, after a long, difficult, sometimes painful and fairly inconclusive attempt, come to the conclusion that 'there is nothing for it but to keep trying'? (Klein, 1976, chapter 14).

The reason lies in values. While recognising that one research team cannot claim to speak for professional peers, it is necessary to say something about the values that underlie our pursuit of this topic. They are about reality, about development, and about integration and synthesis.

Organisations are complex and, like all institutions, have intended (manifest) and unintended (latent) consequences. The methods and concepts of the social sciences have much to contribute in making the latent consequences visible. From this also follow considerable possibilities of prediction. The question, 'If you set it up in this way, the consequences are likely to be of that kind – is that what you really intend?' is one of the key kinds of contribution.

Making administrators aware of the consequences or likely consequences of their policies and actions should not be confused with telling them what are desirable and undesirable consequences. The concern is not *in the first instance* about 'making things more human' or making people behave better towards each other. It is first of all that things should seem to be what they are, that actual policies and operating procedures should match, in their consequences, the values that managers, trade unionists, administrators of all kinds express.

In practice, once the consequences of policy or action are made explicit, inconsistencies between the expressed and actual operating values in an organisation sometimes become obvious. At that stage, the trap is to tell people that they ought to be doing one thing rather than another. It is more important to help them to recognise and work through the discrepancies. Social scientists, like everyone else, have the right to try to influence policy. But it is undemocratic for them to claim special rights, in their role as social scientists. If it turns out that 'tougher' values are in fact the real ones, social scientists may well want to express views about that; but if they have first demonstrated that their concern is for reality, whatever this turns out to be, they will have made clear the distinction between their professional role and their views as citizens, and they will also have earned a greater right to have their opinions taken seriously. As professionals they must know that reality is the only basis for doing anything that will take root. Some of our best friends have fallen into this trap. We recognise that this view may not be shared by all social scientists, but this is where we stand.

Thus the first set of values underlying the pursuit of this subject is about reality. The social sciences have great power to get at how things really are, both through research and through eliciting the dynamics of situations. Without a clear and honest understanding of the realities of an institution, no genuine development can take place.

The second set of values we then wish to lay on the line concerns action, i.e. the direction in which to move from understanding. What do we mean by development? Here our reasons for continuing to believe that the use and application of social science is important concerns the integration and synthesis of different value systems in society and the consequences for mental health – including institutional and societal mental health – if splits and contradictions are denied or ignored.

In many ways Western industrial society has not come to terms with being an industrial society at all. It continues to struggle with conflicting value systems, all of which are important, but which are difficult to reconcile and integrate, and which have internal contradictions. In particular there is one value system concerned with economic growth, development and expansion; there is a second one concerned with the intrinsic value, autonomy and personal growth of human beings; and there is a third concerned with research, the development of knowledge and the exercise of skills for their own sake.

Industrial society has tended to cope with the differences between these values, and the difficulties that may arise in reconciling them, by pursuing them in separate institutions, which have little to do with each other, and it has gone a very long way down that road. Yet it takes no more than a moment's thought to realise that it is simply not true that industrialists are the only people who care about money (and that they care about nothing else), that only social workers care about people, only academics care about knowledge (and that they do not care about anything else), only artists about beauty. All members of society share all of these value systems to some extent; all are in some sense less than themselves while nothing is done about bringing different values in relation to each other, not only between institutions but within the institutions in which we spend our time. It is in possibilities of synthesis and integration that the contribution of the social sciences lies; and that is why this undertaking, with all its difficulties, remains important.

Acknowledgements

Exploring the use of social science involves sponsors, clients and social science practitioners, and this book owes much to many members of these communities. The funding for the empirical work of collecting case studies was provided by the Anglo-German Foundation for the Study of Industrial Society. The Economic and Social Research Council, under Grant no. F0023 2103, provided support for the analysis of the material and the preparation of the book.

Social science practice in organisations can only emerge to the extent that they are prepared to test what it has to offer. For reasons of confidentiality we have not revealed the names of the many organisations in the United Kingdom and Germany who were the clients of social science in these studies. We are grateful to them, as well as to members and staff of the Commission for Economic and Social Change in Germany, for opening their doors and letting their experience inform the work.

We owe much to friends and colleagues in the world of social science practitioners. First and foremost there are those whose work, ideas and approaches feature in the case studies. We have adopted the practice of not identifying the particular practitioner in any case study (sometimes there were, of course, more than one); but, since our debt is so great, we do wish to acknowledge their contribution and thank them for sharing their experience. Those involved in the British work were: Harold Bridger, Bryan Calvert, Leela Damodaran, Christine Edwards, Penny Jones, Denis O'Donovan, Sue Pomfrett, Wendy Pritchard, Derek Pugh, Jim Rose, Alison Rowe, Brian Shackel and Steve Smith.

We are ourselves responsible for the case studies in the United Kingdom. For the German case studies we are indebted to the German team of Edith Rost-Schaude and Rolf Kunstek; we therefore also wish to acknowledge the contribution of their collaborators in the German organisations that provided those cases.

A number of friends and colleagues have generously given time to read and comment on parts of the draft. They are: Harold Bridger, Jon Clark, Christine Edwards, Marie Jahoda, Penny Jones, Eric Miller, Beth Neustadt and Sylvia Shimmin. Sheila Scott helped with editing and shortening the case material.

The preparation of the manuscript has involved many secretaries and several word processors. We are grateful to the former, and especially to Mandy Marshall and Inga Whitehouse, who helped us fight the incompatibilities of modern technology.

Finally, we want to express our gratitude to the unknown person who stole a briefcase containing two of the chapters in manuscript – and returned it intact.

Abbreviations

CESC	Commission for Economic and Social Change
CSC	computer steering committee
CUSSR	Centre for the Utilisation of Social Science Research
DP	data processing
ESPRIT	European Strategy Programme of Research in Information Technology
MbO	Management by Objectives
NEDO	National Economic Development Office
NIIP	National Institute of Industrial Psychology
OD	Organisation Development
O and M	Organisation and Methods
PDD	personnel development department
R and D	research and development
RKW	Rationalisierungskuratorium der Wirtschaft
TCI	Theme-Centred Interaction

1 Introduction

This book has the difficult aim of bringing together systematic research and personal experience and reflection. The systematic aspect is represented by a collection of case studies. The aim of this empirical research was to examine the process by which social science is applied within organisations. We focussed on the utilisation process which occurs when one or more professional social scientists work directly with an organisation. The sample of cases is based on the institutions from which work was being carried out: in-house units, commercial consultants, academics doing applied work and a non-profit research institute. In the course of our work we also came across other approaches to social science utilisation, which were not in the form of specific cases or work with organisations. We present these (five practitioners and a national programme), but they are not included in the main body of the analysis.

Indeed, we did not want to be limited to the systematic analysis of the case material; to try to be systematic is necessary but not sufficient. We also want to discuss what we ourselves have learned from experience in the field. We hope that these two strands will fuse, for that is what professional practice is about. With some roots in systematic analysis and some demands on imagination, it is itself not quite an art and not quite a science. We think it may be akin to a craft. There is, however, little in the way of a craft tradition. The hard work of developing and honing and reflecting on methods is dispersed among small pockets of people, and even more dispersed are those who are in a position to give feedback on what is of greater or lesser value.

The practitioner of social science – we use the term deliberately, though at this stage with some apprehension – needs to achieve some synthesis between the knowledge that comes from research and the understanding that comes from experience and introspection. That requires, on the one hand, dispassionate curiosity, respect for rigour and a readiness to have one's favourite prejudices proved wrong and, on the other hand, empathy, imagination and the freedom to stray. It is a list of requirements which will explain at once why achievement will, in some sense, always fall short of expectation.

The idea of professional practice in social science may well raise some hackles and some cries of 'élitism', so that is an issue we need to confront early: in relation to some professions, such as medicine or the law, non-professional clients are deemed not to be able to do the things the professionals do by virtue of the knowledge they do not have or by virtue of traditional property rights to that knowledge. In some areas these boundaries are beginning to be challenged, but there are, in any case, other fields where the problem simply does not exist. Gardening and cooking also have their professional practitioners, but that does not prevent people from doing it themselves. Both have extensive scientific bases, knowledge of which can prevent mistakes and enhance results, while mere reliance on the scientific knowledge can stultify. In both, some people benefit from professional help and some people do well without it. It does not seem to be such a big deal. The pleasure of it, even for the most experienced professional, is that there is always more to learn.

One theme that recurs in the book is the pervasive importance of funding structures, since he that pays the piper develops pipers. Thus research funding by the Anglo-German Foundation for the Study of Industrial Society brought with it a requirement to do parallel work in the two countries and two German colleagues, Edith Rost-Schaude and Rolf Kunstek of the Forschungsinstitut für Arbeit und Bildung in Heidelberg, collected a number of case studies in Germany. Also Klein, one of the UK authors, has experience of working in Germany in this field and reports on the work of the Commission for Economic and Social Change. There is therefore an Anglo-German thread in this work.

International comparison, however, is not an aspect about which we intend to be systematic. That would require a different and larger research frame and was not the primary aim of the work. Also, at the level of the specific projects in organisations there is no special reason to compare the German cases as such with the UK cases as such. The sample of cases is too small in either country for us to be able to say anything significant about differences in the amount or distribution of such attempts, or about country-based differences in the content of the work done. Some of the cases feature subsidiaries of multinational companies, and may well owe more to company culture than to the fact that they happened in Germany or the United Kingdom.

In any case, the primary aim of the research has been to learn about the processes and problems of social science utilisation. At this level of data collection, therefore, we are simply using the opportunity of the Anglo-German collaboration to obtain more cases and learn from them rather than to set up a systematic comparison. Each of the teams is producing its own accounts, with freedom to draw on the other's material. In our case, we include the German material in the cross-case analysis contained in chapters 10 and 11, but include only very brief descriptions of some of the German cases. Elsewhere, we refer to German experience where it seems that contrast or comparison contributes to a wider understanding of the general topic.

The book is in three parts:

Part I, 'Issues in social science utilisation'. These chapters (chapters 2–4) describe the issues as we saw them before we considered the empirical material;

Part II, 'An empirical study of social science utilisation'. In this part (chapters 5–13) we first describe the historical context of the application of social science, in the United Kingdom and in Germany (chapter 5). Next come brief accounts of the cases in organisation, seven UK and seven German (chapters 6–9). Then come two chapters of cross-case analysis (chapters 10–11). The final part presents some additional case material which is not about organisations. It goes inwards to the individual practitioners (chapter 12) and outwards to a governmental strategy (chapter 13).

Part III, Discussion. In this part (chapters 14–15) we discuss what contributes to successful practice.

Part I Issues in social science utilisation

2 Issues of content: the use of knowledge and the dynamics of action

We said in the preface that application in the social sciences is beset with problems. From the conceptual point of view a major problem is that there are two distinct frames of reference, which the professional needs somehow to integrate. The first is the framework of taking an 'item' of knowledge or a research finding and translating it into use. The second, which criss-crosses and intertwines with the first, is a framework about the dynamics of action. In this chapter we discuss some of the issues raised by these two frameworks.

Knowledge-into-use

The validity and replicability of research findings

The first relevant question concerns the validity of research findings in the social sciences: how 'valid' does a finding have to be before it is legitimate (in the eyes of social scientists) to make use of it, or before it is found useful in practice, which is not the same thing.

From the social science world come ideas, with varying degrees of verification. Maslow's hierarchy-of-needs concept, Herzberg's two-factor theory of motivation, are examples of ideas which in parts of the social science community are regarded as inadequately verified,[1] while in parts of the user community they are seen as useful products of social science. There are probably no findings so respectable as to be completely unchallenged.[2]

[1] See, for instance, Blackler and Williams (1971, pp. 283–303).
[2] The problem of the assessment of quality in science is very usefully discussed by Ravetz (1971, p. 275): 'To give a rough idea of the sorts of assessments that are made, I can distinguish several classes of scientific work, and the standards by which they are defined. The best of all scientific work is that which survives, through all the many testings and transformations, to become genuine scientific knowledge. But this can be known only in retrospect; and so a sober assessment of any new result will not place it in the "immortal" class. However, one can reasonably predict that any given result is likely to yield "enduring facts" which will survive the demise of the original problem: if that problem was a deep and difficult one, and the result is capable of development and extension, then it is entitled to be considered as first class. Now, even a temporary fact is no mean achievement, for its

This absence of consensus about what are valid findings is partly due to the essential incompleteness of all knowledge. It is also partly due to the politics and career structure of academic life: to some extent the identity and worth of one's own work or that of one's team or school are established by challenging the work of others; and this may not necessarily be done by replicating the work, but by using different methods, which are in any case likely to lead to different findings.

There is, however, another consideration which is more intrinsic to the subject-matter: the distinction between an idea and a valid finding may be in principle less fundamental in the social sciences than in the natural sciences because of the greater influence of differences in context. Even in the same historical period different ideas are put forward simultaneously which are not apparently compatible but concerning which one can find evidence if one looks carefully enough. Even more, a different geographical or historical context will affect the evidence on the same idea. Differences in context mean that some investigations are not repeatable, or not repeatable in the same form. Differences in context and time possibly constitute the greatest problem in establishing any fundamental parallel between the social and natural sciences.

This does not imply a total relativism. There are underlying generalities, over which different concrete manifestations cluster. In the field which is generally known as behaviour in organisations, three such underlying generalities, having more than temporary validity, are:

(i) The structural characteristics implied by technology, markets, laws, size, ownership and control systems will have some behavioural and organisational consequences.

(ii) Within narrower system boundaries, the structural characteristics of tasks and work-roles have some psychological consequences for the people doing them; in turn, people will influence the structure of their environment to some extent. The technical and social systems are interdependent.

(iii) Process is relevant as well as content. This implies, firstly, that how things are done, for example, how changes are introduced, will be relevant to outcomes as well as the content of what is done; and it implies, secondly, that groups or organisations can learn to review themselves and modify how they operate.

existence shows that the solution to the original problem had depth rather greater than the explicit statement of the conclusion would guarantee; work which achieves this success is certainly good. Even this grade is not the minimum quality necessary for a result to be worthwhile in the advancement of its field; so long as it meets the appropriate standards of adequacy, and shows its value by being put to use by others, however briefly, in subsequent work, the research which produced it can be considered competent.'

When it comes to application, context again makes replication and comparison difficult. Whether an organisation is the first pioneer to apply a new concept, or the twentieth follower, or whether it is compelled into application because this is decreed by policy or law, is dynamically different and will lead to different outcomes even though the content is the same. On the one hand, the enthusiasm with which something is being introduced may be the most influential factor; on the other hand, sophisticated subjects may become immune to the Hawthorne effect, and some 'change strategies' may not be effective when tried repeatedly.

The usability of findings

Another set of questions surrounds the usability of findings or concepts, even the most respectable ones. It is one of the most dysfunctional consequences of neglect of the development part of the R and D spectrum that the relevance, and therefore usefulness, of even highly valued findings or concepts may not be apparent. An alternative explanation could be that an intervening step is generally omitted. This is the vital step of internalising-and-converting-into-use, which is an act of imagination.

For example, a proposed study was being introduced to the division of anaesthesia in a large general hospital (this study is referred to again in chapter 3). The members of the division explained their policies: they serviced the general operating list, and also provided a service to the departments of obstetrics and gynaecology, dentistry and psychiatry. But their absolute priority was the general operating list – 'If you are scheduled to have an operation you'll have your operation, no matter how short-staffed we are.' The researcher asked, 'Does that mean that I might come across an obstetrician who says, "You can never damn-well find an anaesthetist when you need them"?' With dawning realisation one of the consultants looked up from his coffee and said, 'Good Lord! Yes, I suppose you might.' The concept being applied was a fairly obvious instance of structural perspective. The insight generated by its internalised use was instrumental in getting agreement for the study.

The application of a general finding to particular circumstances itself requires a quality of understanding both of the finding and of the situation. There is a danger that findings may be thought inappropriately to apply in situations which do not match the ones which produced the original research. It is only too easy to draw false conclusions, or to draw correct conclusions from the research and misread the situation itself. On the one hand, therefore, one can say with confidence that our understanding of the functioning of individuals and organisations has increased very greatly during the last sixty years; on the other hand, nobody could claim that the social sciences can supply from stock easy answers to complex problems.

Internalising-and-converting-into-use modifies a finding, or may at least make it look different.

In the absence of general attention from the social science profession to this process of internalising-and-converting-into-use, individual practitioners find themselves doing it privately, in those areas of knowledge with which they are most familiar. In other words, they work out for themselves how to make theory and findings operational. As an example, research on the behavioural consequences of control systems (Woodward, 1970) turns out to be most useful in understanding situations during the diagnostic phase of applied research, and in predicting the likely outcomes of alternative organisational design decisions. This is part of a contingency framework, which is concerned with how the environment affects behaviour choices, and therefore involves looking at organisations in terms of the interplay between behavioural and structural factors. It is not only substantively useful in predicting the behavioural consequences of aspects of structure (for example, technology, markets, and so on), and therefore as an aid to organisation design; it also has the function of demonstrating a scientific – in the natural science sense – way of operating with social and organisational phenomena, and therefore of establishing credibility. Even on the basis of a simple example, like the different behavioural consequences according to whether maintenance is costed with production or is a separate cost centre, people in industry can without much difficulty be helped to enter into this framework, and then to continue to work with it themselves.

Another example of the usefulness of the contingency framework arises from experience of the recent wave of interest in 'job enrichment', job design, and so on. In recent years a number of organisations have tried to decide whether to embark on such an exercise. It helps to understand that, where an organisation is in a rapidly changing market (for example, office equipment), which demands bigger product ranges, shorter product lifetimes and frequent modifications, a flexible mode of production, which also involves more highly skilled and flexible people, is congruent with the needs of the market and increases the organisation's ability to absorb variances (Butera, 1975). Where the market does not make such demands (for example, banking), one may still decide to change work organisation in the direction of greater skill, or greater flexibility, or greater autonomy for work people (or all three). But this will be a decision on ideological grounds rather than functional ones. It will therefore require much greater commitment and consensus, the differences of view between different interest groups are likely to have greater salience, and it may not survive difficulties in implementation. It is a quite different kind of decision.

The skills required to use findings

A further important question about this process of conversion from theory or research results to use is how near to the research base it takes place. Practitioners are themselves users of resources, i.e., of the researches of others. They are likely to experience difficulties similar to those of administrators in internalising the researches of others sufficiently both to be able to make the conversion and to recognise features in the context which will indicate appropriateness. Problems arise when the paths of continuing to develop and modify an idea within a research framework and developing it into use diverge, as at some stage they must if there is to be diffusion. The quality of understanding, knowledge about the limitations of the finding, and awareness of the context within which it was developed, all of which were present during the research, may not accompany the idea into use, especially use by others. This is one of the areas where use implies special training needs.

Findings as products

It is the above-mentioned divergence between the paths of, on the one hand, continuing to develop an idea in a research framework and, on the other, applying it, that underlies the anxiety of many social scientists about the use of 'packages'. There are by now a number of instances of strategies, developed in response to a particular situation, which have been routinised and formalised so that they should be capable of being applied in other situations and on a large scale. Insofar as they involve diagnostic methodologies, they may permit enough input from the local situation to prevent inappropriate solutions; but insofar as they make assumptions about knowledge which the social science community regards as inadequately tested and omit diagnosis of the local situation, they probably exemplify the widest part of the gulf that has arisen between research and consultancy. The distaste experienced by researchers is probably not uninfluenced by the recognition, success and financial rewards which have accrued to some of the authors of such packages, nor by the difficulty they themselves experience in letting go of ownership of a problem area. There is a big dilemma for the social scientist who wants both to see the diffusion of ideas and knowledge and also to exercise methodological caution. The dilemma, and the anxieties that go with it, become clear when one thinks of the phases of the product growth cycle which have been distinguished with regard to the products of manufacturing industry: the 'R and D phase', characterised by high skill and specialised methods in developing a prototype; the 'growth phase', when R and D appears to have succeeded and imitators begin to appear; and the 'mature phase', when the product is established through mass-production methods involving lower-level skills. An important dilemma for social science is whether it should – and wants to – aim to create 'products' analogous to those of engineering science.

The emergence of some products of social science in commercialised form has probably also reinforced the tendency among some people to see applied social science as a succession of passing fads. The research question here would be whether such fads leave behind some permanent residue – in other words, whether what is learned from a passing fashion becomes institutionalised. There are signs that this does in fact happen.

Research as an action strategy

Research is not only a strategy for developing knowledge which may be useful, it is also a strategy for investigating problems in the field directly. Often this is what is in fact meant by applied work.

Van de Vall and his colleagues made a study of this kind of work by examining 120 'applied social research' projects in The Netherlands, 40 of them in industrial and labour relations (Vall et al., 1976, pp. 158–77). They did this by studying the research report and interviewing the social researcher and the policy-maker involved in each project. Interviews with the latter led to five indicators of policy impact and an 'overall policy impact' score for each project. They then related various characteristics of the projects to their 'policy impact'.

The analysis shows that, even within the single framework of research, there are important differences in approach. For policy impact the analysis favours qualitative rather than quantitative methods; familiarity with the organisation's decision-making processes; and grounded concepts of low abstraction and simple construction rather than formal ones. The following are their main conclusions; they find:

> a widening chasm between the values and goals of academic social science and policy-oriented social research. A fundamental difference is that applied social research is guided by the dual norm of epistemological and operational validity. We found that external researchers had more difficulty in meeting this dual standard than did internal researchers.
>
> A second difference relates to the theoretical level of the research results. While academic social scientists are primarily nomothetically oriented, searching for the highest level of abstraction, applied social researchers, seeking to solve a specific social problem, tend towards an idiographic orientation. We found a specific type of theoretical concept – grounded, continuous, and of low abstraction – to be best suited for social problem solving.
>
> A third discrepancy is between the goals of academic social science and social policy making. When confronted with a conflict between method and

praxis, academic social scientists have been trained to choose the first. For the researcher engaged in policy decisions, however, solving the problem will take priority over high correlations and perfect causal models. The increasing emphasis in academic circles upon matters of epistemological validity, methodological rigour, and theoretical abstraction is widening the gulf between the rational goals of academic social science and the incremental praxis of social research utilisation.

Two almost incidental points about this study are striking for the practitioner. One is the assumption that the product of applied research is necessarily a report. The second occurs during a discussion on the applicability of formal or grounded theories: formal sociological theory was 'operationalised [in the study] as quoted from a published sociological source or its author'. In other words, there is an assumption that to quote something in a report is to 'use' it. This also, again, leaves out the intervening steps of internalising and conversion.[3]

The dynamics of action

Methodological caution and ivory-tower perfectionism on the part of academics may be perceived as – and may indeed require – a lack of concern on the part of researchers for the needs of real life, or at least for the needs of their field-sites. A similar lack of concern is implied by their apparent disregard for the dynamics of implementation. A good report may carry conviction, but knowing what to do about it and finding the time, energy, mechanisms and power to do those things is a different matter. Together they in turn help to account for the anti-academic stance taken by some of those who are involved in action. That includes practitioners who come from the tradition of Organisation Development, or OD. This is a body of theory and practice which first emerged from the American business schools. It encompasses a wide range of methods but, originally formulated to appeal to the task-oriented business client, its dominant value has been about change. The concern is with change programmes, change strategies, and the role of practitioners as agents of change.[4] Frequently (though not

---

[3] Critics of social science sometimes do not notice the distinction between formal and grounded theory. Ravetz, in his chapter on 'Immature and ineffective fields of inquiry' uses as evidence of the uselessness of social theory, and the 'eruption of common sense' when need demands, the fact that Talcott Parsons, when analysing post-war Germany with a view to policy recommendation for its social reconstruction, apparently 'used a straight Marxist analysis of class structure with no evidence of the "normative structure" so strongly developed in his purely theoretical writings' (1971, p. 383; quoted from Wright Mills, in 'The Sociological Imagination', pp. 43–4). It is difficult to know whether to be glad or irritated when social science concepts (in this case class structure) have become so well accepted and absorbed that they are regarded as mere common sense.

[4] See, for example, an excerpt from the introduction to the 'Systems' chapter in a well-known text book: 'Practitioners approach a system in terms of its readiness or resistance to change

always) the methods involve process facilitation, tending to emphasise action rather than research, process more than content, and experiential rather than cognitive learning.

It seems to us that the split between research and action has come to acquire some of the characteristics of 'splitting' in the psychodynamic sense. This is essentially a process of psychic economy, in which all the x characteristics of a complex situation are vested in one set of people or one of a pair, and all the y characteristics in another. The goodies are all-good and wear white hats, and the baddies are all-bad and wear black hats, so that recognition and knowing with whom to identify presents few problems. Splitting is very pervasive. One example of it is the attribution of all rationality to industrial organisations, and all emotionality to social science. Indeed, as we explained in the preface, the splitting which has occurred in relation to value systems is why we think the utilisation of social research is important.

In this case, all the values surrounding research, knowledge, thinking and cognitive learning have come to be vested in the role of 'academic researcher' and all the values surrounding development, change, feeling and experiential learning have come to be vested in the role of 'action researcher' or 'OD practitioner'. Splitting of this kind tends to be mutually reinforcing and to lead to a vicious circle from which those who are caught up in it find it increasingly difficult to break out.

Action research

It is important to recognise that, where social science research is empirical, the boundary between research and intervention is in fact not as clear-cut as all that. It is a fundamental characteristic of empirical social research, and a fundamental difference between it and the physical sciences, that the material being researched has consciousness, and reactions and therefore also rights. (In some ways this also applies in the biological sciences, as witnessed by the current debate on research using animals.) Even research for purely scientific purposes, if it is empirical, also involves intervention. Handing out questionnaires, interviewing, observation, are all interventions. They therefore bring with them professional responsibilities for the researchers who make use of them.

For example, although there are differences in professional ethics and cultures, it is usual not to publish or issue reports without also making them available to those who have taken part in the study. More than that, unless there is some overriding reason not to, it is also usual to let those

... Chin ... identifies the properties of the model of an open or closed system in contrast to a developmental model ... the essay outlines the implications of each for *a practitioner's approach to changing human systems.*' (Bennis et al., 1975) (italics ours).

who have taken part in the study comment on reports at the draft stage, both to point out things they think are inaccurate – though the researcher may reserve the right not to accept such comment – and to point out things which, though possibly accurate, are thought likely to cause damage to individuals if made public. It is also usual to make clear that participation in a study is voluntary; and it is also usual to ensure the anonymity of individuals in the way in which reports are formulated.

Whatever the agreements about these things with respect to a particular study, they involve making arrangements: negotiating at the beginning what the clearance procedure will be and setting up the necessary mechanisms, whether they involve steering committees, feedback discussions, distribution of drafts or final reports, or whatever. Any of these are also, of course, interventions and they are, in fact, substantial steps in the direction of action research. Furthermore, a responsible researcher will point out the interventionist aspects of empirical research at the outset. Attitude surveys, for example, even if carried out purely for research purposes, are likely to raise expectations that the matters they bring to light will be taken seriously. It is part of responsible research to alert people to likely consequences of this kind. This also gives them the opportunity of not taking part in the research if they are unprepared for those consequences.

Thus responsibly conducted empirical research already contains the main elements of action research, or professional practice, in social science: the roles of the subjects of the research go beyond the passive role of being investigated; the researcher recognises that research strategies have consequences and acts in this knowledge; account is taken of the possible impact of the research on the host organisation. In addition, if any of this turns out to be unexpectedly difficult, the researcher has to be able to cope with that difficulty and remain detached; not, for example, avenging him- or herself via the content of the reports.

The difference is that, while these things are awkward and possibly irritating accompaniments or side-effects in research, as it were a necessary evil, in action research or professional practice they are the essential core: the people involved in the situation are likely to be drawn into action roles of some kind; the practitioners are concerned with strategies of intervention, and understanding the implications and consequences of different strategies is their main professional tool-kit; having some effect within or on the host organisation is the aim of the exercise (in action research, as distinct from consultancy, this will be accompanied by the twin aim of generating a contribution to knowledge); and an important skill of the practitioner is to be able to 'stay with' the situation, however it develops. The more active and interventionist the role, the more important it is to give to the steps involved in intervention the same quality of serious scientific concern as to the content variables. This means clarifying the conditions under which different kinds of strategy are appropriate, being aware of the consequences of different kinds of strategy, taking responsibility for one's choices, and so on.

The contribution of a clinical perspective

The dynamics of action thus involve the relationship between clients and practitioners, attention to processes as well as to content, and, more broadly, the function which a project or other social science activity may have in the life of the client organisation. The branch of social science in which such relationships have been explored most explicitly and in the greatest depth is psychoanalysis. Other professionals, such as doctors and lawyers, have in many cases taken on board the recognition that the relationship between practitioner and client is relevant to outcomes and plays a part in outcomes, to the extent that it sometimes now features in their training.

However, transferring this experience and knowledge to work with organisations is not straightforward and needs to be done with a recognition of the differences as well as the similarities between these situations. A good deal of work remains to be done in clarifying the relevance of clinical values and experience to work with organisations. It appears to be of four kinds.

1. *Development of the practitioner*

There is no doubt that it helps practitioners to handle themselves appropriately in highly complex, frequently confused and politically and emotionally charged situations if they have had the opportunity to work through and understand their own responses and dynamics, and deal with them. It is also essential that there should be, while work is going on, a locus or forum – whether the practitioner's own on-going analysis, or a trusted colleague or friend or a professional group – where one can discuss what is happening in one's work and its multiple meanings and review one's own reactions in terms of how far they are genuine responses to the events outside and how far they are part of one's own patterns, in response to one's own needs. In the absence of such a forum it is more likely that one's own defences will determine what one sees and how one deals with it.

In the face of being overwhelmed with the complexity of the situation with which one is confronted, there is much rationalisation in this field. It may take the form of defining situations or problems in a way that makes the practitioner's own tool-kit the only appropriate one for dealing with them. (This has been likened to the situation of a small boy who, having been given a hammer, discovers that there are many things that need hammering.) Another defensive strategy is to define the boundaries of the system being dealt with in such a way that awkward or untidy elements, or those which one's discipline cannot handle, remain outside; or in a way that ensures that one's self remains outside. This may look superficially as if it is justified by the role of observer or consultant, but it also has the function of keeping one safe from the dangers of the situation itself, and safe also from the risk of making mistakes. The unassailable immunity from getting it wrong, which most parts of the social science spectrum, from macro-sociology to psychoanalysis, appear to have constructed for themselves in their different ways is, we believe, the main cause of the deep-seated resentment towards social science experienced by the fallible world. It also puts intolerable pressure on young social scientists who, unless they have great inner strength, either have to enter into the omnipotent framework, or experience failure.

A practitioner's 'mistakes' may arise from a choice of strategy, at times when several are available, each of which has costs attached to it. It is, however, possible to make mistakes and to survive, with a professional reputation, provided that one has the opportunity and the capacity for review.

2. *Relevant concepts*

There is also no doubt that some of the unconscious dynamics which are basic to psychoanalytic theory and may be uncovered in psychoanalysis also play a part in organisational life. Splitting has been mentioned. In one of the cases to be described (food processing, case F) a job-design project was partly incapacitated because all the 'be good to people' aspects were projected onto the social science consultant and all the 'efficiency' aspects onto a management consultant. Both felt inaccurately typecast, but the competitive situation in which they were placed made it impossible for them to confront the organisation jointly about what was happening, and the project achieved less than it might have done.

Another relevant concept is 'transference'. This is the process whereby feelings and reactions originating in one situation are unconsciously transferred to another. People in analysis are likely to transfer onto the analyst hopes or fears, good or bad feelings, whose original source is somewhere else, and uncovering this is part of the work of the analysis. Transference happens to academics and consultants, too, but they are not sanctioned – and are not in a position – to interpret it. Sometimes, in the midst of confusion and difficulty, the most important thing is to stand back and ask oneself, 'What are they doing to me?' Counter-transference is the obverse – responses which practitioners have about the client or the client situation, which may originate from somewhere else and which it is very important for them to try to locate.

3. Use of the self

A psychoanalytic perspective helps to clarify how practitioners in different parts of the social science spectrum deal with their own responses. Three ways may be distinguised:

(i) *Denial of the self.* In some parts of the field, the material being worked with is 'hard data', and the aim is to remove the influence of the person of the researcher or practitioner from it as much as possible. The knowledge is all 'out there', and any residual influence of what is 'in here' is experienced as threatening to the validity of the knowledge, and therefore denied.

(ii) *Use of the self.* In some parts of the field, practitioners will make deliberate use of themselves and their own responses. They use themselves like a measuring instrument, asking themselves questions like, 'If this is making me feel angry/anxious/sad/affectionate/muddled, what does that tell me about what is happening out there?'

(iii) *Awareness of the self.* Probably the most common position is that of practitioners who neither explicitly use nor strenuously deny their own responses in a situation. Rather, they try to remain aware of how their own dynamics might be influencing what they perceive and how they react, and to allow for it. Where this does not happen, the fact that detachment is not wholly possible may serve as a rationalisation for not even attempting to be detached.

4. The work with clients

It is here that the model, or analogy, ceases to be useful. While dynamics like splitting, denial, transference and counter-transference, rationalisation and other defences against anxiety are omnipresent, it is not at all clear how such understanding may be used in work with organisations.

For one thing, an organisation is not a patient. Hurling interpretations around is itself a defence on the part of the practitioner. It is very seldom that there is enough coherence in an organisation to make such an interpretation relevant to the organisation as a whole; and then there would be the question of who the client is and how he/it can make use of such insight. Without such a path there is no value in interpreting; it is better for consultants to use any understanding they gain to inform their own behaviour. There are dynamics which manifest themselves in the behaviour of groups (Bion, 1948) and for this reason some consultants choose to work with groups in organisations. But this is not consultancy to the organisation as a whole. It has, of necessity, to leave out of the situation a great deal of relevant data and a lot of the organisation's members.

Secondly, a personal analysis does not make practitioners infallible, and it does not entitle them to behave like analysts. Many personal analyses are, in any case, not very successful. Thirdly, the fascination of exploring personal and interpersonal dynamics may distract people from, or even make them deny the relevance of, the facts of structure and context. In work with organisations this is highly inappropriate (one may also question whether it is always appropriate in work with individuals or groups).

Fourthly, there have been some shifts in values since these ideas were first promulgated. Working in a psychoanalytic framework restricts the practitioner to working with a limited number of people, and the early consultants who worked in this way tended to work mainly with the chief executive or the Board of directors. This is less acceptable in an age which seeks to democratise opportunities for development, as in the Quality of Working Life movement, and which in any case questions the appropriateness of hierarchies (Herbst, 1976).

As we have said, therefore, there is much still to learn about how to make use of a nonetheless highly relevant body of concepts. Nevertheless, it can sometimes make a spectacular difference. One of us was involved in a 'seeding contract', an arrangement with the National Economic Development Office (NEDO), under which firms in a certain industrial sector wanting to explore questions of job design could have four days of a consultant's time funded by NEDO. If this led to further work, the firm would then have to take on the further costs. In one such firm, an initial meeting was held with a group consisting of the managing director, staff from the production engineering and personnel functions, line-management supervisors, and two shop stewards. The consultant's presentation about job design was received courteously, but without particular enthusiasm. Then the managing director said, 'You know, what I would really like to have an outsider do is find out why we were late on the market with [a particular product]. What is it about our organisation that made us miss the Christmas market last season?'

Recognising that it is important to start from 'where they are', the consultant agreed to look at this problem, provided that the NEDO-funded assignment could be carried out as well, and a small study was formulated. A time was arranged when a week would be spent interviewing people who had been involved in the development of 'Product X', the material would be analysed during the weekend, and a feedback meeting would be held on the following Monday morning. At the same time, it was arranged that a feedback and review meeting on the job design work would be held on the Monday afternoon.

Interviews were held with about fifteen people involved in the marketing, design, technical development, production engineering and manufacture of Product X, and two group discussions were held with operators assembling the product. This yielded a considerable amount of material and the weekend, which was spent trying to organise and understand the material and preparing to report on it, was filled with a growing sense of pressure and anxiety.

Eventually, the consultant stepped back from the situation to ask some questions: 'What are they doing to you, that you are spending Sunday, your so-called free time, trying to deal with this impossible task? Knowing that you have taken on more than can possibly be handled in the time? Eating margarine sandwiches because you haven't allowed time to buy and cook food? Knowing that the report is likely to be poor in quality because there just isn't time to do it properly? Nobody has forced you to schedule it this way!' The answer came, 'They have turned you into a mini-version of the company! This is what *they* do. This is what happened to Product X, and it is already beginning to happen to the next product. You have absorbed and internalised the culture to such an extent that you are not analysing what happened to Product X, you are living it!'

It was this experience and understanding that formed the basis of the report back to the company on the next day, margarine sandwiches and all. It formed the context and framework within which the organisation around Product X was then discussed. The meeting was completely successful, and established a credibility which also carried over onto the job design activity. In our joint experience, it is probably the only project in which success was unequivocal. Transference is not only transferring feelings onto the consultant which originate somewhere else, it is also affecting the consultant. Where it is possible to understand and make use of this phenomenon, the two frameworks, of knowledge-into-use and the dynamics of change, come very close together.

3   A framework for diagnosis

Diagnosis exemplifies the relevance, simultaneously, of both the frameworks discussed in the last chapter. In the framework of knowledge-into-use, a diagnostic study provides information which may then be used. In the framework of dynamics of action and change, a diagnostic study provides a 'transitional system', entered into jointly by the practitioner and the client systems, which enables them to explore each other to develop confidence, and to begin to enter into each other's frames of reference. It is a vehicle for 'getting to know you'. Information will become explicit which may not have been so in the past, or may be interpreted in ways that are new. If any of that is disputed, the boundaries of agreement and disagreement should become clear, and with them the possibilities of further action. Learning, and with it change, will take place on both sides.

From the point of view of knowledge-into-use, diagnosis implies using selected parts of the general scientific output to understand some specific phenomenon, which may relate to the organisation as a whole or some of the issues in it. Diagnosticians need to have a background of knowledge to which to relate what they find, and a capacity for scientific rigour in the way they set about finding it. The practitioner as diagnostician is therefore seeking the appropriate social science knowledge to illuminate this context and, simultaneously, creating a means by which client and practitioner begin to understand each other.

However, problems in the field do not align with academic disciplines, and this disparity is one of the causes of difficulty between the academic and the organisational worlds. The issue, both for practitioners and users, is the multiplicity of frames of reference in which organisations have been studied. A situation or problem may be studied from many disciplines or points of view, and each of them may shed some light on it. But it will be a partial light, like the light which has been separated out through a prism. It will not by itself serve for resolution or development. There are many such selective beams by which problems in organisations have been investigaed, with the result that, from the point of view of people in organisations, the welter of concepts, theories and ideas coming from the social sciences is quite bewildering.

Ordering theories of organisation

It may be useful to offer a framework for ordering and relating to this mass of ideas and theories, which appear to be unrelated to each other and merely competing for attention. Once they are seen as having a place in a broader framework, it should be easier to select points of entry for diagnosis and to make judgements about diagnosis itself.

Theory is about explanation, and attempts to develop theories arise from a deep need to make sense of the environment. But just as organisation theorists attempt to make sense of the complex environment that is organisations, so their output itself presents a complex environment of which anyone who wants to use it has to make sense. The following is an attempt to do this. It comprises four broad levels.

Level 1.   *Persons affect organisation*

The most direct and immediate explanation of the experience of an organisation is likely to be in terms of the people in it. If one's superiors were less autocratic or more far-sighted, if one's peers were not so competitive, if one's subordinates were more able or more committed, one's experience of the organisation would be different. And, indeed, it would. There is some truth in explanations at all of these levels.

At this first level, there exists a great deal of research and theory about personality and personal development and some of it has been used in devising methods of selection and training. Those who favour this level of explanation are therefore likely to look to selection and training for solutions to organisational problems.

However, they do not always make the appropriate links between cause and effect. During the Esso project, many managers had explanations for some of the problems the company was experiencing: as a subsidiary of Standard Oil, New Jersey (now Exxon), and part of a world-wide organisation, the UK management did not purchase the raw material, but had to process whatever crude oil it was optimal for the wider system to send. Without control of raw material purchase, it was not possible to use unit profit as a measure of performance, and difficult to devise other measures. It was therefore also difficult for managers to know personally when they were doing well.

Again, the building of a large new refinery a few years previously had involved recruiting a large number of young graduates into the lower levels of management. Some years later, this had resulted in a diamond-shaped age structure: a relatively large number of middle-level people around the age of thirty were competing for a small number of senior posts, with uncomfortable and sometimes distressing results. Or again, competition had recently sharpened, with a number of new small oil companies appearing in the market and this too, of course, had consequences.

Yet, having described a situation and given this kind of explanation of it, managers would quite often sit back, reflect for a moment, and conclude: what we need is bright people with ideas. Clearly, the solution did not align with the analysis of the problems.

Level 2.   Relationships affect persons

The influence of individuals is important, but individuals are not limited to one behavioural strategy. They have a repertoire of strategies available to them and which one they select will depend on a number of things, including how they themselves are treated. Thus interpersonal relations, the effect of the group on the individual, and the behaviour of groups as such represent the next level of explanation. These, too, have been the focus of much research, as well as experimentation.

The body of literature at this level is enormous. From the Hawthorne experiments of the late 1920s (Roethlisberger and Dickson, 1939), through the study of the morale of an Air Force Unit in the Second World War (Patterson, 1955), to studies of supervisory style in industry in the 1960s (Likert, 1961), the impact of the social context on individual attitudes and behaviour has been documented again and again. Those who are drawn to this level of explanation will look to behaviour modification for solutions, and there are many forms of training, many ways of giving feedback about behaviour, which attempt to achieve this. Often they are aimed at shifting behaviour towards some culturally acceptable norm, perhaps that of being more 'democratic' or 'participative' in relation to others. More rarely they are aimed at helping people to understand better the roots and dynamics of their own behaviour, and become, as it were, more truly themselves. In any case, social process is here seen as a causal factor, sometimes as the principal or only causal factor, explaining the problem or situation being considered.

Level 3.   Situations affect relationships and roles

However, it is coming to be recognised that social processes, too, are subject to external influence. A managerial style which is appropriate when a new field of endeavour is being explored may not be appropriate when a fire breaks out. Batch production manufacture requires many managerial decisions per day; process production requires few, many decisions having already been built into the design of the plant. The implications for managerial style, and the personal qualities needed to survive and be successful in these situations, are different. In addition, people who have been influenced by programmes that modify behaviour may not be able to sustain their newly acquired behaviour when under stress. An autocratic supervisor is easier to relate to than an inconsistent one.

Time presents a good illustration of a situational constraint which affects relationships. In the organisation of newspaper production, the time when the paper has to be 'put to bed' has a pervasive impact on most aspects of the organisation and its activities and relationships. When a research department working to a six-monthly or annual time-cycle has to relate to a production department working to a weekly cycle the people involved are likely to find each other insensitive to need and difficult to relate to, and may well attribute these difficulties to personality factors. Geographical location is another such situational factor. When people from different functions or departments are geographically separate, there is more chance of incomplete information leading to fantasy in their perception of each other than when they are near.

There is not much research literature isolating these situational factors and tracing their effects, but there is a body of research and writing at the next level, which considers what gives rise to such situations, i.e. structure.

Level 4.   Structure affects situations

Structure is defined differently in different disciplines. The term is used here to indicate those things which, although they may be influenced in the long term, cannot be influenced in the short term and therefore at any particular point in time create the environment within which organisations and their members have to function.

As regards society as a whole, for example, people may influence the size of the population to some extent with their decisions about family size or emigration. In the short run, however, a country's demographic structure, including its age distribution, with the profound effects that has on resources and the provision of services, and consequently also on politics, is part of the environment within which families have to function.

As regards organisations, the factors which have such pervasive effects have already been mentioned: ownership, the legal system within which the organisation operates, the characteristics of the markets within which it operates, the level of scientific and technical development and therefore product technology and production technology, and size. Control systems have a similarly powerful effect, but of course mainly arise within the organisation. Many of these effects and connections have been researched, and at this level, too, may be found some of the key concepts and literature.

The discussion has thus moved from a psychological level of explanation to a contingency level. At each level there are researchers and practitioners at work, and diagnosis is often taken to mean whereabouts, within a particular level or framework, an organisation or a department or a problem is located.

There is little doubt that currently the most popular levels of diagnosis and consequent action in the behavioural sciences are the first two. It may be that this is because selection and skills training on the one hand, and human-relations-type training activities on the other, actually seem to offer some hope of change. Managers feel able to do something in these areas, while, on the other hand, gaining an understanding of structural influences may leave them intellectually convinced but feeling either helpless or required to take on something more fundamental than they feel able to handle. As some of these connections become better understood, however, there may be a willingness to move into areas of influence which were previously thought to be inaccessible. Certainly it is coming to be recognised that technology is a matter of choices and that technology design itself can be influenced (Rosenbrock, 1979, 1983).

But the real fun in diagnosis, in any case, lies in moving between these levels. In any given situation or problem there will be some factors which lie in personality, some in the nature and quality of human relations and behaviour, some in situational constraints and some in underlying structures. Both for the person in the situation and for the professional observing it, organisational diagnosis may well involve scanning up and down the scale to assess, firstly, the relative contribution and importance of each level in that particular situation and, secondly, how they may be interacting. That then usually presents a wide range of possibilities for action and development.

An example of diagnosis

An example may serve to illustrate the interplay of factors at different levels in the search to understand organisational problems. It concerns the role problems of hospital anaesthetists.[1] The professional association of anaesthetists had some concerns about its membership. Its research and education committee sponsored four studies, mainly focussing on the fatigue aspects of the job; but one study was commissioned to explore role and organisational aspects. This illustrates the interplay between the different levels of structure, situation, and social and personal dynamics.

It was decided to carry out an exploratory case study of the division of anaesthesia in a district general hospital, which had 850 beds. In the

[1] A detailed account of this study is published as an occasional paper by the Association of Anaesthetists of Great Britain and Ireland (Klein, 1980a).

division of anaesthesia there were fourteen anaesthetists, seven men and seven women. Unstructured interviews, averaging about two-and-half hours, were conducted with all the anaesthetists, with two consultant surgeons and with a senior nursing officer. In addition, about fifteen hours, spread over a week's operating lists, were spent in theatre, observing the work there.

Unstructured diagnostic research of this kind yields very rich data. But the richer the material, the less easy it is to quantify and with such small numbers that was not, in any case, the purpose. After a considerable time spent in assimilating and trying to understand the material, with its many apparent contradictions and inconsistencies – it was most important to be able to tolerate the complexity and not to try to reduce it – a deliberate attempt was made to refer to the diagnostic framework described.

A search through the material for level 4 facts of structure that might exert influence at other levels yielded three:

  the scientific and technical content of anaesthetics and the way in which this had developed;
  the fact that a patient comes into hospital for surgery and not for an anaesthetic;
  the fact that an anaesthetic is a relatively bounded, short-cycle event.

These three – there were, of course, others – all had the quality of being given, at least in the short term, if not altogether. It then turned out that much of the material indeed fell into place behind these structural facts, bringing into play explanations at the other levels, for example the following.

Consequences of the bounded, short-cycle nature of the event

An anaesthetic is not only a fairly short event, it is one with fairly clear-cut boundaries. It has a high proportion of technical and a low proportion of interpersonal content, at least as far as interaction with the patient is concerned. This has implications for level 1 phenomena, because it helps to define the kind of medical practitioner who may be well suited for the role of anaesthetist. There seems no doubt that these characteristics help to select who enters the specialty. Tight boundaries mean, for example, that , 'There's not much paper-work; you don't clerk patients, you don't take samples, that sort of thing.' The bounded nature of the work is what makes it possible not only for married women, but for anyone who wants to pursue outside interests, to work part-time.

The short cycle of the anaesthetic itself means that one can experience a completed service for patients quite often, and it also provides fairly quick feedback about how well one has performed – 'It's nice to put a patient to sleep and then he wakes up and he's talking to you and you've done something for him. One moment they're asleep and then they are talking to you.' 'It's extraordinarily satisfying to have taken the patient through one of the most difficult times of his life safely and properly, and then they wake up and they don't even remember going to the theatre. That's one of the best things about it.' It was pointed out that an anaesthetist may give between 30,000 and 40,000 anaesthetics in the course of a career.

By unambiguous is meant the fact that, once the patient is awake and breathing safely, the anaesthetic has been completed whatever other problems the patient still has. Some people did not want the long-term care of the patient or the ambiguities of ill-health – 'It's very much an open-and-shut sort of job. You meet the patient, you assess him, you put him to sleep, you go and see him once afterwards, hopefully, or twice. It's a unit, a complete entity.' 'I like finishing with them and then getting new faces.'

'In the house job – there is a ward full of problems, and the next day they're all there again, whereas in anaesthetics I come on in the morning – the patients – they've got me, they've got my undivided attention for an hour or two, and then they go back to the ward. It's not the same with a stroke or with some problem that I've made ten phone calls about.'

On the other hand, there was some room for interpretation, depending on individual personality. What has been described was a rather bounded, closed system. If these aspects were not what appealed, the boundaries could to some extent be extended, and people then spoke of research, or pain clinics and intensive care, and in terms of places where, 'They already look after them for twenty-four hours, fluid regulation for instance, and only then the surgical team takes over.' Also the broader management of the patient – 'Some places have a pre-operative clinic where you chat with the patient, see if they are allergic to anything, and so on. I hope this will spread. It would need more posts but you would learn more by managing the patient.' Taking the whole history was then perceived as an opportunity to learn rather than the chore of clerking, and the patient's long-term progress as a necessary feedback.

This leads to the final issue under this heading, that of the high technical and low interpersonal content of an anaesthetic, and therefore the vexed question of 'patient contact'. Here, too, there was some room for individual differences to express themselves. This even influenced techniques, for instance, whether the anaesthetist considered it kinder to give heavy pre-medication or to deal with patients' fears by talking to them.

Consequences of the fact that the earliest decisions concern surgery

That patients come into hospital for surgery and not for an anaesthetic is indisputable. This structural fact could be traced as having major implications at level 3 for one of the most important role relationships in the operating theatre, that between the surgeon and the anaesthetist. Surgeons derive their authority from the fact that it is they who decide on the operation and perform it, and it is they who carry the overall responsibility for the patient. In the last resort, as one surgeon put it – 'You don't say, "I'm going to do an anaesthetic list next Tuesday, find me a surgeon."' In addition, some have an authority stemming from personal eminence. This authority then carried over onto a whole range of matters in some of which its appropriateness was less obvious and where others could experience difficulty and resentment:

> surgeons not only devised timetables and operating lists, they modified them at short notice and sometimes failed to make them known. They scheduled work to suit their own requirements, and did so without consultation – 'Surgeons can really be outrageous. They can be so demanding and rude and thoughtless ... this business of putting patients on the list without the courtesy of saying, "Can you manage?" They put eight hours' work on and don't dream of saying, "Have you got a long list?" They assume that you are there as a service.' 'It's supposed to be ready at 5.00, but ... I ring up at 8.00 or 10.00 and there's no list yet';
>
> in private practice surgeons had the power of patronage, so one was dependent on them to get work. (However, one instance was quoted where a syndicate of anaesthetists was set up to control their own access to work);
>
> there was a general assumption that the surgeon's time was more valuable than the anaesthetist's. It was he who must not be kept waiting – 'You've got ten minutes, then they start looking through the porthole';
>
> it was the surgeon who determined the general atmosphere in the operating theatre. Surgeons obviously needed to work in the way that suited them best, and they varied greatly. The atmosphere in the theatre ranged from formality and silence to the surgeon beating a tattoo on an old lady's bottom as a signal for starting. In any case, the anaesthetists were constrained to take their cue from the surgeon and not the other way about;
>
> with their limited knowledge of anaesthetics, surgeons could have unreasonable expectations – 'One surgeon actually said, "You should be able to anaesthetise any patient if the heart is beating and the patient is breathing"'; they could make unreasonable demands – 'If everybody's in a hurry and you say you have to wait four hours because he's had a meal, they say, "What does it matter if it's only two hours?"'; they could fail to realise what was being achieved – 'If

things go well, you are hardly there. If they go badly, you are not doing your job well'; they could make inappropriate requests – 'Some surgeons believe in blood, that blood is good, and they give too much'; they could seem indifferent to problems outside their own sphere – '(a patient with heart trouble) … it's not *his* problem patient, it's *my* problem patient'.

Consequences of the scientific and technical content of anaesthetics

As regards scientific and technical developments, enormous strides had been made in recent years in the development of new drugs, new methods, and new equipment. Anaesthetics had expanded in scale and complexity, and had become 'a real science, as well as an art'. Examinations were becoming more difficult. There was even a possibility that the qualities of modern anaesthetics could be exaggerated or too much taken for granted – 'They [surgeons] get a bit blasé. They think that anaesthetics've got to such a pitch they can go on for ever.'

In turn, developments in anaesthetics had had a number of consequences.

1. Greater separation from surgery

In the 'old days', surgeons had known about anaesthetics and sometimes administered anaesthetics themselves. Exceptionally it could still happen that 'some old-timer might tell the anaesthetist what anaesthetic to give, and it might be out of the ark'. But the knowledge and methods, at the same time as growing, had established themselves as clearly different in kind from those of the surgeon. An operation used to be a single undertaking, it now tended to be two distinct undertakings. Surgeons tended to opt out of knowing about anaesthetics. They were interested in the result – a safe and stable patient – but not in the choices and strategies involved in getting there, and this could be a cause for regret – 'There was a partnership between the surgeon and the anaesthetist. You were looking after that patient together, you would exchange ideas about the patient. Now it's different; you are looking after different ends of the patient. The surgeon doesn't know about the anaesthetic side of it, there is more of a conflict therefore.' A surgeon said, 'Anaesthetic technique has left me behind. I don't really understand now, if he tells me what he's doing … and I'm not really interested.'

2. Greater professional standing for anaesthetists

At the same time as leading to greater separation from surgery, the distinctive nature of the scientific and technical content of anaesthetics had brought a sense of independent professionalism for anaesthetists, as well as high status, expressed in consultant posts. This had led to a more complex relationship with surgeons, both at the level of the specialty in general, and at the working level. When GPs had done anaesthetic sessions in local hospitals, the question of competition for leadership would not have arisen, nor would the surgeon's right to dominate the scene and make the rules have been questioned.

3. Changes in surgery

Developments in anaesthetics had meant that more complex and difficult surgery could be carried out – 'We can keep the patient alive while they do those fantastic things'. It also meant that routine surgery had become easier – 'They don't need such dexterity any more, because with improvements in anaesthetics we can keep the patient under for six to eight hours while the surgeon fumbles about ...' 'I've anaesthetised for simple hernia, which should take forty-five minutes, and I've sat for three or four hours because the surgeon's not very good.'

4. More patients can be anaesthetised

Developments in anaesthetics had meant that not only could more types of operation be performed, but they could be performed on more types of patient. Patients with various kinds of ill-health, either associated with or independent of the reason for operation, could be successfully anaesthetised – 'You very rarely turn a patient down, however ill he is.' However, there was a cost in worry for the anaesthetist.

One of the people interviewed admitted to being worried the whole time. A second was in two minds whether to give up the job for this reason. A third, fairly recently qualified, said that although with time the anxiety was getting less, 'I still wake up in the night imagining procedures. I wake up and think the oxygen's run out or something.' A fourth said, 'Sometimes I see a patient who's going to be operated on Monday morning, and I can worry all weekend about that patient.'

It was an important aspect of medical policy that the pre-operative examination of patients should be carried out by those anaesthetists who were going to treat them, so that they could prepare their strategy and know what to expect. In the hospital under discussion, this policy was carried out, but many of the anaesthetists referred to other hospitals where it was not. It seems at least possible that, where anaesthetists do not make a practice of doing the pre-operative assessment, this may be a defence against anxiety – '[Where I come from] the consultants don't go to the pre-med, because if there's a problem they wouldn't sleep.'

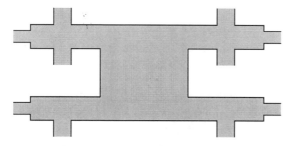

Figure 1   *Layout of operating theatre complex (a)*

So why was the policy sustained in this particular hospital? The operating theatre complex, although old, was well designed. With the exception of an accident and emergency theatre and the obstetric theatre, all the theatres were centrally located in one place, opening onto a common concourse, from which also opened the recovery room, and coffee and changing rooms, as in figure 1.

The advantages of this arrangement were frequently stressed – 'It's not so at the Y where I do some sessions. I feel very cut off there, and isolated.' It had a number of consequences. Firstly, it was easy to continue the teaching of junior staff, since it was easy for senior staff to be present when needed and to slip out and leave juniors on their own when things were routine.

Secondly, one could very easily ask a colleague to stand by for a while if something was complicated. The anaesthetists recalled an earlier time, when one theatre had been located in another block and a registrar would be on his own there, no matter what happened.

Moreover, doctors had almost certainly also gone home directly from that building, again no matter what had happened. For a third consequence of this layout was that it provided the opportunity to discuss technical issues with colleagues both before and after operations, and therefore also to work through some of the anxiety. This analysis suggests that an additional structural factor, the layout of the building, had consequences for level 2, the impact of social processes on individuals. The shape of the building where the operating theatres were located was facilitating a form of social support among the anaesthetists which was important in helping them manage some of the most difficult personal aspects of their role. It seems very likely that this was the institution, or the means, which made it possible to sustain the policy of examining patients pre-operatively.

When a draft report on this study was sent to the Association's research and education committee, one of its members, who was head of the division of anaesthesia in a large teaching hospital, telephoned the

Figure 2   *Layout of operating theatre complex (b)*

researcher. In that hospital the operating theatres all opened onto a long corridor, as in figure 2. He said, 'You know, this is interesting. This morning I had a woman patient I was worried about. But I'm the boss, I'm not supposed to get worried. I have one woman colleague I don't mind admitting it to. But she was working at the other end of the corridor, and going all that way for help would have been a big deal. Anyway, I couldn't leave the patient that long.'

To come back, therefore, to the framework for organisational diagnosis and the interplay between different levels: the structural factors of scientific and technical developments in anaesthetics had led to great advances, but had created situations and relationships which affected roles. In particular they had brought some psychodynamic consequences for anaesthetists in the form of anxiety. The architecture of the building made it possible to work through this anxiety by means of social and professional support from colleagues. This in turn made it possible to sustain medical policy.

From this diagnostic study one may see that a single level of analysis would not have captured the range of factors that produced critical effects for the anaesthetists. A study of, for example, the way that people affect the situation might have led to better selection criteria and made a contribution, but it would not have shed light on the nature of the relationship between anaesthetists and surgeons. This kind of analysis displays the range of factors which are having an effect and the interplay between them, and gives the people in the situation the choice of which they wish to pursue or are in a position to pursue.

4 A practice profession

Diagnosis is a link in the transition from research to use. It combines the methods and frameworks of research with the values of use. As far as the actors are concerned, the transition is from the role of researcher to the role of practitioner. Practitioners are people who are not merely concerned with finding things out, but who do something with the things that they or others have found out. Or anyway, who do something! In our case studies we have one person who is clearly in the role of a researcher handing over findings, and a number of different kinds of practitioner.

In one sense, professional practice in the social sciences is not new, since social scientists have been working in practitioner roles for a long time. However, it is new in the sense that the 'real', respectable, research-oriented social science profession (at least in the United Kingdom) has not generally acknowledged it, has not paid attention to the issues involved and the dynamics of implementation, does not train its students for it and often pursues its own consultancy activities as a guilty sideline. Universities do not often have institutional means for dealing with the fees which are paid for help obtained from social scientists, and this is a good indication of its illegitimacy.

One reason for this is the uncharted nature of the scientific issues involved, for those who have been trained only in the methodologies of research. This contributes to the process of splitting which has been described (see p. 14), which allocates the pursuit of knowledge to a research community that does not get involved in development, and development to an OD community which does not get involved with academic research.

As a result, venturing into professional practice requires considerable courage. For one thing, social scientists who work as practitioners expose themselves to the criticism of their research-oriented colleagues, without having equivalent institutional or professional support systems. For another, direct contact with members of organisations carries particular risks. In their relations with social scientists, members of organisations – operators, managers, any members – have the basic advantage of not having to justify themselves or their primary activities. They can ignore social scientists, misunderstand them, despise them. Moreover, if one ventures into an action role, consulting or helping with some experimental change, there is always the chance that this may go wrong, the advice turn out to be mistaken or rejected, the experimental change to be disappointing. Such lack of success is likely to be quickly apparent and to have to be faced and dealt with on the spot. None of these dangers are faced by academics who remain safely behind desks and in libraries. The feedback cycle for inadequate theoretical work takes much longer, often more than a lifetime.

In all this, and because of the general separation from the academic, research-oriented social science community, there is lacking a professional role model for social science practitioners. At least some of the differences between what appears to be possible in the use of social science and what actually happens in practice must be due to the incomplete nature of the models and assumptions that are being used.

Professional models

In an initial approach to this topic by one of the present authors (Klein, 1980b), it was suggested that, since the social sciences have not so far produced a role model that arises out of their own subject-matter, all the models to which social scientists refer derive from other professions, with whose situation that of applied social science overlaps to some extent, but never 100 per cent. Many of the difficulties which are then encountered in practice arise from this 'to some extent'. The models referred to are the medical or clinical model, the engineering model, the business model, the political model and the educational model (this last not included in the earlier discussion).

We would now like to develop this discussion further. Since the existence of social science practitioners is a fact, we would like to consider some of the elements contributed to this practice role by medicine, engineering, business, politics and education. The practice of these professions provides not so much models as sources of experience on which social science practitioners draw and whose contribution they have, somehow, to integrate.

Clinical aspects

The medical or clinical model has been very important in the development of social science consultancy and action research. It has perhaps been represented most strongly in the work of the Tavistock Institute of Human Relations, which grew out of the Tavistock Clinic, which in turn is strongly rooted in clinical and psychoanalytic concepts and values. The first social scientist to work full-time as a consultant with an industrial organisation in this country was Elliott Jaques, who was a psychoanalyst by training. He made the earliest, and still very influential, attempts to formulate something like professional principles for this role (Jaques, 1951): for instance, that consultants need to remain independent, i.e., cannot be captured or let themselves be manipulated by either side in a dispute; that they do not make private reports about people to others; that they do not reveal what they have been told without permission. Such principles are not taken out of the air, but are based on knowledge about the consequences for clients and their problems if the consultant acts differently.

A number of things follow from the medical or clinical model:

(i)   *One does not sell products.* In medicine there is a strong taboo about advertising and selling. It rests on the wish to protect the patient from being exploited. Otherwise a doctor might persuade patients that they need treatment (and should pay for it) who are not in a position to judge this for themselves.

(ii) *The absolute confidentiality of information given in private.* Other models also treat information as confidential, but the principle does not have the same priority. For instance, in the 'business' model the reason for preserving confidentiality is that, once one loses one's reputation for treating information as confidential, one is less likely to obtain new contracts. It follows that those members of an organisation who are not in a position to award contracts may not need to be treated with the same care. Consultancy in the medical sense is something quite different from management consultancy.

(iii) *One does not make judgements.* A doctor treats a broken leg, even if it is the leg of a thief or a murderer. Here there is, of course, a difference from the situation of medical science, if only because the concept of 'health' or 'ill-health' in an organisational sense is very unclear, and often a matter of opinion. Nevertheless, it does have a message for the action researcher: psychiatrists cannot accept patients for treatment if they cannot at least accept them as individuals to the extent of keeping separate from the treatment any moral views they may have about the patients' actions. If action researchers have fundamental objections to an organisation's primary task, they are unlikely to be able to empathise enough to work on its problems.

Engineering science aspects

This is the model of research-into-application. Practitioners who draw on this model need to have the skills of diagnostic research and some knowledge of empirical research findings, including the research findings of others. Since they will not have such knowledge comprehensively, they also need some access to resource systems to advise them and some sense of when to use and when not to use libraries and information retrieval systems.

We do not believe that the step of internalising findings and converting them into use, which was discussed earlier, is essentially different in the social and the engineering sciences. Engineers, too, have to spot the relevance in a finding, the potential for use in a situation, and the modifications needed to bring the two together. When describing their processes, experienced engineers are not afraid to use the word 'flair'. The difference is that they hardly ever document these processes, with the result that there is an element of myth about taking findings off the shelf and applying them, just like that.

Where this myth influences expectations about the use of social science, there is unease about the emphasis which many social scientists put on the processes and roles involved and, instead, an attempt to eliminate their influence as much as possible. The search, then, becomes one for outputs that may be classed as products and which are considered more reliable and more 'scientific' in the natural science sense. It is within this model that legislation was conceived in Germany requiring 'scientific findings about the workplace' to be applied (see chapter 5). There are certainly some areas in the social sciences for which this model is relatively appropriate; but there is a danger that social scientists, who may be intimidated by the great theoretical and practical achievements of the engineering sciences, also try to work within this model when it is not appropriate, or may be pushed in that direction. This tends to lead to premature generalisations, which the next generation then overthrows. It also leads to the reductionist quality, and the rather strenuous denial of humanity, of some of the work described as 'human factors'.

The scientific aspects of knowledge-into-use and the dynamic aspects of the process can come into conflict, and the practitioner who tries to hold on to both is walking a difficult road. One of us once lost a major consulting assignment for saying, 'I don't know' in answer to a question during an early project meeting. The meeting had gone well until a senior manager asked whether the project being discussed, as well as creating better-designed jobs, would also tap hitherto untapped motivation and enhance productivity. The truth of the matter was that one could not know. However, what the questioner needed was not scientific prediction but reassurance in his anxiety about moving into the unknown. Failing to get it he, and with him the management group, lost confidence in the project.

The organisation's chief executive had wanted the project and was disappointed. The incident continued to trouble him for a long time. Referring to it several years after it happened, he burst out with a frustrated shout of, 'Your bloody integrity!'. With greater experience it is no doubt possible to meet the questioner's needs without compromising scientific integrity; but hanging on to both can be difficult.

What happens more often is phases with different emphases, such as a 'research loop' in a consulting project. Even here, however, it is necessary to hold on to dynamic and scientific aspects simultaneously. In the banking case (case B) to be described, a research loop was just a little too long and a little too interesting in its own right. A steering committee, which constituted the link to consulting aspects, was disbanded while the research was going on and this left the resulting report without an owner. Although useful work went on for another seven years, it was not as effective as it might have been.

Business aspects

Social scientists have to eat and pay off mortgages. If that is accepted, then the way in which they are funded has to feature in the discussion. We can locate here the structural component of the 'splitting' described earlier. In general, research is financed from public funds and consultancy by the people or organisations benefiting from the work.

Attitudes and behaviour follow these structural facts: research seems to have a built-in commitment to not being useful and consultancy can become very market-oriented. On the one hand, there are no sanctions to prevent the proper requirements of academic freedom from shading into a complete absence of a sense of responsibility towards the society which is providing the funds, at the same time as academics feel morally superior to those who have to demonstrate credibility to some more direct user. Some academics appear to believe that money, although inherently dirty, is somehow sanitised when laundered through public funds. On the other hand, some social science consultants have become primarily marketers. In this model the results of social science are products like any others and the social scientists business people like their clients. They seek out clients and advertise and sell their wares. This conflicts powerfully with clinical values, which require that people should not be persuaded that they have problems and need help when this is in someone's financial interest.

Because of the importance of funding as a structural influence, we used the funding structure of institutions as the basis for sampling our case studies. There is a clear need to develop ways of multiple funding. However, attempts we ourselves made to persuade the then Social Science Research Council to consider dual funding, so that work could be done which had a research component, paid for out of public funds, and a usefulness component, paid for by the user, failed.

Political aspects

No-one nowadays would claim that there is such a thing as a value-free view of the world. But there are differences in the role that personal values play in the work of social scientists and practitioners. In one tradition, the value judgement is made when one decides whether or not to engage with an organisation. After that, the social scientist's task is to help the client organisation clarify its own values, become aware if it is in fact operating within them, and deal with areas of conflict. Social scientists can only help in this way if they can distance themselves from the problem under discussion and be accepted by all members of the organisation as being non-partisan. Other social scientists, in contrast, openly declare that they are on a particular side.

There are differences in the degree to which the social sciences have become politicised in different countries, and in different professional cultures within countries. Those who have strong political views have generally limited themselves to analytical critique and refrained from consultancy or active intervention in organisations. This is not, however, always the case. There is a model, based on a pluralist theory of organisation, where the consultant takes one sub-system of the organisation as client and rejects the others. It could be said that psychologists who devise tests without concerning themselves how they are to be used are doing the same thing.

It is sometimes argued that there is no such thing as detachment. Political and other values have always influenced both the selection of topics for research and the interpretation of findings. But it has generally been accepted that what happens in between the selection of topics and the interpretation of findings needs to be detached if it is to be credible and, indeed, if the conclusions drawn are to have any power. The more controversial aspects of politicised research concern precisely that which happens 'in between': for example, the roles and methods which researchers adopt, the parameters and data which they take seriously or do not take seriously, and where they decide to set system boundaries, i.e. what they consider to be within the system and therefore susceptible to change, and what they consider to be the environment and therefore given. All of this also applies to action researchers.

A pluralist view of organisation implies that the organisation is not seen as a significant entity contained within significant boundaries. Rather, it is a temporary container for members of interest groups or professional groups such as trade unionists, or managers, or computer specialists, and so on, whose links with those professions and reference groups are stronger than their links with other parts of the organisation, so that the 'skin' round the organisation is relatively thin. The implication is that there are significant system boundaries around society at a macro level, while significant sub-systems are the strata within it. Social scientists working with this perspective are likely to concentrate on global variables and to reject findings, for example, which point to different consequences of the division of labour in different technical circumstances. They will tend to focus on the relationship between employer and employee and not, for example, on the relationship between different functions such as design, development, marketing and production. They are likely to take structural variables more seriously than cultural ones (in work organisation, for example, the effect of ownership and power more than the effect of engineering training and the models of man that are inherent in it).

Until recently, working with this perspective has precluded adopting action roles in organisations. As suggested earlier there are now, however, some exceptions to this. For example, as part of the German Government's programme to 'Humanise Life at Work' (*Humanisierung des Arbeitslebens*) a research team carried out an action project with the operators of one department of a firm manufacturing screws, bolts, and so on. By means of off-site week-long seminars with the operators, and other educational and consciousness-raising activities, the team aimed to encourage the workers to develop their own ideas for the improvement of their working conditions, and the project was substantially successful in achieving this aim (Fricke, et al., 1979). However, the project also revealed limitations that are encountered when action research is approached from a pluralist, societal perspective.

Firstly, the approach was costly. Since the aim was not merely to stimulate ideas but to see these through to implementation and to sustain the greater independence and self-confidence of the workers involved, a research team of several people (working with only one department in the firm) required government support for several years. Work of this kind is unlikely to be funded by the firm itself, and therefore needs large-scale public or societal support.

Secondly, the kind of changes made were limited to working conditions, involving ergonomic aspects and the installation of a rest-room. Changes involving broader aspects of work organisation would inevitably have meant collaborating with other departments and other levels in the firm.

The researchers found eventually that systemic aspects of the firm had to be taken more seriously than they had expected. By the end of the project the foreman of the department was complaining bitterly that he had been cast in the role of the one who always had to say, 'Yes, but ... '; members of the works council were complaining that they had not been sufficiently informed and involved; members of other departments resented the privileged situation of their colleagues; management, insofar as they had not always been ready to implement the suggestions that had come up, felt that they had been treated merely as the enemy. At the beginning, the researchers had interpreted such responses as stemming from the personality characteristics of the people involved. Later, they were forced to see them at least to some extent as aspects of roles which were not only roles in a system but systemically linked with the roles of 'their' operators.

The operators in the department had at first been perceived, not as a sub-system of an organisation but as a microcosm of a social class. In a subsequent project the researchers recognised that, in order to further the interests of this microcosm, they would have to take some systems aspects of the organisation on board as well, and they planned, for example, some management- and supervisor-training activities.

It is important that the value stance of a practitioner be made explicit, so that members of a client organisation can be in the position of making real choices. One way of obtaining this explicitness is to consider how practitioners define the boundaries of the system they are working with. Considered in this light, many apparently 'radical' social science activities turn out to be rather conservative, and vice versa.

Educational aspects

All change and development implies learning (and, sometimes more importantly, unlearning) and in nearly all circumstances the use of social science in organisations involves some learning on the part of members of the organisation. One of the functions of the practitioner is to provide educational support for this process. The amount of time and effort devoted to education is one feature that distinguishes social science practitioners from their engineering science counterparts.

There are many reasons for client learning as part of a change or development process, and many kinds of learning. An obvious one is the development of specific, task-oriented skills where the change in question involves the design of jobs and new forms of work organisation. These skills may range from the current widespread need to develop competence with a keyboard, or use a visual display terminal, to the need to master the control processes of large and complex plant such as a nuclear power reactor. Even where there is no overt change in work organisation, the training needs of operators in such situations are frequently underestimated, if the operators are to be able to understand what is happening and intervene when something goes wrong, rather than respond routinely to signals. (There is also a need for institutional or societal learning about such things, since they have been highlighted by research for a very long time (King, 1960).)

A second kind of learning is that needed to gain understanding of interpersonal and group processes. In that case the learning is not specific to particular situations but permeates organisational life.

In both these instances the educational aspect is self-evident, and there may be explicit training activities. In other cases it is not so self-evident or explicit. Organisational change of almost any kind involves learning and unlearning. If, for example, it leads to different structures or procedures or different kinds of work, then the decision processes involve the articulation of alternatives and examination of the consequences of alternatives. Working through these processes, with or without some external facilitation, helps people to internalise the conclusions and own the results, and is a form of learning.

Finally, there may be teaching and learning in the concepts and methods of social science itself. Elements of theory, methods of research, diagnosis and design, the management of change, ways of reviewing and improving group functioning, may all be taught if the organisation wishes to internalise such methods in order to become independent of professional, or at any rate external, practitioners. Since this is the stated objective of many practitioners, the transfer of learning through education may be central to their activities.

The techniques used for teaching are varied and have developed from a number of traditions. Formal skills teaching comes from the training side of industrial psychology. It usually involves a mixture of theory and practice. Experiential learning approaches rely almost exclusively on conceptualising from practice. Many of the 'packages' used to apply specific social science concepts contain specially constructed teaching components. The teaching associated with participative design and with the transfer of social science methods is perhaps least formally recognised and least systematically developed. Learning and internalisation sometimes take the form, during a transitional phase, of relating to practitioners as a model, or using them as a 'ghost'. How would they have responded to this or that? What would they have said or done?

The role of educator in the professional life of the social science practitioner is subject to a number of continuing issues. One is the question of whether teaching is undertaken 'in-house' or in a separate training venue away from the client's premises. A related issue is the problem of transferring learning from the training exercises to the work setting. An old issue receiving renewed attention is the question of whether it is better to provide a formal basis and conceptual framework for teaching or whether practical involvement, 'sitting-by-Nellie' 'on-the-job' training is more effective. From a time when the formal, systematic approach was dominant, the reality of 'on-the-job' training (even in management training) has now won many adherents.

Many of the issues have to do with the extent to which practitioners and clients recognise the centrality of the educational role. Clients seeking the implementation of specific organisational solutions may not appreciate the educational implications and may not provide practitioners with the resources necessary to fulfil this role systematically and thoroughly. Similarly, many practitioners may see themselves primarily in action, 'engineering', roles and may themselves underplay the education needs or be uncertain how to identify and fulfil the learning requirements. It seems that the 'trainers' (the industrial psychologists and the OD specialists) identify themselves to a very large extent with the educational role, while other kinds of practitioner are uncertain about the degree to which they are educators and the form of teaching they need to provide.

This dilemma emerges as a crucial issue for professionalism in the so-called 'gate-keeper' problem. In many professions, for example particularly in medicine, a central principle is to preserve for accredited members (trained via accredited courses) the knowledge, methods and skills within the boundaries of the profession. Teaching given to clients is marginal: the patient with heart disease does not learn the techniques of open-heart surgery. Whatever the reasons for this approach, it has the function of preserving a range of problems as the sole province of the professional. What then do we make of a profession that spends its time trying to transfer its knowledge to the client so that the practitioner becomes unnecessary to the client in the future? Guard the gates and you have a clearly defined professional territory; open the gates and it is everybody's territory. If social scientists guard the gates too assiduously, they may not permit the internalisation that leads to utilisation, while even the idea that such gates exist may be bitterly resented. Finding a way of coping with this dilemma may be one of the fundamental issues in the maturation of social science as an applied profession.

Part II An empirical study of social science utilisation

5 The research programme

The aim of the empirical research programme was to examine the process by which social science is utilised within organisations. In particular, the aim was to examine different approaches and outcomes in different client organisations.

In examining the relationship between social scientists and organisational clients we decided not to pick our sample according to the type of work being done. This was for two reasons: firstly, because a case would need to be examined in some detail before one could determine the category of work being done, and secondly, because the categories are often not clear-cut. Instead, we decided to select our cases according to three kinds of institutional base from which work is generally carried out: in-house units, where the social scientists are employees of the client organisation; external, independent commercial consultants; and external consultants based in academic institutions. It seemed likely that the base from which the work is done would have a pervasive effect on the utilisation process. Somewhat outside this strict framework, however, we have included three pieces of work from a non-profit organisation doing action research, which is thus on the boundary between an academic and a consulting institution.

In looking at the utilisation process, we adopted the case-study approach. We sought a specific example of the work of the social scientist and explored its origins, the degree and type of collaboration and the outcomes. In the UK cases we collected two kinds of data: unstructured interviews with the professionals and the central figures in the client organisation, and the documentation in the case. With this data we prepared a narrative of the case which interviewees could confirm or correct until an agreed record was obtained. The German case material was supplied to us by the German team.

The case studies

There are seven case studies from the United Kingdom and seven from the Federal Republic of Germany. We had hoped originally to publish a volume of the full case material and a volume of analysis and discussion. However, the economics of publishing make this impossible and we include in this volume shortened versions of the cases. The cross-case analysis contained in chapters 10 and 11 is based on the fuller material and the reader will find in it references to data which are not in the abbreviated descriptions. One of the German cases, case J on guest workers in the motor industry, has been published in full (Kunstek, 1986).

In addition to the seven full cases, the UK team has some data about the mode of operation of five UK practitioners, some of them in units involving one or more social scientists. These are examples we came across in our search for full cases and which it was impossible or inappropriate to develop into full-length records of specific pieces of work. Nevertheless, we were able to collect information about the approaches of these practitioners and thus to enrich our data in a broader sense. We present them in chapter 12.

As well as the case studies in organisations Klein, one of the UK team, had the opportunity of studying the work of the Kommission für wirtschaftlichen und sozialen Wandel (Commission for Economic and Social Change, CESC) in Germany. This was not an example of social science applied to a specific organisation; rather it was a strategic attempt, on a governmental scale, to harness research for economic and social policy. We include an account of it because of its intrinsic interest and because it has no parallel in the United Kingdom. We find of particular interest the fact that it demonstrates many of the same issues and dynamics as the cases at the level of organisations.

As is usual with such research, we have adopted the convention of not disclosing the identity of the client organisations or of the consultants and their organisations.

The historical context

Before presenting the case material it is important to look at the background to actual present-day attempts at social science use. There are marked differences in historical development, scientific tradition and government policy in the United Kingdom and West Germany, and they influence what happens. While we did not set out to make cross-national comparisons, the differences in context serve to illuminate the general topic. Another reason for presenting them here is their striking complementarity. It would be good to be able to move a little nearer towards having the best of both worlds.

The British scene

In the rather pragmatic tradition of social science in the United Kingdom, the usefulness and applicability of research have seldom been far from the minds of social scientists and those who have financed their work.

Between 1915 and 1965 there existed a strong and consistent thread, linking sponsors and researchers in the belief that research and problem-solving were mutually enriching. It is both ironic and sad that two world wars served to strengthen the link. The tradition began with the setting up of the Health of Munition Worker's Committee in 1915, with its remit of investigating the influence of hours and conditions of work on the output and health of workers. It continued and broadened with the studies of the Industrial Health Research Board (still relevant to current problems but mostly forgotten) and the creation of the National Institute of Industrial Psychology (NIIP), both in the 1920s. During the Second World War, substantial research divisions in the armed services did work which was problem-centred and through it also developed some of the people who later carried a problem-centred orientation out into civilian research institutions.

Stansfield produced a valuable account of research sponsorship during this phase (1981). After the war, he writes:

> the general public was aware that science and 'the boffins' had played a big part, especially through radar, in winning the war; people looked forward to a better post-war Britain, to be created in the spirit of developments such as those represented by the 1944 Education Act and the National Health Service, and they saw science and the use of science in industry as a big factor in making industry more productive and in improving the quality of life, both at work and elsewhere. An Advisory Council for Scientific Policy was established. This, already in 1947, stressed the use of 'the natural and social sciences', and 'the contribution which might be made by a review of existing knowledge of human factors affecting productivity and by making available Government funds to enable valuable research in this field to go forward'.

As a result, the Government set up a Committee on Industrial Productivity with a Human Factors Panel under the chairmanship of Sir George Schuster. Stansfield records that this 'pressure to develop the social sciences did not come primarily from social scientists; it came from biological and physical scientists who felt held back by the weakness in this area alongside their own developed disciplines, and also from potential users who were aware that their needs could not be met as things were'.

Under the auspices of the Schuster Panel, the NIIP carried out research into methods of foremanship (1951). Joint consultation was the subject of two projects, one conducted by the NIIP (1952) and the other from a sociological standpoint by Liverpool University (Scott, 1952). The Tavistock Institute of Human Relations made a major study of the human effects of technological change in the coal mines, which gave rise to the development of socio-technical theory (Trist and Bamforth, 1951; Trist et al., 1963).

The Tavistock Institute also launched the pioneering studies in the

Glacier Metal Company. This was the first instance of a full-time social science consultant working with a UK firm (Jacques, 1951). The fact that the consultant was a psychoanalyst brought new types in insight, knowledge and new techniques to bear on the human problems of industry. Not least among them was the realisation that the mere uncovering of a problem and making it explicit can in itself be part of the solution. The Glacier study was also breaking new ground in that it was looking at problems of organisation and the proper definition of roles and relationships within a company. Overall there was a shift after the war from looking at the worker to looking at management problems or whole organisations, for instance the ways in which organisations adapt to change.

Common to this work was a philosophy of detailed, empirical research and of the interplay between research and practice. This was summed up by Sir George Schuster when he reviewed the work of the Human Factors Panel in 1952 (Ministry of Labour and National Service, 1952):

> As I see it we are at a stage where, for the better understanding of problems in human relations and human behaviour, the great need is for accurate factual observation of things which are actually happening in industry, for the collection of clinical material – of evidence on the way in which various influences are working – and the proper collation and interpretation of that evidence, so as to ensure that methods and policies can be considered in the light of that evidence and not under the influence of prejudice, hasty generalisations from inadequate data, individual hunches or superficial popular opinion. Observational studies of this kind can be regarded as 'scientific' if 'science' is used in the widest sense – the Baconian sense – in which it includes any orderly empirical study of the natural world.

The Schuster Panel included industrial members, both employers and trade unionists, as well as academics. So did its successor committees, leading up to the Human Sciences Committee of the Department of Scientific and Industrial Research. Up to 1965 these were the major Government sponsors of research and, in spite of the difficulties experienced in this tripartite commissioning of work, it ensured that researchers were reminded to relate theory to fieldwork and research to its use. Journalists were commissioned to produce short, simple accounts of research reports and these received wide circulation. (Department of Scientific and Industrial Research, 1957–67). There were many meetings and conferences bringing researchers and users together. Increasing support came from the experience of usefulness, not from an a priori belief in the importance of social science. Much of this is probably now forgotten.

The tradition described created a degree of respect for and knowledge about the work of social scientists, and led to the setting up of the Committee on Social Studies, chaired by Lord Heyworth, which reported to

Parliament in 1965. It recommended, and achieved, the setting up of a permanent institution for sponsoring research, the Social Science Research Council. It also had two other indirect but clear consequences:

(i)   The creation of a Centre for the Utilisation of Social Science Research (CUSSR) at the University of Technology, Loughborough, under the direction of Professor A. B. Cherns.

(ii) The decision of Esso Petroleum Company to develop and explore the application of social science by appointing an in-house social sciences adviser.

An important characteristic that these two initiatives therefore had in common was that they developed towards the end of a particularly rich and fruitful period of research in and about organisations. The work of Woodward (1965), Burns and Stalker (1961), Lupton (1961), Klein (1964) and the work of the Tavistock Institute, seemed to hold great promise of usefulness. In both ventures (each of which had both action and research purposes) the main research question was 'How?' How was all this richness in the social sciences to be utilised? These are the questions to which both the final report of the CUSSR (Cherns and Clark, 1972, pp. 15–18) and the account of the Esso work (Klein, 1976) address themselves.

It is also relevant to note that both attempts were less than successful and may have been based on too great, or too simple, an optimism. The Social Science Research Council, too, eventually ran into political difficulties (Rothschild, 1982). Whatever the reasons, reflection suggests that the tradition described may in fact have substantially ended with the work of the Heyworth Committee. The late 1960s were a time of substantial growth in teaching and research in university social science departments, and it was a time of growth in the number of experiments and attempts at application being made by industry. It would be a mistake, however, to see these two trends as part of the same development. Possibly the most important aspect of them was a growing divergence between what was happening in the universities and what was happening in industrial application.

As regards university research, a large part of the work done under the auspices of the Social Science Research Council between 1965 and 1982 was processed by committees based on academic disciplines and staffed by academics, many of whom did not share or identify with the history that has been described. This had important consequences for the evaluation of research proposals. A recent commentator has said, 'It seems the only thing that mattered in psychology was whether the methods were good enough, and in sociology whether the ideology was good enough.' Those social scientists whose concern was for use and application came to be increasingly isolated from their professional peers.

In industry, as was already observed in the account of the Esso work, many of the assignments beginning to take place under the generic title of 'applied behavioural science' did not come from a research base at all. The fastest-growing sector was of assignments based on training, usually experiential training, which emphasised interpersonal skills and behavioural change. These assignments were frequently introduced by consultants, some of whom developed standardised forms of intervention designed to be applicable in all situations, and which came to be known as 'packages'.

Such assignments came directly from, or were indirectly influenced by, the emerging American tradition of OD. There was considerable controversy between the research/contingency orientation and the OD/ behavioural change orientation, one such controversy being documented in Klein's *A Social Scientist in Industry* (1976 chapters 8, 9, and pp. 236–41).

By 1979, a study carried out for the Chemical and Allied Products Industry Training Board (McLean et al., 1979) identified more than eighty people 'engaged in organisational change' in the chemical industry alone. They are described throughout as 'interventionists' and their activities as 'planned change'.

The researchers tried to understand the patterns they had found:

> Part of the explanation for the inconclusive 'change' programmes may perhaps lie in the theoretical models and concepts of OD which contribute a number of built-in delays. One in particular is the linear model which stresses 'education first' and the concept of 'readiness'. This implies that people are not naturally ready for change but must in some way be processed or educated by change experts into a state of understanding and acceptance before the actual problem-solving or change effort can be carried out.

From their data, the researchers deduced an evolutionary development:

> We can now speculate on possible ways in which organisation change may have developed in organisations. Here is one.
>
> (i) An early emphasis on organisation-wide educative programmes (initiated by internal and external experts) which heighten levels of awareness of human interaction and demonstrate its patterns and complexities but also its relevance to the way in which a company operates..
>
> (ii) Growing dissatisfaction with such programmes by managers on the grounds that they may have more relevance to solving personal problems than organisational ones.
>
> (iii) The development of problem-oriented workshops using outside experts to help explore some of the actual work-based problems concerning relationships.
>
> (iv) Projects in which managers address interpersonal issues as an integral aspect of day-to-day operations, sometimes at the prompting of an

internal expert acting as process consultant but with gradually decreasing reliance on his/her presence.

The research raised questions about the match between the strategies postulated in the theoretical OD literature and the experiences of people in the field and their struggle to find appropriate concepts. But there is no question that change is the object and relationships and behaviour the substance. Academic research had moved away from a concern for use and application, there was no professional training for application and no other institutionalised concern for it, and the gap had come to be filled in other ways.

Through the 1970s and 1980s, the OD movement continued to grow both in development of in-house OD networks in organisations and in the provision of social or behavioural science services from management consultancies, some large firms of this kind, for example, offering consultancy on the 'management of change'.

This was the historical evolution of the splitting which was described in chapter 2. On the side of the institutions concerned with social science funding, the need for usefulness and help from the social sciences was expressed in the setting up of a number of problem-oriented institutions. But the response, and indeed the terms of reference of the actual funding, were always in terms of more research. A Technical *Change* Centre was set up, to carry out *research* studies, and was closed again. The research councils introduced several relevant initiatives, for example forming a Joint Committee between the Economic and Social Science and the Science and Engineering Research Council to fund linked studies; funding a Work Organisation Research Centre; funding a Programme for Information and Communication Technologies which in turn created a number of centres researching the impact of these technologies on society. But in all of these, researchers were being funded to do more research. The only exception was a small unit originally set up within the Department of Employment and called, for the sake of respectability, the Work Research Unit, which has been actively concerned with dissemination and application. A continuing problem remains the institutional barriers which discourage academic work on practice. Recruitment and career development, for example, depend on research reported in academic journals and good applied work earns little credit.

One feature of the 1980s has been directed research programmes which bring academics and industrialists together in research consortia with the purpose of linking theory and practice. A major example was the Alvey Programme for Information Technology. However, by the time the need to deal with the split positions brought by researchers into such consortia was explicitly recognised, and strategies for dealing with it being formulated (Klein and Newman, 1988) this programme, too, was discontinued.

Two features cut across this picture: firstly, at public policy level there has continued to be social research intended to inform policy-makers in national and local government. Secondly, there has been some resurgence in empirical research which can provide valuable insights for the organisations studied (for example, Buchanan and Boddy, 1983). But such work is hardly ever conducted in an action-research framework, with the organisation's needs as prime focus. The conceptual and methodological issues surrounding utilisation and practice have not regained academic respectability.

The German scene[1]

Both historically and in terms of scientific traditions, the German context is quite different from that of the UK. For one thing, the years before and during the Second World War created a major discontinuity in social research. When university departments were built up again after the war and research traditions and different 'schools' evolved, their main focus of interest was theoretical and methodological. There was not the same history of involvement with the problems of practice, and among academics there was no experience of collaboration with users. There was no action research. Where social scientists did empirical work at all, it was to gather data for theory verification.

However, research studies of this kind were sometimes used as a basis for consulting, occasionally at a managerial level but mainly at a political level. Their function was one of feedback. In this framework the Rationalisierungskuratorium der Wirtschaft (RKW) during the 1960s had a section for social research, and the region of North-Rhein-Westphalia established a programme in the Sozialakademie of Dortmund to carry out researches on social situations in general and work situations in particular, with a view to feeding back into the political process.

The thrust towards more direct use and usefulness of the social sciences came later and from a different source. It was Government, and particularly some of the programmes of the Social Democratic Government, which stressed the need to base social policy on research and to influence the world of practice with the methods and findings of social science. For a long time, this societal demand for usefulness was in large part resisted by the academic community. It is relevant to point out that the social sciences have been, on the whole, more politicised on the continent than in the Anglo-Saxon world. Thus, while some social scientists might resist using

---

[1] We are indebted to our German collaborators, Dr Edith Rost-Schaude and Mr Rolf Kunstek, for some comments on and modification to this section.

their skills to solve problems on grounds of methodological purity, social scientists associated with the 'left' would also be unlikely to want to help optimise the functioning of systems at a lower level than that of society as a whole and would, by the same token, be unlikely to be accepted in action roles in organisations.

However, while a certain amount of political controversy has surrounded the social sciences, there is in German society a much greater respect for science, and for knowledge in general, than there is in the United Kingdom. This is allied to certain models of science and of scientific method. So for example, as indicated earlier, there is a clause in the Company Law of 1972 which requires that 'proven scientific findings about the workplace must be applied'. This sounds strange to British ears, where research involving people at work has been very context-specific and where the emphasis in application has been on cases and experiments, often mediated through the person of the social scientist, rather than on the broad application of generalised 'knowledge'. This legal requirement is clearly influenced by a natural science model which requires general laws, free from the fallibility and variability of human interpretation and intervention. The clause in Company Law in turn has had considerable influence both on the sponsorship and the nature of research carried out since it was passed. Large-scale financing of demonstration projects is justified if the expected output is likely to be generally applicable knowledge, and research design is also more likely to be geared to that aim.

Thus it is initiatives at national policy level which have characterised the German scene, more than initiatives at organisational level. Within organisations, OD activities began to develop during the 1970s. Even more than in the United Kingdom, they were independent of social science research in the universities and tended to fill the gap left by the academics. When our German collaborators looked for case studies, these were therefore the kinds of cases they found.

Apart from the legal framework already mentioned, we know of two national policy initiatives in Germany: one is the CESC which was set up in 1971 with the remit to commission research which should serve as the basis for a proactive and future-oriented social policy. An account of the work of this Commission is given in chapter 13.

The second major Government initiative is the programme to Humanise Life at Work (*Humanisierung des Arbeitslebens*), which was initiated by the Government in 1973 (Bundesministerium für Forschung und Technologie, 1974). Under it, organisations which were prepared to do something to 'humanise' life at work could get substantial Government subsidies, on two conditions: firstly, they had to have the agreement of their works council for the proposed work; and secondly, they had to allow the projects to be researched. When a project was approved, the organisation concerned could get approximately half the project costs back from the Government, and there would be research groups involved who got the whole of their costs. Between 1974 and 1989 just under DM1.3 billion was spent in this way. Grant applications were assessed by committees consisting of employers and trade union representatives as well as academics and civil servants. During 1989 the programme was being restructured under a new title 'Work and Technology'.

Given the legal framework and the scientific model on which it is based, part of the aim was to subsidise such researches and experimental models as would generate generally binding criteria, and knowledge which should serve as the basis for norms and standards for general application, and to fill gaps in 'proven scientific findings'.

The format of the programme was designed to maintain some kind of parity of power and influence between employers and trade unions. Thus the agreement of the works council of any organisation taking part was required, and there is an equal number of employers' and trade-union representatives in the various committees reviewing grant applications. Each side, however, has regularly, from the beginning, complained about the too great influence of the other and this debate has also been carried on within the organisations where projects have taken place, as well as within the political parties and Parliament.

The debate has also included complaints about the role of the social sciences. For one thing, the sheer amount of money being spent on them has been criticised. For another, employers and the conservative party complain that social scientists aim to use changes in production systems in order to revolutionise the whole of society, while the trade unions complain that social scientists are too distanced and academically oriented. In 1982 the format of the programme was changed so that social science institutions no longer receive grants in the programme independently, but only as sub-contractors of the organisations in which projects take place, i.e. they have to be acceptable to those organisations. Some social scientists feel that this is an ideological selection process, through which (a) fewer projects will take place since, in cases where there is a difference of opinion between management and works council about a social scientist, the particular project will not go ahead and (b) it may turn out that only those social scientists who are willing to subscribe to economic and engineering norms will get opportunities to work in the programme. These issues are currently still under debate.

Apart from its substantive content, which we do not attempt to assess, the programme has had a number of side-effects relevant to this study: one is the spread of 'work structuring' activities of one kind or another, including outside the formal humanisation programme. Some of the German cases in our sample are of this kind. Another effect of the format to date has been that, through the obligatory researches accompanying the various projects, a number of German social scientists gained experience of working in organisations and lost their fears and, in some cases, their objections. At first, in spite of strong pressure from the committees making the project grants, the 'accompanying researches' were just that – research studies accompanying the projects rather than advisory or consultancy inputs. With increasing experience over a number of years this began to change, although social scientists venturing into action-research roles still risk considerable criticism from their professional colleagues.

Another side-effect of this programme is a growing concern about the issue of multidisciplinary work. The dominant framework of the university system and career structure has traditionally been the subject-discipline. During the 1970s the CESC, in its role of research sponsor, tried and failed to bring together into a problem-oriented framework the different disciplines concerned with *Arbeitswissenschaft* (the science of work – ergonomics, work study, occupational medicine). The first of the projects in the humanisation programme involved five distinct research groups in four institutes, each carrying out accompanying research strictly within the boundaries of its own discipline (industrial sociology, educational sociology, ergonomics, production engineering, psychology of learning) and refusing to move outside them. Now, several years later, the demand for interdisciplinary work is beginning to come from researchers themselves.

Thus the lines of development in the two countries seem to be crossing: at a time when a tradition of empirical and problem-centred work seemed to have been substantially interrupted in the United Kingdom, it began to develop in Germany.

Issues of classification and evaluation

Classification

The history of the use of social science in the two countries suggests that the case studies show many different influences. As stated earlier, we are not using cross-national comparison as the main basis for analysis: while there clearly are differences between the countries, the number of cases is small and does not necessarily exemplify them. What we have done is make a *post hoc* appraisal of the cases and use one dominant characteristic of their content as the basis for categorising them. This might be about targeting a particular kind of outcome, sometimes with a particular kind of method, or dealing with particular problems being experienced by a group. When the case studies are classified in this way, some differences between the countries nevertheless do show up: all the cases in category 2 are from

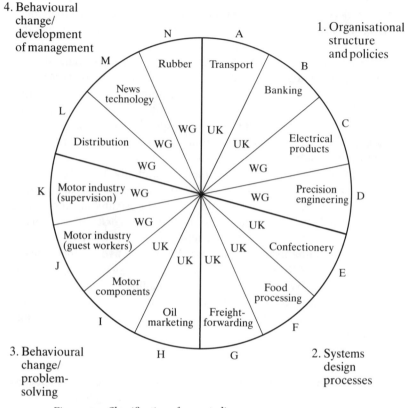

Figure 3   *Classification of case studies*

the United Kingdom, and all the cases in category 4 are German. In the other two categories they are mixed.

The classification we arrived at is shown in figure 3.

(i)   *Organisational structure and policies.* In four of the cases the target of the intervention was strategic problems leading to changes in organisational structure and policy. Two of these cases were from the United Kingdom: examining the role of supervisors in a nationalised transport industry with a view to implementing policies to improve local management practices (case A), and examining branch banking in a systematic way with the long-term aim of providing better customer service (case B). There were also two German cases of this kind: one in an electrical company was part of the 'Humanisation of Life at Work' programme and was an attempt to create flexible working structures in a number of production departments (case C). The other was a programme in the precision engineering industry to counter the shopfloor deskilling effects of moving from a mechanical to an electronic form of production by introducing a job design scheme (case D).

(ii) *Systems design processes.* Three cases were interventions in the processes by which organisations made major technical systems changes. They were all UK cases in which the consultants attempted to give more prominence to human and social issues in the development of new technological systems: the design of 'green-field' factories for confectionery (case E) and for processed food products (case F) and the design of a computerised system for freightforwarding (case G).

(iii) *Behavioural change/problem-solving for specific groups.* In four cases (two UK, two German) the direct target was the behaviour patterns of specific groups of employees in order to deal with specific problems they faced. In the first of the two UK cases, groups were assisted to examine the role of marketing in the future, given dramatic changes in the oil industry (case H), and in the second, groups examined the structure and mode of operation of a motor components factory, given a near-disastrous history of poor industrial relations (case I). In one German case this led to designing 'learning shops' for guest workers (case J) and in the other training was devised for supervisors in the motor industry (case K).

(iv) *Behavioural change/development for management.* There are three cases in this group, all German. These were in news technology (case M), in distribution (case L) and in the rubber industry (case N). The objective was to use strategies for the training and development of management, which were considered to have universal application, in an attempt to make fundamental changes in management culture and structure across the organisation.

Evaluation

In the next four chapters the cases are presented in these four categories. All of them have been shortened from the original accounts, some more than others, but we have tried to ensure that each category contains at least one relatively long account. The degree to which they have been shortened reflects in some measure the amount of empirical detail that was available. As stated earlier, the analysis in chapters 10 and 11 is based on the original fuller material, so that the reader will find some references in it to data which are not in the abbreviated descriptions.

Following the presentation of the cases in each chapter, a commentary is offered which begins the process of analysis. Since it relates to sought outcomes and their achievement, the remainder of this section examines the methodological issues surrounding such evaluation.

The initial question we asked of each group of cases was what had they achieved. We examined the cases for outcomes in an attempt to show what happens when social science is applied. This was not undertaken in the spirit of 'selling' social science, i.e., examining whether or not it is cost-effective. Rather, it was done to show the types of outcome that can be achieved, the types of outcome that are difficult to achieve and the routes that lead to the different end products.

We based the analysis on a simple paradigm. Firstly, you analyse what outcomes each case sought to achieve and then you examine what actually happened. Even such an apparently simple and obvious approach is fraught with methodological difficulties and surprises, which gives some important insights into the difficulties of evaluating social science enterprises.

The commentary at the end of each chapter examines the beginnings and ends of the cases (goals and outcomes). It says little about the complex of events that lie between. These are analysed in the two subsequent chapters (chapter 10 and 11), which look more closely at what social science is being utilised and by what methods, and what factors facilitate and inhibit this process of utilisation.

The following factors have to be taken into account in evaluating the outcomes of the cases and the role of the social scientist practitioner in the achievement of these outcomes.

1. *The changes of sought outcomes during projects*

Although each case established a broad objective for social science intervention, there are many variants in the cases with respect to the stability of this objective. Factors affecting this stability are:

(i)   The initial objective may be very specific or rather general. To review branch banking is a broad objective, leaving until later the question of specific action objectives. To derive a role for marketing is more specifically action oriented.

(ii) Objectives may be reviewed and changed in the course of the project. In all of the cases projects moved through different phases with criteria being reviewed, new goals being set, and so on.

(iii) The initial objectives may have been agreed with one part of the client organisation. In undertaking the work, however, it is usually necessary to involve other parts of the organisation which entails further negotiation of the objectives, and this often modifies them.

(iv) While an overt objective may be agreed for a project there are

usually other, covert objectives held by both the client and the practitioner. Commonly for example, clients had a secondary objective of
testing the value of social science interventions using the overt objective as a vehicle. Similarly, social scientists are perpetually in the
business of demonstrating the value of their emergent disciplines.

2. *The place of the case in the life of the organisation*

While the cases are longitudinal studies they constitute only a short phase
in the life of the organisations. Events before the case shape the outcomes
that can be sought. Chapter 11 examines the facilitating and inhibiting
influences of these factors. Similarly, many of the outcomes may not reach
fruition during the course of the study and we could only ask our respondents to predict the next phase of each story.

3. *The dynamics involved in applying social science*

There is not a one-to-one relationship between social science knowledge
and what is implemented. Indeed, many social scientists would feel that
they have failed if this were the case. In most strategies it is fundamental
that social science is in some way 'internalised' by clients – individuals or
organisations – so that they 'own' the knowledge. At the individual level
this may happen via experiences which help people to 'rediscover' social
science concepts. At the organisational level it may mean taking in relevant
staff or training those already there. Either way, clients will apply the
knowledge in their own way, which will probably not be a faithful
interpretation of a specific aspect of social science. They may also feel that
the action and its outcomes are a result of their labours and may well object
if it is attributed to some other input. A fundamental problem for the social
scientist is that the greater the success in enabling the client to internalise
material, the less control or even knowledge the social scientist has of the
outcomes, i.e., what is done with the material. This, in turn, has a
fundamental consequence for the evaluator: if a change occurs in structure
or in behaviour as a result of client action, to what extent is it attributable
to the social scientist? Does it matter? It is of no consequence to the client
but may affect the sense of worth and career of the social scientist.

4. *Multiple change processes*

A social science input is hardly ever the only change process going on.
There may very well be major 'outcomes', for example, the opening of a
new factory, but this is the result of many different inputs. In some respects
social science is at its most effective when it is diffused widely across all the

parallel activities needed for a major outcome, i.e. it does not make a contribution to a specific aspect of a major change but has a systemic influence. If it has this effect, it practically defies evaluation to parcel out the relative impact of social science or compare it with other influences.

5. Relevant outcomes

It is not always easy to establish the outcomes which are to be regarded as the indicators of the achievement of objectives. Is a structural change, for example the creation of an autonomous work group, to be regarded as the outcome or should it be the consequences of that change, i.e., does it improve productivity, increase job satisfaction, and so on? Is it enough that a workshop leads to heightened consciousness of group dynamics or should the evaluation seek evidence of greater ability to manage group dynamics as a result? While it is easy to establish that x workshops were run with y participants, it is much more difficult to assess the cognitive and affective changes that occurred within participants and the consequent effect on their behaviour.

Having regard for these and other factors, we did not attempt systematic, quantitative assessments of outcomes at a specific point after the intervention began. We did not have the considerable resources necessary to undertake this and we were not convinced of its desirability. We relied instead on the subjective reports of social scientists engaged in the cases and of key members of the client organisations. Where it was available, these respondents were able to report the result of internal evaluation exercises, but this was only in a minority of cases. We were less concerned to obtain quantitative assessments of the degree of success of outcomes than to obtain descriptive accounts of what had occurred and how various outcomes related to one another. Following the issues listed above we were particularly interested in the following questions:

(i)   To what extent were original sought outcomes pursued?
(ii) What other objectives appeared on the agenda and to what extent were they achieved?
(iii) To what extent was it possible to link outcomes with the social science input or to social scientists as interventionists?
(iv) To what extent were there discernible spin-offs from the intervention, for example, client staff carrying ideas beyond the departure of the social scientist, developments away from the site of initial change, and so on?
(v)   To what extent were the methods and procedures brought to the client by the social scientist institutionalised within the organisation so that they survived after the project ended?

6 Cases in organisational structure and policy

Four cases are presented in this chapter. The role of supervisors in the transport industry (case A) and consultancy with a bank (case B) are reported from the United Kingdom. From West Germany there is a case in electrical products (C) which formed part of the national programme to Humanise Life at Work and a project from a precision engineering company (case D) involving a change programme without direct social science intervention.

The theme that is common to these four case studies is the intention to make major organisational changes or implement policies of major strategic significance to the organisation. In the transport study (A) the role of supervisors was examined with a view to implementing policies to bring them more clearly into the management structure. In the banking case (B) diagnostic studies of branch banking were undertaken with the intention of rethinking the organisation of branches. In the electrical products case social science inputs were planned in order to determine organisation changes to improve the quality of working life. In precision engineering the company had to make job-design and organisational changes to move from the manufacture of mechanical to electronic products.

The transport, banking and electrical products cases all involved external social scientists working as consultants to the organisation. In the precision engineering case the company used social science concepts and methods but without the aid of social science practitioners. The transport, banking and electrical products cases are presented at some length and the precision engineering case is reported in a shorter form. At the end of the chapter a short analysis compares the objectives and outcomes in these four cases.

A. Passenger and freight transport: the role and motivation of supervisors

The client in this case was a very large nationalised industry with a complex organisational structure covering the entire country. The case study describes two investigations of the role and motivation of supervisors. The nature of the collaboration was heavily influenced by the history of the social scientist and by previous dealings between the company and the social science community.

The social scientist

This was a sociologist working in an educational institution. She had worked on a variety of research studies of industrial life and had particularly noted how difficult it was to fit complex organisational behaviour to the formal models of the academic community. She had undertaken a number of applied studies, in which she had made her own attempts to analyse and explain what she observed, before being asked to take on this consultancy assignment.

The company's strategy for social science utilisation

The Board had established a strategic studies unit and one of its members took the portfolio for human resources. At one time this director had been the senior personnel manager in the company and he called a high-level seminar to identify priorities for personnel research. Three areas were identified, the availability of labour, the achievement of change and the motivation of staff. The director established studies in each area using external resources. He had a particular approach and strategy for these collaborations:

> I personally tend to be research oriented. I believe that the method of solving a problem is basically the scientific method. So throughout the work, I've tended to use research people and research methods to help me. I have found there are academics all over the country who are longing to get into industry to use it as a laboratory. My policy has been to find three or four and having judged that they are good and that we can work with them, to stick to them. Otherwise you've got to teach every new person all the details of your industry from scratch. If you use the same person each time, they are accumulating more background knowledge all the time.

The studies of staff motivation began with managers and were undertaken by another consultant. The next stage was a survey of the 7,000–8,000 supervisors in the company and the director offered it to the social scientist. She was at the time looking for a nationalised industry in order to obtain comparative data on local democracy to relate to another industry she had been studying. The study of supervisors offered just the opportunity.

The main study: line supervisors

The director and the social scientist planned a survey of the attitudes of supervisors in the main line function of the industry. The study was conducted by the social scientist, assisted by two members of the client's staff. It was planned that she would provide the sociology methods input while her two internal colleagues provided their detailed knowledge of the company.

The director commented about the project-team composition:

> It has really been ideal to have someone with an academic/research background with people who really know how the company works and can explain technical terms and relationships at work which would not be clear if the academic was working alone. After the idea of always using the same consultant, this dual working is the second general principle upon which I operate.

The consultant also found it a useful partnership, but not without its difficulties:

> Both of them saw themselves as learning from me and the exchange was good. The company is very complicated and it is difficult for an outsider to familiarise herself with the industry sufficiently to do a good study. What I had was all their experience and knowledge at my disposal in exchange for me trying to train them to do social surveys. It was, however, quite delicate and I had to be a bit careful because they were not students. I was a woman and not much older than them and, on occasions, they found it difficult to accept that I did know best on methodological issues. But it worked.

The consultant planned and carried out detailed pilot studies in four locations, interviewing supervisors, their managers and their trainers on matters of job description, job satisfaction, relations with others, and so on. She had anticipated that this pilot investigation would become the forerunner of a more structured survey which could be administered at a much wider sample of locations. In practice, however, she was asked to prepare a report on the basis of these data.

Results

The findings provided a wealth of detail and a main problem was expressed as follows in the project report:

> The main problem that emerged is that the majority of supervisors do not think of themselves as members of the management team. There are a number of reasons for this: amongst the most important are the background and age of supervisors, their relationships with local and higher management, the nature of their duties and the conditions under which they work. The effect is that supervisors do not act like management. They tend to take a narrow, parochial and essentially short-term view of their work. Even when they would like to operate in a more managerial fashion, local attitudes of both staff and management can conspire to prevent this.

The survey found that supervisors were generally happy in their work and found considerable satisfaction in the intrinsic responsibilities of the job; it had variety, autonomy, responsibility, interest and involvement in the running of an industry in which they had great pride. However, there were many reasons why they felt isolated from management and tended to take a narrow view of their responsibilities.

The general feeling within the project team was that supervisors had tremendous power over the effectiveness of day-to-day operations and if they could be given a real sense of having an important role in management, it could materially improve the performance of the business. The reasons for them feeling outside management were disparate; if something could be done about each of them, the effect in combination might be significant.

Preparation of the report

The project team prepared a report on the survey which was delivered to the director. The first draft was prepared largely by the consultant and her team, but subsequently it went through a number of re-drafts strongly influenced by the director. The final report had a particular structure which the director felt he could use with his senior colleagues. The report was sixty-two pages long with five appendices and was organised as follows:

(i) *Management brief:* a four-page summary of the entire study, printed on coloured paper. The main problem was expressed together with a list of eleven major findings which were directly related to ten recommendations calling for specific actions, for example, a review of practices in promotion, the need to make training more practical and the need to increase informal consultation between supervisors and managers.

(ii) *The main report:* a full discussion of the survey and its aims and methods with well-documented findings.

(iii) *Appendices:* these included a checklist of items relating to local managers' policy towards supervisors. Examples from this thirty-item checklist are:

Do my supervisors have excessive spans of control?

Do I take enough interest in the training and development of my supervisors? Do I give them realistic projects and show an interest in the results? When supervisors return from training courses, do I help put into practice that which they have learned?

Do I consult with my supervisors before a local consultative meeting? Do I make sure they are told of the outcome in good time?

Do my supervisors hand over properly at the end of each shift?

The director commented upon his approach to the structuring of the report:

> I laid down a structure I have found useful in my industrial work which is a short introduction (to explain how it came to be written and its purpose) and then a little description of its methodology (because it's quite new to most managers). This is followed by a summary of the findings (because people are impatient readers) and a summary of the recommendations. If we can get people to read that far we've won. Following that there is a discussion section which can be at length so that the interested person can read it fully. The other requirement, because even with that structure people are pretty lazy, is a management brief or summary in which you give the gist of it.
>
> I say to all consultants that I don't just want an interesting report, I want a useful one: it must make positive recommendations which we can apply. I also insist on the numbering of paragraphs because, when you have a discussion round the table and someone says there is a point they don't like, they can refer to point 2.2.1 (b) and everyone can find it.

The consultant had some difficulties with the way the report was constructed but felt that, overall, it produced a document that would be read widely within the company:

> I didn't disagree with anything that was said but, as a trained sociologist, I would not make these sweeping generalisations on the basis of four sites. I would have been more cautious. But managers would not understand my caution. They want you to tell them what to do. But if you do that you may mislead them so I try to give them an understanding of a different perspective on their position and to make suggestions on how they might cope with their problems.
>
> The director taught me a lot about how to put a report together for use in the company. He drew out a checklist for local managers which has been very popular and I would never have thought of doing that. He also pointed out that I should make very clear that what a study of this kind does is to indicate how people feel about things and, whether or not the basis of their belief is accurate, it is their beliefs that govern the way they are going to act. For example, the supervisors feel they are badly paid but the response of management is that they are not badly paid if you look at the statistics. But if they believe themselves badly paid, it will affect their motivation.

Dissemination of the report

When the director received the report he took responsibility for disseminating it within the company and seeking support for the implementation of its recommendations. As a senior executive he was able to bring the report to the attention of higher management. He also discussed the findings with each member of a number of senior policy-making committees and subsequently presented the report in committee meetings. The authors of the report, the consultant and her two company colleagues, were not asked to present the findings. The director commented upon this division of responsibilities:

> My role is to present the report to these very senior committees, which is something I can do best because I am talking to people of my own level. Occasionally we have used academics to do this and it works well in discussions of four or five people but they don't understand the conventions and tactics of arguing the thing through with a bigger group in a formal committee which may be quite hostile at the beginning. Probably the biggest contribution I personally made to the acceptance of this work was the initial 24-hour seminar at which the top people laid down priorities for this work. In presenting the report I could always say that we were asked to do this by the chief executive and by the Board member for personnel.

The consultant had reservations about this arrangement but accepted its logic:

> I would have liked to have presented the findings myself or at least to have been present. The director was able to defend it properly and knew the right answers. The political situation is such that if it comes from a researcher it can seem to be threatening. The way a piece of consultancy is received has often nothing to do with its worthiness but with the political situation.

Outcomes from the study

In addition to the dissemination and implementation of the report other developments resulted from the study. One was a request to the consultant to evaluate the progress of implementation. A second was a request to study workshop supervisors, another type of supervisor not included in the initial study. The director felt that the positive response to the report and the variety of outcomes that resulted were indications of a job well done:

> It was marvellous that the chief executive asked me to ask the consultant to come back and study whether the recommendations had been put into effect and were effective. It went further than that when he asked for a similar study of workshop supervisors. So for these reasons you can see why I rate this a very successful piece of co-operation.

The consultant was also pleased with the reception given to the report, but had some reservations about the resulting developments:

> It is probably the most widely read report I have written and I keep getting more requests for it. I thought the other requests were good ideas, especially the workshop supervisors study. I felt I had four good cases and if I could add

a workshop one, there would be an academic paper there. But in a way my plans have been upset because the idea was to do a really super pilot study and get them so interested that they would want a full-scale study. Then I could follow through my initial plan of taking a sub-sample of my industrial-relations sample and looking systematically at the supervisors. But the report from four locations is now accepted as the last word on this kind of supervisor. So I have queered my own pitch by making it so good in their terms that they don't see the need for further research on this kind of supervisor.

There is also something else I now realise. If I constructed my structured questionnaire from this report and did my large sample, all it would do would be to modify the conclusions and identify more precisely the location of trouble spots. But in terms of ideas and thinking, I would produce no more because it is all there.

The study of workshop supervisors

The opportunity to study workshop supervisors arose when it was planned to introduce internal work study consultants in one location, to establish whether improved working practices would improve productivity. The director felt a simultaneous study of the supervisors in the location by the consultant would be advantageous. While not entirely happy about working with internal consultants of a different discipline, the consultant undertook the study.

The study was undertaken in a similar way to the previous one and on similar topics. It was made clear that it was a separate exercise from the work of the internal consultants. It showed, once again, that the supervisors found considerable intrinsic value in their work, but they were quite young and could not distance themselves from shopfloor staff and identify with management. There were also problems of organisational structure: the degree of decentralisation and conflicting requirements from two higher levels of management. A report was constructed in a similar form to the earlier one, and its recommendations were widely accepted and acted upon. In this instance, the consultant played a part in presenting the findings to management.

Outcomes for the client and the social scientist

The client

The director regarded the consultancy relationship with the consultant as a particularly valuable piece of collaboration. He felt that the combination of his influence, her knowledge of social science methods and the local knowledge of the people she had worked with had been very successful.

While there had been some tough discussions about the recommendations in the reports, they had been widely disseminated and acted upon. He attributed this to a number of factors:

(i)   The style and influence of the chief executive. One of the things he said soon after joining us was that he would like to see far more links with the universities and he has always been supportive of this work.

(ii)   The Board member for personnel is a very enlightened chap and he has given as much support to this process as his time pressures have permitted.

(iii) I'm exerting my influence from a senior position and as someone who at one time held the top personnel job in the company. That helps a great deal; you just have more clout because of your history. A social scientist who worked in the company previously did so in a much more junior position and could not exert this degree of influence.

(iv)   The quality of the field work where, using a person like the consultant, we get a good intellectual input, help on methodology and acceptability to staff, and often the unions.

(v)   The single most important thing I did was to hold the 24-hour seminar before we got cracking. So we got the support of all those top people for our priorities.

The social scientist and the research institute

The social scientist also considered her consultancy collaboration with the company to have been valuable and successful. She attributes this to having a good sponsor, highly placed, who was sympathetic, understood academics and stayed in post throughout the studies. He was able to put people at her disposal to help her understand the organisation and he also arranged access and disseminated the results.

From this study and other work, the researcher has also had to consider how far to go with intervention in the decision-making process. She has concluded that her role should be limited in this respect:

> I see myself as providing information upon which managers can take better decisions rather than being involved in the decision-making process myself. If you believed decisions were made on a rational basis within the organisations then you could see yourself being involved. But they are not; people fight out what's going to happen in political ways and you, as an outsider, are not part of it.

But the consultant's work on industrial democracy, especially in her other studies, means intervention poses particularly awkward questions:

> In my study of the balance of power between management and unions I have a lot of sympathy for both sides. If you do a very good analysis of the power of the unions, that can be used by either side to the benefit or detriment of

both sides. So in disseminating your results you say, 'Because of the sensitive nature of what I am doing, both sides must have a copy of any report.' I am effectively saying, 'Here you are, I relinquish my responsibility. I have not tipped the scales by giving one side information to manipulate the other, so my conscience is clear.' That is where I am at the moment, but I know it's not as easy as that. Managers, for example, are much better at using this information because the unions are either not interested or don't know how to use it. So giving them both a copy of a report may not be treating them equally.

The consultant also found that this project highlighted some of the difficulties and stresses of being based, as she was, in an academic institution. She felt there was a very low commitment in her academic institution to any kind of commercial enterprise and especially to contacts with industry. Even when she transferred to a polytechnic, which she had thought would be more supportive of this kind of work, she still encountered many problems. She found that there were few people with external grants and therefore no procedures set up for buying equipment or recruiting secretarial staff. She also found conflicting demands between her teaching and research. The consultancy work also created problems because there was no procedure for clients to pay the polytechnic direct, which meant that she could not use polytechnic facilities to do the work.

This project exemplifies the transition of a social scientist who was committed to research that was empirical and grounded, and was discovering the new territory that application and use of findings led to. It also shows how emphasis on professionalism in research was providing a good match with a client who wanted to control diffusion and application.

B. Banking: organisational and socio-technical analysis in the context of long-term consultancy

Origins and start of the project

The client in this case was one of the four clearing banks in the United Kingdom. The consultancy relationship lasted eight years, during which time it waxed and waned, and encompassed a range of different activities. All of these in one way or another followed from a major diagnostic organisational study; but in its central focus that study was not taken up in the way that had been envisaged.

The consultant was based in an independent research institute and first met the bank's personnel director at a conference:

> Settings such as conferences can provide opportunities to begin an exploration of skills and competences which are free from the anxieties that beset 'buying' and 'selling'. I didn't even know who this was until I looked up the list of delegates afterwards.

A few weeks later, the personnel director made contact and explained that he had, for some time, been considering how to get some kind of contribution from the social sciences to the work of the bank. It was not a matter of specific problems, but of a general sense that here might be something worth exploring.

The first question, therefore, was how to continue and extend the mutual exploration, but still without any major commitment. The consultant had no knowledge of banking other than being a customer and to the question, 'What can you do for us?' could only reply, 'I have no idea – is there some way I can begin to get to know you?' A contract for one week's work in the personnel division was agreed. Exploratory interviews would be held with members of the division, and the consultant would then meet with the division for a day, during which the perceptions of the organisation arising from this study would be discussed, and there would be a general presentation on the uses and applications of social science. This was framed under the headings of Occupational Psychology, Ergonomics, Human Relations and Industrial Sociology as areas of professional activity, and stressed the interdependence of social and technical factors in any particular situation.

For the consultant:

> the kind of diagnostic exploration that this small study involved provides one of the greatest pleasures of the job. When you start to work in a setting which is new and different you're allowed to ask stupid, or anyway naïve, questions. The pleasure lies in rediscovering that there is a framework of analysis which actually works, even on strange and new data; in other words, that the questions begin to get less stupid. When you begin to test the framework out, with the jigsaw-puzzle question, 'If this is happening over here in the way you describe, does that mean that such-and-such may be happening over there?' and the answer is a slightly astonished 'Yes', that is one of the most satisfying experiences in the whole business.

A basis of some confidence having been established with the personnel division, the next question was how to begin to use the new resource. An opportunity arose a few weeks later, when the bank set up a working party on customer service, which the consultant was invited to join.

The customer service working party was set up by the domestic (i.e., branch) banking division and included people from personnel and management services divisions. It was a direct result of the emphasis that had already been established on the interdependence between social and technical factors in a situation that the personnel division had decided to join in this work.

The consultant once again had to say that she did not know what might constitute an improvement in customer service, beyond having an intuitive sense that it was not likely to be only a matter of the pleasantness and courtesy of the cashiers. It would be necessary to understand a good deal about how branch banking functioned before one could see where service to customers might be slipping and how it might be improved. The first major piece of work, therefore, commissioned jointly by personnel division and the customer service working party, was a study of the work and life of a branch.

A study of branch banking

A strongly multidisciplinary team was assembled, with experience ranging from clinical psychology through sociology and social psychology to computer ergonomics. It included two members of a university department, subcontracted to the research institute. It was immediately obvious that socio-technical concepts could not be used in the usual sense of a social and a technical sub-system, since here were not two sub-systems but three: not technical arrangements and staff, but technical arrangements, customers and staff. The team set out to look for the interdependencies between these three systems.

The proposal was discussed with staff representatives from a national trade union and a local staff association. They agreed to the study but said that, if a resource of this kind was to become available to the bank, there were other, more important, problems to look at. For example, the process of clearing cheques between different banks involved factory-like tasks of great repetitiveness and monotony and something should be done to improve these. It seemed that this might become the next assignment, and that a pattern might emerge where work would be done alternately on problems suggested by the management and the staff sides. The personnel director said that, if such a pattern did develop, he was prepared to pay from his budget for alternative assignments to be carried out for the staff side:

> It seemed a very good way of dealing with the perennial problem that the first contact – whatever happens later – is initiated by management, often because the staff side either doesn't know that the opportunity exists or doesn't have the power to invoke it.

However, by the time the study of branch banking was complete, there had been elections for new staff representatives and a different set of officials did not take up the option which had been discussed – 'It was, as so often, the problem of hand-over'. An element of 'alternating' had, however, been incorporated into the first study. The staff representatives had expressed concern about how the system of representation was experienced in the branches. Some questions on this issue were included in the interviews and a separate report about it written for the staff representatives.

A detailed study was carried out in four branches around the country. It involved in each case in-depth interviews with customers and staff, observation of activity in the branch, tracer studies of letters and phone calls, description and analysis of work procedures, 'shadowing' (i.e., following round) the sub-manager, description and analysis of the computer system. All this yielded a great deal of material, and preparing a report took more than three months.

The report was in two parts: a brief, summarising discussion and a much longer source document which showed how these views were arrived at. The organising principle was how the experiences of staff and particularly of customers that were encountered had been, and could be, influenced by the policies and systems of the bank. For example, there was an instance of a man who had broken down and cried at the memory of having had a cheque dishonoured by a new branch manager who did not know of his long business relationship with the bank; managers were moved around much more frequently than before. Another man had discovered that charges were to some extent negotiable; infuriated by the sense of arbitrariness, he systematically persecuted his branch manager. The summarising discussion was under two headings, 'Work systems and the customer', and 'Policy and the customer'. The following is a fragment from 'Work systems and the customer':

> Many people, both customers and older staff, say that there has been a change in the nature of banking ... They attribute the change variously to the greatly increased number of accounts being handled, the employment of younger and less experienced staff, and changing attitudes at the top – 'In the old days the local manager used to be the person to whom a widowed lady could turn for assistance. Now they are still trying to do that, but the principal concern is with profit.'
>
> The change is seen as being [among other things] from personal to impersonal ... This dimension we find to be very much a function of the working systems.
>
> Physically, the most frequent and characteristic contact between customer and bank is at the counter in the branch. This contact in itself is briefer, colder and less personal than contact in a shop ... On the other hand, references to the Post Office were made rather often, usually by those (customers and staff) who said that the bank is getting 'more like' the Post Office. So what does 'more like' mean?
>
> In the Post Office each transaction is self-contained. The bank has the customer's 'account', i.e. a number of transactions of different kinds, related in a continuous way over time. An 'account' is an entity that develops a kind of personality of its own, more than the sum of the individual transactions, somewhat separate from the customer whom it represents, and sometimes more real to the staff than he is.
>
> There are valued accounts, dud accounts, accident-prone accounts. When

he opens an account, the customer hands over an aspect of himself. This involves both a fear of losing control of it, which is why there is concern about the stubs on chequebooks, narrative statements, returned vouchers, all of which help one to retain some control; it also involves the hope that this aspect of oneself will be looked after.

Opening an account also means that one has 'joined' the bank, i.e. one has become a member of an institution in a way in which one cannot become a member of the Post Office. (A little more could be made of the 'opening ceremony', when an account is first opened ...) Thus it is the existence of the account that makes the difference from relationship with the Post Office and coherent servicing of the account that indicates care. Friendliness at the counter is important, of course, but staff in the Post Office can be friendly too ...

Interaction between customers and staff in the branch ... is the starting-point for long sequences of highly interdependent tasks, and therefore cannot be simply determined by the personal characteristics of the front-line staff on the counter. Computerisation has led to the setting up and automatic handling of a large range of facilities for a large number of accounts. In the process there has been an enormous saving of clerical labour, much of it tedious and error-prone. On the other hand, there has been a loss of coherence and wholeness, which are derived from the relationship between the various transactions that constitute an account.

If a customer phones to say that a credit is in the post, there is no way for the system to acknowledge this fact (and the letter drawing attention to an overdraft will still arrive). If a customer writes, making several separate but related points, they may (or may not) all be dealt with, but the relationship between them will be lost, since they will require separate handling and are likely to be dealt with by different people. Again, human ledger-keepers would remember relevant items they had entered, when something new happened in relation to an account. The manager knows when an account goes overdrawn, but he does not know why, and he may react tactlessly or inappropriately. He can call up a profile of the account, but it will not tell him the trends, the reasons, or anything other than the cash facts – like a passport photograph, it gives a few visible cues but little of the reality; calling-up an enquiry on the computer can be done without any other member of staff knowing about it, so what memory staff do have of the account does not get drawn on as much as before.

In fact, staff do ... fill in some of the gaps, but ... it is not easy – customers are less real to them than they used to be, their account numbers are more relevant than their names, one no longer knows their spending habits and is therefore less likely to spot an anomaly, etc ...

What appears to have happened is this. Since computerisation ... a large wave of effort has succeeded in getting a range of facilities and services established on a systematic basis. In the process, the customer has become split. Different customer requests are associated with different relations with the bank and dealt with by different work systems. Service is understood as response to a customer need, rather than response to a customer ... The next wave of effort should be directed at putting the customer together again.

Looking back at the study of branch banking, the consultant points out that it raises some very difficult questions about how to handle a 'research phase' within an overall framework of application, and especially about the function of written reports:

> I now think that, during the study, we veered a bit too far into a research framework, as if research had been the main task. As researchers we lose out because it is unlikely that the full study can be published. As a consultant I, in particular, became so immersed in the complexity, difficulty and fascination of the analysis that I neglected to maintain and develop the relationships and institutions necessary for making use of the diagnosis afterwards. When the report was ready, I discovered that the customer service working party had been disbanded and realised that I had made an important mistake in not maintaining continuing contact with it. This left personnel division as our main client, with a considerable problem of what to do with our findings.

The bank had 3,500 branches, grouped into 80 areas and 7 regions. The personnel director invited each regional manager to send an area manager from his region to a seminar about the study and report. The regions would then be left to make their own decisions and arrangements about dissemination and follow-up. This meant that what happened in a whole region would be determined by the response of one of its area managers, but the personnel director did not feel that he had the power and authority simply to circulate the report; he was in any case concerned to strengthen the autonomy of regional management. The team know very little about what local reactions were. In one area they were invited to a number of branch managers' meetings to discuss the report, and they sometimes by accident, in subsequent years, came across some direct consequences. But:

> We're inclined to think that the study did not have much direct effect. We know for certain that it contained many more ideas and possibilities for development than have been made use of. Nevertheless, everything that happened in the next seven years was, directly or indirectly, a consequence of that study. It gave us a basis of understanding how the bank functioned, it served to demonstrate our bona fides, and it provided a springboard for a number of subsequent activities.

Activities following the study of branch banking

1. Relationship with the organisation and methods department

This department had represented the management services division on the customer service working party and therefore had an *a priori* interest in the study. The most direct as well as the most lasting consequence of the study of branch banking lay in the work of this department, with whom the team developed a continuing relationship. They took, and continued to take, the study of branch banking as a basic source document. They sent personnel division a list of over fifty points they had picked up for action and development, and a strong recommendation to distribute the report to all branches, and were very critical when this was not done. They also undertook their own branch survey project:

> We were at first a bit surprised at this, but it was essentially a process of internalising the new concepts and ways of looking at things to which they had been introduced and integrating them with their own specialist and technical knowledge. This process has continued and still goes on today. In fact it seems to have consisted of two processes going on side by side: on the one hand there has been some erosion and attrition of the concepts, and on the other hand there has been renewal and continuing learning.

The O and M group developed proposals for a fairly radical reorganisation of branch banking activity, involving the concept of town identity, the grouping of branches into networks, the concept of customer liaison officers and the separation of service tasks from routine processing tasks. This latter the researchers saw as 'erosion' of the new concepts, accompanied as it was to be by two-tier recruiting, i.e., by assuming that staff could be classified as 'career people' and 'job people'. Another form of erosion arose out of the interaction of O and M with other parts of the bank. They had branched out from the traditional narrow version of what constitutes a 'system' in the O and M sense, into considering the implications which the needs of customers and staff had for organisational change. This meant, firstly, that they ran into cultural problems and, secondly, that they ran into boundary problems *vis-à-vis* other departments in the bank, and *their* systems:

> There was a period of discouragement and depression [in that group] during which I wondered seriously whether we had caused damage: if a culture change is effected in one part of an organisation, the people in that part of the organisation become vulnerable in a much more serious way than outside consultants, who can always withdraw if their ideas are rejected.

But in the course of time these ideas did come to be accepted and new forms of branch organisation were implemented on a trial basis. It is difficult for the team to assess whether and to what extent the systems that were later implemented contained traces of the original values and concepts. It is also difficult to be clear about their parentage, since there were other contributory factors (changes being implemented by other banks, the cost of office property).

> In the minds of the O and M group, however, the ideas are still live, and expression of them can be detected in various of their activities, down to the selection of equipment. They say that the idea of 'putting the customer

together again' has been a central influence in much of their subsequent work. They continue to use the study as a source document. At the same time they say that many of the problems highlighted in our study remain unsolved.

With regard to reinforcement and renewal, two members of the research team acted as consultants to the O and M group for some time, attending meetings and running seminars. Members of the O and M group also developed an independent relationship with the university department from which two of the team had come. This involved a number of activities: training, recruitment of one of the department's graduates, a study of the computer enquiry system, and participation in subscription research.

2. Training for sub-managers

The study had revealed two problems concerning the role of sub-managers in a branch: firstly, although branch work was labour-intensive, managing staff and organising their work was seen as a fairly low-status activity. 'Real banking' was about lending, and sub-managers saw their largely administrative role only as a stepping stone. Secondly, they were in consequence not trained for it. It was decided to commission a training module for them, focussing on human relations and work organisation.

Two courses were run on a pilot basis in one area, and went well. However, although reports on the course design were very positive, it was not taken up and repeated. The team believe that this kind of training, particularly as it was designed by outsiders, presented a threat to internal training specialists.

The thirty-two sub-managers who had attended the course decided to go on working together as a group. Once a month they rented a room in a local pub, met for lunch, and worked on common problems afterwards. The consultants were twice invited (as guests) and felt that much more was probably being learned during this follow-up work than during the original, very brief, course. This follow-up institution continued in being for several years, until the original members had moved on.

3. A study of overseas branch

A presentation to the Board about the domestic branch banking study led the general manager of the bank's international division to ask for something similar. However, while in the domestic banking network the same work was replicated in each branch, the fourteen departments in the centralised overseas branch each did different work, ranging from routine clerical operations to the highly skilled buying and selling of currency and securities. It would not be possible, in a reasonably short time, to carry out detailed analysis and diagnosis of the whole operation.

The project that developed was led by the general manager (administration). Four departments were picked for an initial study, their managers and the division's personnel manager forming a project committee. The study highlighted a number of issues and led to a request for a comprehensive attitude survey.

Drafts of a questionnaire were discussed with the project committee – 'This time we were keenly aware of the need to keep this committee in being' – and with staff representatives, both groups making modifications. The administration and quantitative analysis of the questionnaire were sub-contracted to a market research organisation and on the basis of their analysis the team drafted a report.

The general manager (administration) had become very interested in the study, mainly as a result of the exploratory phase. However, his health was poor and, at about the time the draft report was ready, he died. Because he had been waiting with such interest for the findings, a copy was sent by his staff to him at his home, only about ten days before his death and he even tried to get some changes implemented at that stage.

Two senior managers (a job grade) were assigned to take over his work on a caretaker basis. They had not known about the project, and when they discovered its nature and content they were appalled. There was a series of very stormy meetings, firstly about whether to circulate a report at all and then about its contents. Eventually the Board member (the original sponsor) was drawn in. He proposed a three-tier committee structure to handle the findings: representative committees within departments, a 'middle committee' between departments for issues involving comparability, and a senior committee:

> I was asked to be a member of the senior committee, but this meant that I had no direct contact, because it didn't meet for the first two years. I was sent the minutes of the other committees. The first wave showed that staff were highly critical of the project report, and felt that it was not worth the money that had been spent. This was very painful; I knew it to be true of the highly truncated report that had eventually been agreed. After that, the attention of the committees turned to substantive issues. The committees had my name attached to them. It was very strange that a lot of people who had never heard of me were using my name as an adjective to describe a committee or an agenda.

In spite of some attempts to wind them up, the committees continued in being, largely due to the commitment of a new senior manager in overseas branch. He read the original full report, and the original one on branch banking, and saw them as an opportunity for implementing some ideas which he had had for a long time, but for which he had found no outlet:

The irony is that, even after this man in turn moved on, the committees continued in being. A new personnel director regards this institutional consultation structure as the big success story of our involvement with the bank. To us it felt as if we had had very little to do with it.

Comparing this with the effect of the study of branch banking, the consultant felt afterwards that the technically better work had had less impact than the technically less good work. In each case the result was the product of a combination of technical content and the power of the sponsor.

The final phase

After six years of the consultancy the personnel director had retired. His successor kept the relationship alive for two more years via a retaining fee but contact was slight. The main activity during this phase was the work of the implementation committees in overseas branch, and one new project.

4. Work structuring in a subsidiary bank

The bank had a small subsidiary bank affiliated to it. When the question of harmonising its computer system with that of the parent bank began to be discussed, a group of personnel and management services managers took the opportunity to consider also the whole question of the organisation and design of work:

The main thing about this project as it developed was the autonomy of the in-house group. The initiative for the kind of direction that should be taken came entirely from them, influenced in general terms by the literature on job enrichment, and as regards banking to some extent by having read our original report on branch banking. They came to us for project discussions, for advice on methodology and some training in methods of research, for occasional back-up support, and sometimes to talk through drafts of documents. But we had no direct contact with their clients.

They did a diagnostic study and then went on to implement some changes in work organisation. The main feature of these was that a small group of clerks in a branch came to look after a designated group of customers in a relatively comprehensive way, rather than carrying out separate transactions. The project aims of flexible and multi-skilled working worked out very well; aims concerning autonomous working had to be modified.

Discussion

The exploratory way in which this collaboration between a social science organisation and a client organisation began meant it would have been unreasonable, even if anyone had thought of it, to expect institutions for taking on and implementing diagnostic findings to be set up from the beginning. The consultant realised afterwards that links with the commissioning institution (the customer service working party) were essential, but might not have had the power to keep this in being when the client organisation decided to disband it. One clear finding is that a study which the social scientists believed to be of high quality, but whose sponsor either had relatively little power or did not want to exert power, had less impact than a poor-quality report whose sponsor had the power to set up institutions to handle it. Another finding is that far-reaching and problem-centred findings were difficult to use, since their implications were diffuse and would affect a number of departments, which were already aligned according to other criteria.

There must nevertheless have been a substantial amount of internalisation. In 1989, nine years after the end of the consultancy relationship, the team were once again approached by the O and M group to contribute to a further reorganisation of branch banking activities.

C. Electrical products: the role of external social scientists accompanying a work structuring programme

Background

This case describes the role of a group of external, academically based, social scientists who carried out 'accompanying research' in the framework of the German Government's subsidised programme to Humanise Life at Work.

The overall project was a very large one, to change work structures in seven plants of a large electrical manufacturing organisation. The company had decided to take part in the humanisation programme from the beginning, and the aims of its proposed project were as follows:

  to create flexible working systems in assembly, which should facilitate the optimal co-operation between people and technology;
  to create new forms of co-operation which should facilitate an optimal collaboration of all those involved in the production process;
  to design training concepts and procedures which should make it possible for workers to take on increasingly complex tasks.

The frame of reference was above all to create flexible new work systems in which technology and organisation would react together in such a way that they would be able to respond to the dynamic of technical developments as well as to short-term and long-term trends in the market for products and the labour-market. A central premise was to maintain profitability, since the position within international competition and the pressure of markets on prices would not permit neglecting economic points of view in favour of humanisation points of view.

The company's central industrial engineering department, with the help of the humanisation programme's administration, began to search for suitable scientific institutes and researchers, who might make a contribution to these aims through 'accompanying research'. This was obligatory as part of the funding conditions. Eventually, the following research groups were involved in the project as external agents:

> an engineering institute which was to improve manufacturing organisation and which, secondly, had a research group offering a contribution to the development of training and induction programmes in the framework of work-pedagogy;
>
> an ergonomics institute which was to cater for the design of the working environment and of working methods (tools, and so on) based on ergonomic principles;
>
> a sociological institute which was to investigate the processes of co-operation and interaction in the framework of conflict theory;
>
> a social science institute which was to be concerned particularly with the design of the new work structures from the point of view of their learning content and the scope they offered for learning and development.

The account of the present case is undertaken from the experiences and the point of view of this last-named institute and its researchers.

The scientists taking part in the project were relatively independent of the firm, since their work was financed 100 per cent through the humanisation programme. The firm itself had undertaken an obligation to work towards the objectives of the programme, since it had accepted a 50 per cent subsidy towards its project costs from the programme.

Within the company, the central industrial engineering department took responsibility for the project. Apart from this, the relevant staff departments within the individual plants were responsible for relationships with the social scientists working there.

Development of the project

The company defined the projects taking place in the seven different plants as having the following objectives:

> work structuring through group work (product 'loudspeaker');
> higher qualifications (training) through the process of working (product 'car radio');

job enlargement through the assembly of a whole product by a work
group (product 'car radio');

increased productivity through flexible work systems in sub-assembly
(product 'sub-assemblies for colour television set');

the development of flexible work structures in the assembly of small- and
medium-sized batches (product 'universal electrical tools');

the development of flexible work structures in mass production (product
'dishwasher');

developing models for task-oriented workshop planning (product 'chips
and diodes').

The whole project was to be accompanied by the interdisciplinary
research community, described above, in three phases:

(i)   A planning phase, in which the team developed criteria for the design
      of the new work systems, alternative plans, and processes for reach-
      ing decisions.
(ii) The phase of introducing the new work structures.
(iii) Evaluation.

The roles of the social scientists were to be different in the course of these
three phases. In the planning phase they were to take on the role of
consultants and of contributing planning alternatives; in the implementation phase, the role of 'change agent' or social-scientific helper; and in
the evaluation phase the role of classical evaluation research. This differentiation led to a number of conflicts, which created great difficulty both for
the method of working and the status of the work of the social scientists,
and which plays a substantial part in the account which follows.

Planning

At the beginning of the project the first problem for the social scientists lay
in the fact that members of the organisation wanted to have socio-technical advice about the design of work structures relatively quickly, i.e.
without a detailed prior analysis of the initial situation. They did, however,
admit that it was necessary to get to know the situation and to reach
agreement in global terms about the premises for the restructuring of work
systems.

The social scientists approached the demands of the task of consultancy
in the planning phase with very complex theoretical concepts. Knowledge
and findings from industrial sociology, social psychology, psychology and
educational psychology were scanned and tested for their applicability. It
became clear fairly quickly that there was a large gap between the
knowledge available in learning theory, socialisation theory or social

psychology, and the demands being made upon it under the heading of 'proven findings' in work science. Altogether one could say that the social scientists' naïve initial attempt to find criteria for innovative changes from theoretical social science knowledge was unrealistic and doomed to failure.

When the social scientists attempted a basic statement of their own position, they landed among the tensions created by the conflict of interest within the organisation. This can be very well illustrated by an attempt to introduce increased opportunities for participation or autonomy as an additional goal into the planning of the work. While top management found it in any case very difficult at the beginning to include this kind of objective, a particular kind of conflict also arose for the trade union representatives. On the one hand, they supported the inclusion of wider participation among the goals of the project, on the other hand, their own centralist/bureaucratic administrative culture resisted a too far-reaching devolution of opportunities for decision-making downwards.

Here was a first problem already in the planning phase: according to the rules of participative project design, both the foreman of the particular production department under discussion and a representative of the people involved were invited to the planning teams. But it turned out very quickly that these people not only felt insufficiently informed to take part in the process of design, but also were so put off by the language of the professionals taking part that after a few meetings they could not follow the proceedings any longer and left the team.

It was very clear, particularly in the first phase, how strenuously all the people taking part tried to find an adequate role in the total process. The social science researchers had two problems in particular: one was the demands that were being made on them to be consultants and the other was the question of whether they should behave in a neutral way or, in the framework of the whole co-operation, should take one group as client. The sociologists in the team tended to take up worker-oriented positions, the social psychologist tended to want a neutral role.

However, the dynamic of the team showed relatively quickly that, when the role of the social scientists was defined from outside by the groups within the company, it tended to become worker-oriented. On the one hand, there was a tendency to regard social scientists as a necessary but irritating requirement of the Government's programme, on the other hand, the elected representatives of workers were somewhat suspicious *vis-à-vis* the social scientists, since from the beginning of the project they always saw them in co-operation with senior people in the organisation. At the same time, the engineering institute was taking the lead in devising strategies for deciding between alternative forms of work organisation which had the appearance of rationality but in which the worker representatives were always disadvantaged because outnumbered.

This complex of problems during the planning phase lost some of its salience when it emerged that new work structures, with the accompanying requirement for higher training levels among the work people, brought with them demands for higher levels of payment. Both within the project teams and between the negotiating partners at national level there were long debates and negotiations on the question of whether the higher rates should be paid already at the beginning or only when the higher level of skill was actually reached. A third view became apparent during the debates about this question in the planning phase. Some members of the company, and above all those who felt particularly committed to the humanisation idea, thought that workers, too, should demonstrate that they valued the non-monetary advantages of the humanisation programme by refraining from demanding more money. Only in this way would it be possible to get away from the old orientation of payment as the central issue.

This conflict about pay was at times so tough that it became clear quite early on that this was one of the most central areas that would have to be decided at a general level in the framework of the whole humanisation programme.

Implementation

From the point of view of the social scientists, the implementation phase began with a disappointment. While the general philosophy during the planning phase had been that an interdisciplinary team should arrive at an optimal solution or new design of work structures in as rational a way as possible, it turned out at the end of the planning phase that the real decision processes were taking place behind closed doors among the management of the company.

At the beginning of the implementation phase it also emerged that, because management was not prepared to go through a systematic and comprehensive strategy for introducing the change, the work people involved did not feel that they were part of the process and did not identify with the decisions that had been taken. Already at this time unsuccessful attempts on the part of the social scientists to take part in the introduction of the changes showed that the company saw the role of the scientists only as that of external agents whose knowledge they would try to draw on and use, but whose values and potential for decision-making would be carefully excluded from the process. Whenever there was a problem, if social scientists were drawn in at all, it was as advisers to management after the decisions had been taken.

Evaluation

For this reason the social scientists concentrated strongly on their role as classical evaluation researchers. They worked out concepts for analysing documents, for interviewing workers and supervisors, for observation and the analysis of workplaces and technology, and they tried to capture the effects of the complex changes which had been made through a classical before-and-after research plan with control groups.

Apart from methodology the required interdisciplinary collaboration was a second problem area. According to the values of the scientific community, anyone who wants to make progress needs to demonstrate his own unique results, and therefore the researchers, who had been brought up in these traditions, practised strategies for defining their boundaries. Only much later did they get to know ways of proceeding which could have been used jointly with other teams to reach better results. Demarcation strategies between the different groups of researchers went so far that themes like, for example, 'stress' (in the ergonomics sense) were treated by different groups with almost the same concepts and with compatible methods completely separately. Only in one case did a social science team succeed in arriving at open collaboration with an engineer and this led to the only respectable interdisciplinary piece of work in the whole project.

Outcomes

A main purpose of the project, with its aim of restructuring a number of work systems, and which took altogether something over six years, was to collect experiences and arrive at models which would be of use for other companies in the Federal Republic. It was of course also assumed that the company itself would retain and continue to develop the new work structures. This began to happen in one of the plants already in parallel to the experimental production department that was the subject of observation. Members of the company who had gained experiences in the humanisation project tried out elements of the work structuring philosophy in a production department in another location and with which the social scientists had no contact.

Thus experience in the organisation developed under a variety of conditions, and were at first evaluated only in the experimental department. During the project there was still a central industrial engineering department. This central department systematically collected information both from the project itself and from the attempts being made in the company outside the project, and tried to disseminate it throughout the whole organisation. They also saw to it that researchers were not the only people giving lectures and presentations at congresses and other public occasions about the results of the project.

However, towards the end of the project the whole constellation of the organisation changed. The beginning of the change was seen in a tendency to dismantle the central industrial engineering department and to lessen its independent status. Together with this tendency there appeared a systematic 'cleaning up' of the newly structured production processes, in the sense that those which were economically successful were retained but those which were not so successful were dismantled. This development was accompanied by changes in the market and in technology development, so that certain products which had been subject to experimentation and change in production methods disappeared from the repertoire.

The problems of the social science group that have been described reflect in large part the problems of inexperienced researchers who entered the process with the norms of the scientific community and who came out of it with new understandings about the role of their own knowledge in organisational life. On the whole, it has to be said that the mutual learning process between social scientists and industrial practitioners turned out to be so complex, and that there were so many areas of conflict within the industrial process itself, that the success of the work structuring procedures tended to fade into the background compared with this kind of activity. This has to be said especially in view of the long duration of the project and the very high expenditure of public money for the design of new work structures in the various plants of the company.

Nevertheless, it is clear that a mass of knowledge and material has been created; this could not be taken into the process in a direct sense, since the various parties taking part were too preoccupied with coping with the process itself. Therefore the knowledge and findings will become useful and usable for future work structuring endeavours only long after the end of this project.

D. Precision engineering: work structuring in the context of broad organisational change

Background to the project

The organisation in this case was a German subsidiary of an international company, mainly manufacturing weighing machines. The origin of the project lay in the fact that the firm was converting its manufacture from mechanical weighing machines to electronic ones. This brought with it new demands on the training and qualifications of the staff. These new demands were embodied in a polarised new task structure: some of the staff would have to acquire new and higher skills, mainly in the area of planning and at an abstract/logical level. At the same time, others – mainly the women employees – would be asked to accept de-skilling kinds of work, mainly in the assembly of printed circuit boards for the electronic weighing machines.

In this situation of dramatic (and destructive) change, the management and the works council together decided on a fundamental transformation of the whole system of production and work. Some of the members of the works council were, in terms of their own jobs, members of junior and middle management (chargehands and foremen). Because of this, a very harmonious collaboration developed; all the initiators of the project shared the basic ideas, as well as a readiness to collaborate, to a high degree.

Project strategy

The aim of the management and the works council was to combine comprehensive work structuring with ergonomic measures to improve the workplace, and with focussed personnel development strategies. Consistent with the company's 'house style', all this should be carried out through the close co-operation of management and the works council, and without bringing in anyone from outside. The only influences from outside were a system for enabling people to evaluate proposed solutions for work organisation; and a psychologist who helped to design training measures. The change programme involved a principal project manager, drawn from top management, working together in steering committees with a range of sub-project managers from the various areas in which solutions were to be developed.

The main objectives of the project were first discussed at a works meeting. These were:

(i)   Comprehensive *work-structuring measures* in the form of:
       generally enlarging freedom of action and decision-making;
       changing job content (*job enlargement*) in a way that led to tasks which took six minutes being aggregated together into tasks that would achieve the assembly of a whole instrument in two hours;
       job enrichment in the sense that inspection and repair tasks were added in with assembly work; and
       planned and focussed *job rotation*, aimed at the systematic acquisition of higher skills.
(ii) Comprehensive *strategies for personnel development*, intended to include individually tailored development plans for each worker.
(iii) Improvement of *ergonomic conditions* in the work systems:
       environmental aspects (including the colour of the walls and furnishings of the workrooms) could be specified by the work groups themselves;
       the work groups would develop and take part in deciding the design of working arrangements (tables, chairs, fixtures);
       workers should be able to move about more freely, achieve vari-

ation in the type of demand being made on them, arrange their own pattern of rest pauses and develop their own forms of communicating with each other.

(iv) *Working hours* should be as flexible as possible and unusual working hours such as shift work should be avoided.

(v) *Pay* should be in the form of a flat time-based payment system without incentive schemes.

(vi) Finally, a system was introduced which was intended to motivate workers to clean up waste material: they were allowed to sell copper waste which occurred during production, and use the money for social purposes such as a works outing.

Each department met to diagnose its own situation, and developed its own solutions. General guidelines combined production-oriented and people-oriented criteria. Since each group was able to carry out measures for itself, and a system of responsible group leadership from the ranks of the employees themselves had been developed, acceptance of the scheme was very high. The employees recognised that work structuring and personnel development really did develop to their own advantage.

Because of this, and because the project had the unqualified support of both management and the works council, the aims of the project were achieved to a very high degree. These had been to adapt production successfully to the new demands of the electronic age, to increase the job satisfaction of employees and to lower the rate of labour turnover.

Conclusions: objectives and outcomes

The original objectives in these four cases were fairly broad and some progress was made towards them in all cases. In the two UK cases empirical investigations were undertaken before specific change objectives were formulated. In the transport example (A) the role of the supervisors was researched and as a result policy changes were made by senior management to improve the support given to this role. In the banking example (B) the original objective, of demonstrating an approach that could be useful, had been met. However, when it was applied in diagnostic studies in branches the results did not lead directly to integrated policy decisions. The findings were fairly widely disseminated within the bank and were used for a range of specific purposes, for example to assist in the planning of pilot studies by an O and M department, to develop sub-manager training, and so on. There may have been an impact on the longer-term strategic planning of branch banking by senior management not known to the researchers. In case C, the electrical products company, considerable changes were in any case made to introduce flexible working structures into manufacturing plants although, in some cases, these were subsequently deemed uneconomic by management and withdrawn. In precision engineering (D), a range of changes was introduced, from changing the colour of the walls to enriching jobs so that shopfloor staff took more responsibility for planning and inspecting their work. In each of these cases, as the projects progressed new objectives were negotiated but they remained within the original terms of reference. In the transport example, the social scientist moved from researching one type of supervisor to researching an entirely different type. In the bank the social scientists engaged in further work to follow up the findings of the original study, for example, to develop training, to research the use of computer systems and to investigate attitudes in the overseas branch of the bank. In the electrical products case the other objectives for the social scientists were to work out their role and methods of operation with respect to the client, the trade unions and the four other research groups in the project. In the precision engineering case there was no social scientist directly associated with the change programme and individual departments were encouraged to define their own further objectives.

In the three cases where social scientists were present (A, B and C) there are clear indications of a separation between the role of the social science practitioners and the roles of client staff as the project progressed. As client staff internalised the results of diagnostic studies and as the project neared action points so the clients took the lead and the social scientists took a back seat. In the transport example (A) this was a very clear distinction because the senior manager who commissioned the study took the consultant's report, derived action recommendations from it and piloted them through policy-making committees. The social scientist meantime was requested to engage in a further piece of research. In the bank case (B) the consultants worked with a number of groups to translate findings into action recommendations but subsequent work was done largely without them. Informally they did a good deal of advisory work; formally there was a tendency to use them further in a research role. The changes made in the electrical products case (C) were largely established and implemented by management with little direct support from the social scientists. In this particular case the social scientists were more familiar with empirical research methods than with action research and were still trying to formulate appropriate methods while these actions were taken. In all three cases, it should be noted, the social scientists were external to the client organisation.

In the precision engineering case (D) ideas were used which were current in social science, for example about job enrichment and the process of change, without a social science change agent. The action programme was planned and implemented entirely by internal staff without formal qualifications in social science.

There were indications in all these cases of some attempts being made within the client organisation to develop skills in relation to social science and to some extent to institutionalise aspects of the work done. In the transport case, for example, the consultant taught internal staff the research methods so that the ability to conduct such surveys should be available internally. In the banking study the O and M staff subsequently undertook a study similar in many respects to the original one and they employed an ergonomist in-house to undertake specific types of human factors work. In electrical products the implementation of flexible working structures was introduced in plants not involved in the humanisation project.

In the precision engineering case the change programme spread through the departments of one plant, although each followed its own path in the form and degree of change undertaken. We have no data on whether the change programme spread to other plants.

The reaction of the practitioners in the three cases involving social scientists was one of some disappointment. In each case there was considerable progress towards the intended goals and each appeared to make a lot of initial progress. However, to the practitioners it appeared that the projects never fulfilled all their promise and, while there were changes, they tended to be too little in too few places. In fact, the organisations in these three cases were large and substantial, and pervasive changes would have taken considerable resources. The disappointment of the practitioners appears to relate specifically to three issues:

(i)   *Loss of involvement.* The social scientists anticipated close working with the client through the action phases but this did not occur. As a consequence they experienced very little direct effect upon the actual changes made.

(ii) *Fragmentation.* As the projects progressed so the integrating concepts tended to be lost and different facets of action were often pursued by different people, and in an unconnected way.

(iii) *Institutionalisation.* In the view of the social scientists, not only were the findings not directly applied in many instances but only in minor ways were the more general learnings of the studies and the methods of social science institutionalised for subsequent use within the organisations. To the regret of the social scientists, it looked as if much of the learning would be lost. Although some features of the work were institutionalised, it was the loss of the rest which disappointed the social scientists.

7 Cases in technical systems development

The three cases in this chapter are all from the United Kingdom. They are all examples of social scientists making a contribution to the development and implementation of major technical change. In two of the cases the change concerned the closing of an old factory and development of a new one: case E is an account of the process which led to the opening of a new factory for the manufacture of confectionery and case F describes the development of a new factory for automated food processing. Case G is taken from the freightforwarding industry and describes the systems development process employed to introduce a major computerisation programme in a branch-based service organisation.

In all of these cases the social scientists were external consultants to the organisations making the changes, two from an independent research institute and one from a university department.

E. Confectionery: contribution to the design of a new factory

Background to the project

This project was about a contribution to the design of a new factory, from the point of view of job satisfaction and work design. The client was a family firm, manufacturing sweets and confectionery. The company had a history of solid growth, and employed some three thousand people. At the time the project began, it had four factories. In 1977 it was decided that one of these, in London, could not be adequately refurbished within the existing building and site and should be replaced by an entirely new factory elsewhere.

The personnel director had previous experience of the work of the consultant. This was an industrial sociologist who had moved from research to application, with a particular interest in work organisation. He visited the consultant to ask for a contribution to the development of the new factory in the area of work design. The way he put it was, 'We would like, for once, to get the social and psychological aspects taken care of at the design stage.' He had already, some years earlier, introduced a form of

OD to the company which was based on managers exploring their personal relationships with each other.

The consultant had some misgivings about that kind of background, but the opportunity was a unique one:

> My first thought was that here was an opportunity, for the first time in my experience, to get involved early enough. Usually questions about job design are asked too late and job design work which I had experienced myself, and of which I had read, was almost entirely re-design, within fairly narrow constraints and with limited options. Therefore, although the assignment was an interesting one, I had to make it clear that methodologically it was to me unknown territory. It would involve designing jobs for people who would not appear on the scene until much later and so was very different from improving existing jobs with the benefit of the experience and contribution of those in them.

Some design activities

A project group at Board level had been formed and when the consultant first met this group, in June 1977, a site had been acquired outside London and planning permission for the new factory obtained. At this meeting the group was beginning to discuss the choice of architects and the general shape of the building. It was clear that the prospect of an entirely new factory was acting as a focus for a powerful vein of idealism in the company. Not only did they want the jobs in the new factory to be satisfying, they wanted the architecture to be innovative and human in scale, and to make a distinct contribution to the built environment.

Two concepts for the new factory were being debated: on the one hand, the concept of a large, hangar-like structure within which there would be freedom and flexibility to arrange and rearrange things; on the other hand, the concept of a 'village street', with small production units, as well as social facilities. Within a few minutes of joining the group, the consultant was confronted with the question, 'What do you think – large hangar or village street?'

> I had, of course, no basis for an opinion, and realised that we were in a dilemma. The concept I intended to work with was that of a production process as a socio-technical system, i.e., one where the human and technical aspects are interdependent and need to be considered simultaneously, with the human aspects and needs playing a strong role. To translate this concept into practical reality, one needs to understand the manufacturing process and its technology in some detail. So within ten minutes of joining one of their meetings for the first time, I had met the major methodological difficulty in design – that of phasing. The company felt that they could not even begin to talk to architects until they had some idea of the basic shape of the building

they wanted; one could not sensibily discuss the shape of the building without some idea of the production layout; and I could not contribute to discussion about the layout from the job design point of view without a socio-technical analysis of the production process, which needed time. At that stage I had not even seen the manufacturing process.

At a second meeting the consultant worked with the project group to list job design criteria, discussing priorities among them and relating them to production criteria. The consultant had the opportunity to spend a day in the old factory looking at the production process, but when she attended the third meeting of the project group, she was still far from really understanding the details of the production system. She had learned that the first of the products to be manufactured on the new site, a mint, consisted almost entirely of crushed sugar with some additives, which was then compressed into a tablet and packaged. Instinctively, she went back to basics:

> I was groping for a more detailed understanding, and said: 'Look, I still haven't understood the process properly – suppose I'm a piece of sugar, I've just been delivered. What happens to me?' Somebody said, 'Well, the first thing that happens to you is that you get blown along a tube. But there is a physical limit to how far you can be blown.' I said, 'OK, what happens next?' And somebody said, 'Next you get crushed into a powder.'
>
> In this way I talked my way through the process in very great detail, role-playing the product. For example, I heard myself saying, 'All right, so now I'm a granule – what happens next?'
>
> 'Next, we drop mint oil on your head.'
>
> 'Might you miss?'
>
> 'Yes, we might.'
>
> 'How would that be discovered?' And so on.
>
> I checked back a number of times to ask whether this was just a game or whether it was useful, but they assured me that they were finding it very useful. The product was a fairly simple one, which they had been making for a long time, and their ways of thinking about it had become rather set. Now, these ways of thinking began to unfreeze, and they began to discover alternatives and to say to each other, 'It doesn't have to be like that, it could be like this, if such-and-such conditions are met.'

In particular, some things which had been customarily thought of in sequence could, it was found, be done in parallel. This meant that the logic of the production process was not necessarily a straight line and this, in turn, meant that one could think in terms of a short, squat building. This was the eventual shape of the 'product house' which emerged out of this process.

The consultant realised afterwards that her own strategy had instinctively been about leaving options open. Once the factory was staffed and experience of the work system beginning to accumulate, there was more chance of reviewing and revising it in a short, squat building than in one where the logic of the layout led to long, straight lines.

During these design activities and partly through the work which had been done on design criteria, it had emerged that there was a very strong value – not to say ideology – in the company, concerning autonomous work groups and team working. This emphasis was strong and, in the consultant's view, somewhat romantic, in that group working was expected to solve a wide and diffuse range of problems. She found herself putting emphasis on unaccustomed ergonomic considerations and other 'mundane' aspects of work to try to maintain some balance.

The next phase of involvement was with the management team which the company had been recruiting to develop, and later run, the new factory. A residential seminar with them included consideration of a rough model for the proposed product house. The team had invested £200 in Lego bricks and had worked very hard to produce a first tentative layout. This they presented, with the question, 'What do you think of it?' In a way that was similar to the earlier experience, it seemed unreliable to translate the arrangements of the layout by a sheer act of imagination into the work experiences that might be going on around it.

> I said, 'I'm not very good at reading drawings, I can't really think my way into this. What is actually happening down there? Suppose it's seven-thirty in the morning, what is going on?' One of them said, 'All right, I'll be a press operator.' Another said, 'We don't know if we're going to have press operators.' Gradually, they took on roles according to the tasks that needed to be done, and then someone said, 'OK, it's seven-thirty in the morning, the bell's gone and the doors are open ...' He was interrupted – 'What do you mean, bell? Are we going to have bells?' And there followed a long discussion on clocking-in. Their optimism and enthusiasm about the consequences of autonomy was unbounded, and it was I who found myself playing devil's advocate – 'Suppose a work group has a member who is persistently late? What will they do? How will they demonstrate it if there is no clock to give them the information?' The outcome of this discussion was that there should be space on a wall to install a time-clock if it turned out that the work groups themselves wanted one.
>
> By midday we had, in this way, worked our way through the start-up and first hour or so of production. In the process, a number of things in the layout were changed and it was interesting to see how difficult it was to undo even as ephemeral a decision as the arrangement of a few Lego bricks, given the hard work that had gone into their original arrangement.

A study of the old factory

Although the factory was to be new, the basic production technology would not be radically different from that in the old one. The consultant suggested that it would therefore be relevant to make a study of the work system in the old factory, once the pressure of deciding on the shape of the building was gone. Although jobs in the new factory had been offered to all staff in the old one, many knew that they would not be able to move to the new site for domestic reasons and would therefore in time be made redundant. It was very touching, therefore, to discover how ready staff were to think and work on possible improvements 'to make it better for the other girls'. The study yielded thirty-five pages of comments and suggestions. For example, at one point in the process, when the mints were finished, they came sliding down a chute at the left of an operator, and were carried from left to right along a belt, on which they were shuffled into rows, before being moved into a wrapping machine which wrapped them in rolls. The operator monitored this process, picked out any that were broken or jammed, made sure that the wrapping machine was supplied with paper and glue, and so on. There were eight of these arrangements spaced along the room, each one involving a chute, a moving belt, a wrapping machine and an operator.

In the course of the study, one of the operators developed the idea that it would be much better if the equipment was grouped together in pairs, four pairs of belts running parallel and attended by four pairs of operators, instead of eight single ones. 'I'd have a mate, opposite me', she said. 'We could talk. And we could help each other out. When I go to the toilet, I wouldn't have to switch off, because she could watch mine for a bit.' What actually happened was that, when the supervisor was not looking, operators switched the equipment off in order to visit each other, since the work was isolated, with each operator looking at the back of another operator, several yards away.

Management liked the idea, but came back some weeks later to say that it had been impossible to persuade the equipment manufacturers to make the equipment so that some ran from left to right and some from right to left, with the controls in the mirror position, as they would have to be if operators were to face each other instead of looking at each other's backs. The reason had been the cost of re-design and the special development and retooling required.

> It was, of course, no kind of technical challenge; but it was a challenge to seeing the operator and her work-role as part of the system, rather than something to be added on afterwards, and this was the difficult boundary. It was a boundary which management itself had not at that stage really crossed. I don't know with how much conviction, as an important purchaser of equipment, the request was made. I did discover, more than a year later and by accident, that the engineer who had been sent to negotiate with the manufacturers on this issue thought that he was doing so because, if the lines were grouped in pairs, it might be possible to have one operator monitoring two lines.

Three points are worth noting about this: first, that engineering training, with economic criteria as the dominant ones, is very deeply ingrained. Secondly, that even in this company, which was making a heroic effort to give greater priority to human criteria, the message had not got through to all the staff. This, I felt when I discovered it, had been to some extent my fault. My early work on values and design criteria had been with the Board-level group. When I later met the site team I missed the significance of the break in continuity. It was the same company, but it was mainly not the same set of people and there was a need, which I did not fully appreciate, to start again at the beginning. The third point to note is that the break in continuity of thinking would not even have come to light if we had not, at a later stage, done some research about the building process, unconnected with the main project.

Outcomes

The process of designing, planning and building the factory took much longer than anyone had expected. Much of the delay was due to industrial relations problems in the building industry combined with, in the company's view, the nature of the management contract with the architects and, in the architects' view, the company's insistence on choosing the builder. The consequences were bad for industrial relations since, for two-and-a-half years, the people in the old factory who were to be made redundant did not know when this would happen.

Much of the activity during this time was not connected with work design and the consultancy relationship became sporadic. The consultant was paid by the day and felt inhibited about initiating visits and work. She was therefore not present during many phases which had no overt and explicit 'human' aspects but during which decisions affecting work organisation were in fact implicitly made. During this long period the framework which regards the work system only as a social system was reinforced, and the social systems aspects of work design highly developed, while sociotechnical aspects became eroded. This was because 'Organisation Development' in the sense of concern with social systems and group relations, introduced by the personnal department, was already institutionalised in the company before the project began, while thinking about the interdependence between social systems and technology depended on input from the consultant.

Thus there was general agreement among the participants – and independent research has confirmed (Wall et al., 1986) – that, when the factory started production, the group-working aspects worked out very well. The considerable problems that were experienced were all in technical and production areas. The management team later said that, in their great enthusiasm and commitment for developing the work-group concept, they probably did not give enough attention to these other aspects. On the work design side, packers in the new factory are still sitting looking at each other's backs, as they did in the old one. The noise level is high and the principle of feedback and overlap of roles between different operations was lost in the course of the design of the building. Another idea which had been lost sight of by the time the factory opened was that of leaving options open. The consultant believes that there were several factors which contributed to this, the main one being that in the designing, planning and building of the plant, there was such a welter of things to take care of that an abstract concept like keeping options open would have had to be very strongly internalised to remain alive and be remembered, as many hundreds of decisions were taken:

> When a colleague and I later ran a seminar on socio-technical design, he spoke of 'minimum critical specification' where I had talked of 'keeping options open'. Although the audience preferred 'common-sense' terms, I can see now how such terms are easy to accept without translating them into practice whereas my colleague's phrase provided a hard principle against which practice could be measured and evaluated.

Later developments

Relationships between the company and the consultant remained friendly, and there was occasional contact. At one stage the works manager developed a pattern of sending tapes on which he discussed what had been happening, particularly during the start-up phase, and what his own experiences were. It was a kind of compromise between having a consultant and not having one. He later allowed these tapes to be used for the benefit of managers in another company undertaking a similar green-field development.

Two years after the start-up, the consultant was invited to do training in the company 'in the socio-technical methods you used with us'. It was a surprising request, and to test whether it was serious, a half-day presentation at senior level was made first, followed by a two-day appreciation course. This included a small simulation exercise, manufacturing paper aeroplanes by different methods and comparing the experience. For the production director, the experience was one which he later said made an 'indelible impression'. It came from realising how stressful a short time-cycle, with tight controls, could turn out to be. At one point, one of his aeroplanes was rejected by 'quality control'; without comment he slipped it in again and this time it passed. In great anger, he threw it at the 'inspector' and shouted, 'Now I know why there are problems between production and quality control!'

The production people in the company decided that they wanted training in socio-technical analysis and design to become part of the training for all managers. It was left to the personnel department to follow through on this decision. As far as the consultant knows, this did not happen.

One reflection about this project is that an organisation's enthusiasm for innovation may make them bring in a range of innovations which are not necessarily congruent with each other. The innovations then become part of the political dynamics of the organisation.

The project also shows some of the ambivalence which clients experience towards help, both wanting it and being afraid of such powerful needs. Thirdly, the method of payment for consultancy, and its institutional consequences, had important implications for the outcome.

F. Food processing: job design and industrial relations: a contribution to the design of a new canning plant

This project concerns a social science contribution to the design of a new high-speed canning plant. The project as it developed had two strands: one concerned plant and job design, and the other concerned industrial relations. At first these were quite distinct. Later they came, for a time, closer together. The project can, in a sense, be seen as a history of trying to bring plant and job design and industrial relations into relationship with each other.

Background

'Foods Ltd' was a subsidiary of a large multinational organisation and was engaged in processing and packaging food products. It had three factory sites. One of these (site X) was becoming uneconomic to run and had begun to make a loss. This was thought to be largely because of technically outdated and labour-intensive methods. It was decided to build a new high-speed canning plant at one of the other two sites (site Y) 30 miles away.

In the summer of 1979 a steering committee of directors of Foods Ltd was beginning to discuss plans for the new cannery with parts of its network within the parent company. On the personnel side, the parent company's employee relations adviser suggested to the personnel director of Foods that the new cannery would be an opportunity to pay attention to the design of jobs as part of a strategy to improve industrial relations, and suggested a possible social science consultant, located in an independent research institute.

The preliminaries

At a first meeting the technical director of Foods expressed a strong wish and value that jobs in the new cannery should be rewarding and satisfying, so that the people there should be happy and that industrial relations, in turn, should become more positive. On the other hand, it soon became clear that the engineering background of the Foods staff made them hope for standards and specifications for making 'good' jobs that could be taken off the shelf. They were disappointed when the consultant said that there were no ready specifications, and that the main route towards arriving at 'better' jobs would lie in the design methodology.

At one level the Foods people quickly came to accept this reasoning; but when the project was being reviewed three years later, the technical director said wryly, 'I was looking for someone to tell me what colour to paint the walls.'

The industrial relations strand of the project was dominated at the beginning by the fact that a plant was to be closed, involving the loss of several hundred jobs in an area where there was already high unemployment; and that, although a new plant was to be built, it would employ fewer than the old one, would be in a different location and few of the people at site X would benefit from the creation of the new jobs at Y.

The announcement of these plans was scheduled for November. In the meantime there was a phase of mutual education between the consultant and the management. For example, in a seminar the consultant described simulation and the testing of alternatives as a way of arriving at design decisions in a new situation where there was no operating experience to draw on. There was some discussion about whether models or larger physical simulations might be practicable, as transitional systems, a means for trying out ideas. Although it would involve costs, the costs it might eventually save were likely to be greater. Later, as time went on and people became busier, the sheer time and trouble required to build a model came to appear increasingly burdensome.

The Foods project engineer internalised very rapidly the job design concepts and methodologies. He and the consultant visited another canning company where considerable efforts in the direction of job enrichment and autonomous work groups had been made. The purpose of the visit was for him to learn about these developments and for the consultant to begin to learn about canning technology. The consultant could not, at that stage, be introduced to canning within Foods itself, because 'the Plan' had not yet been made public.

In advance of the public announcement about the closure of X and the proposal to build at Y, company staff had prepared a strategy which, consistent with the company's culture of 'tough' and 'adversarial' industrial relations, consisted of anticipating every possible response and move that might be made by the trade union side and preparing clear-cut moves and steps and statements for every eventuality, at the same time linking these to a timetable.

When the consultant saw the strategy document:

> I discovered that there was no mention of the nature and quality of jobs in the Plan, its announcement or in the strategy. This surprised me greatly in view of the importance for industrial relations that the technical director, as well as his colleagues, had seemed to be attaching to these ideas. It seems likely, with hindsight, that it is here that the seeds of eventual relative failure should have been recognised: after this, job design considerations always had to be inserted against the combined weight of timetable, cost estimates, trade union preoccupations and suspicions, and company culture and politics. Seen in this light, it is perhaps a miracle that anything happened at all!

The initial trade union response to the announcement was not as strong as had been feared – there was no strike – but it was, predictably, preoccupied with the fate and the terms and conditions affecting the people working at X. Thus once the Plan was announced, there was for a long time no opportunity to raise another new topic, that of job design.

Three trade unions were involved in the company: a general union to represent the process operators, an engineering union, and one for the supervisors and junior managers. As it developed after the announcement, the trade union position showed some differences between the approaches of the three: broadly speaking the engineers, whose members would be in the least unfavourable position in the X labour-market, were mainly concerned with obtaining the best possible terms for their members who might become redundant; the supervisors' union concentrated on the number of jobs which might become available for their members at Y; and the general union concentrated on trying to prevent the closure from happening.

This meant that, for several months, they refused to negotiate with the company about anything at all, and it therefore also meant that it was not possible to do any exploratory work in the X cannery, or to talk with them about the design of jobs in the new plant. Discussing jobs in the new plant would have implied accepting that the old plant was going to close.

The waiting period

There then began a protracted waiting period during which the main activity was discussing strategy. The choice seemed to be between having the consultant work secretly in a back-room capacity with the engineers, or waiting until the problem with the general union should be resolved so that she could work openly with the trade unions.

The steering committee's sub-group on personnel matters, of which she became a member, unanimously thought that she should wait until she could work openly. Three years later, some members of that sub-group thought that this had been a mistake – 'If you had been prepared to swallow that principle and work as a management toady, (a) you would have had more influence, and (b) we would have ended up with a management group that understood the concepts better.'

The consultant says:

> In the light of what happened later I can understand that conclusion. However, faced with the same dilemma and without knowledge of what happened later, it is inevitable that I would make the same choice again.

Discussing strategy was, of course, not the only activity during the waiting period. Some other developments were as follows.

1. The project team was getting on with making decisions about suppliers of equipment and with developing a layout for the cannery. The consultant was not involved but the project engineer, who had taken on board concepts such as the value of roles overlapping and people collaborating for a perceptible end product, was a member of the steering committee sub-group as well as the project team and this influenced the layout. He also produced a list of technical constraints in preparation for job design activities and began to experiment with role descriptions, writing a tentative job description for one key operator in terms of the experiences involved as well as the tasks to be performed.

2. The steering committee was getting on with its work. Sometimes they asked themselves, 'What would the consultant think?', and made correct guesses. The use of a ghost seemed a useful device in the process of internalisation.

3. In May the project engineer was transferred out of the company in a career development move. In the logic of the cannery project, this signalled the transition from basic design to more operational concerns. In the logic of the job design project, however, it was a great loss of continuity of development. The project engineer had become the in-house 'holder' of the concepts. In spite of later efforts, there was never again anyone in-house who was identified with holding the knowhow and concern for job design. The works manager of the Y site now moved into the project in an active role, heading the future operational team.

4. The parent company's management services subsidiary began to be involved. The engineering project team resisted for a time, but when it came to an operational level the works manager came to use the consultancy input on a wide range of personnel matters:

> The frame of reference of this consultancy was about minimum cost running. The language, however, turned out to be about behavioural science concepts, organisation development, managerial style, etc. When the opportunity arose, much later, to discuss this, it was claimed that the aim was to harmonise the two sets of values. But using the language of one set of

values for the tools and concepts of another is not the same as harmonising them!

5. Some of these strands came together and surfaced in a somewhat bizarre episode. The parent company's consultants had developed a layout proposal which was different from that of the in-house project team and there developed a debate about the relative merits of the two layouts. It clearly had both realistic components about the characteristics of the two layouts, and political components about the source from which they came.

The consultant was invited to a meeting and asked to decide between the two layouts:

> When I think about it, this episode still contains for me an element of craziness. My experience of canning at that stage consisted of one half-day visit to a cannery and a total of perhaps five or six hours looking at drawings … I have often wondered since then what would have happened if I had met the company's expectations and confidently selected a layout. I would dearly like to know if it would have been implemented.

The consultant offered a method for deciding between the layouts, if job design considerations were to be the deciding factor. This involved giving priority ratings to a number of job design criteria, and then scoring each of the layouts on each criterion. The method turned out, however, to be vulnerable to partisanship where the sample was small, and it did not reveal a clear advantage either way. What it did reveal was that both layouts gave cause for concern and the consultant suggested that one criterion for selecting between them should be which one was more susceptible to upgrading.

Management began to form the view that their consultant was not decisive enough.

6. In May there appeared to be an opportunity to break the deadlock. There was a small line in the existing factory at Y, making a product for which the market appeared to be growing. A second line was to be built and the personnel director proposed that it should serve as a training exercise in job design. This would give the company practical experience of this approach on a small scale, and also did not have any redundancy implications. However, the market situation changed and the second line was not built.

The full-frontal phase

By July the tension surrounding the timing of the project was great. In some ways, i.e. as regards basic design and equipment purchasing, it was rapidly becoming too late; in other ways, i.e. as regards collaboration with the union, it was still too early. The personnel director decided to cut the

Gordian knot and proposed 'going full frontal'. A timetable for an announcement was worked out, involving letters to the full-time trade union officials, meetings with the X and Y department heads, meetings with middle management in both factories and three meetings with trade unions (one with each of the unions but jointly between the two factories). The general union did not accept the invitation but all the other meetings took place at the beginning of September.

With the agreement of those who had taken part, the consultant prepared a 'First Progress Report on a Job Design Activity at Foods Ltd.' This was circulated to all who had been invited, including those who had not come. It began by reiterating why such an activity was felt to be necessary:

> Traditional ways of designing plant involve two processes:
>
> (a) engineers concentrate on obtaining the most reliable equipment and production methods, which to many engineers means those methods which leave least to human intervention. They work to criteria about output, quality, costs, etc., and they want variances to be controlled automatically where possible. The only area where they are required to pay explicit attention to human criteria is that of safety.
>
> (b) at the same time, trade unions attempt to protect the interests of their members in terms of the numbers to be employed, their grades, pay, conditions, etc.
>
> In these processes, neither party has traditionally paid much attention to the content and meaning of the jobs that are being created and yet both know that work is a very important part of people's lives.

The report went on to summarise what had happened at the meetings, including doubts that had been expressed about the genuineness of management's intention. It ended by saying that the consultant would be available for a week in each of the two factories to see anyone willing to discuss these matters further. The consultant recollects:

> During the first part of my stay at Y I heard nothing from the general union's convener. But on the last day (Friday) I received messages indirectly, to say that she intended to talk to me. Since she was working on the afternoon shift and would not be on site until 2.00pm I arranged to take a later train back to London than I'd planned. She didn't come and when I realised this I, in turn, sent her a message: it was that I had interests, too, and that if I had known she didn't intend to come I would have caught the earlier train as I was going out that evening. On getting this message she came, and we had a long conversation.

That conversation contained two threads: one was that this was a management whom one could not trust, any co-operation was likely to be abused; the other was that impoverished jobs were indeed a problem, some short-cycle repetitive packing jobs in the existing plant were so dreadful that some of her members were clinically depressed; it would be wonderful if something could be done about this.

In a second progress report the consultant proposed that a Y cannery job design committee should be set up. The works manager announced that the company accepted the recommendation and invited the three trade union groups to do the same, and to nominate two representatives each. They accepted.

The job design committee and the job design steering group

The Y job design committee functioned for about eight months.

> It may be an obvious point, but one could not involve the actual operators who would be working in the plant, because they did not exist yet. At least there was a representative system.

At the same time, there was set up a superordinate monitoring and holding institution, the job design steering group. This included the parent company's employee relations adviser, the Foods Ltd technical and personnel directors and the works managers from site Y and the company's third factory. The consultant proposed some overlap, such as observers from the job design committee to the steering group. There was no objection to this, although later events prevented it from being implemented:

> Although its life was short, the job design steering group was possibly the most strategically important of the institutions that were created in the course of the project. For a short time at least, there was an institutionalised, systematic and policy-level means for planning, deciding and reviewing the activities connected with job design.

At the first meeting of the job design committee the general union representatives spoke openly about the difficulty of making a contribution, since they were new to canning and were not engineers. The engineering and supervisory union groups wanted to talk about the number of jobs that would be created in the cannery rather than the quality of the jobs, and there was much argument on the lines of 'We can't talk about job content until we know numbers and structure', 'We can't talk about numbers and structure until we know job content.' A pattern emerged in which meetings dominated by 'numbers and structure' alternated with meetings in which work was done on job content issues. For example:

1. The job design committee did the exercise of putting job design criteria in order of priority. They selected one which showed both high priority and high consensus – 'being able to influence one's own pace of work' – to explore with the engineers. Going through the layout sys-

	Method	Capital cost	Labour cost	Job design aspect
1	1-m sleeve on m/c	Nil	1 person	20-second cycle
2	3-m sleeve on m/c	Low	1 person	60-second cycle
3	carousel	High	1 person	12-minute cycle

Figure 4   *Comparative analysis of work methods*

tematically from the point of view of pacing revealed that, at the stage where lids were put on the cans, an operator would be locked into a 20-second job cycle. Alternative methods were explored, and were compared systematically on capital costs, labour costs, and job design aspects, as shown in Figure 4.

At some capital cost an arrangement leading to a 12-minute cycle was selected and installed.

2.   Two control systems engineers were involved in the planning of the cannery. They became interested in the ideas of job design, and one of them made a presentation to the committee:

> This showed up a problem which dogs this subject and which is not sufficiently highlighted in the literature. He said that at that stage the control systems could still be designed in almost any way the committee wanted. He liked the idea of working as a service to the operators who would later be doing the jobs. But once the floors were laid, with channels for the cables, it would be very difficult to change. The representatives, at that stage, did not have enough knowledge of the process to be able to be very specific about what they needed.

However, some useful meetings took place between the representatives and the control systems engineers about the design of visual display terminals, the placing of mimic panels, and so on.

3.   To help the learning process, the representatives asked for some job design work in the existing plant. Preliminary work was done but by the next meeting the committee was in its other, negative mode: there was no point, nothing could be improved without big investment which would never be sanctioned, and so on. Later, whenever the suggestion for a trial run or work on other jobs in the plant came up again, senior management always pointed to this experience as grounds for not agreeing. They also did not agree to the construction of a model of the cannery as an aid in developing work roles.

4.   A series of visits to other organisations was planned, and one took place.

5. A residential training course was planned for the committee. Before it took place, members of the committee filled in a job satisfaction questionnaire, about their own work experiences. It was planned to analyse and feed this material back as part of continuation and follow-up afterwards.

The course appeared to go very well. However, on the last day, as the application of the learning to the plans for the cannery became more and more specific, difficulties began to emerge. At the end, the general union's representatives said that they were withdrawing from the project.

The final phase

There was a good deal of on-going business to keep the committee going, even in the temporary (it was hoped) absence of one of the unions. The consultant was to be away for a month and the works manager wanted to keep the committee and a number of planned activities going. The personnel director thought that the union might be willing to accept help, in confidence, with whatever problems it was experiencing with the job design activity and the consultant wrote to the convener offering such help and saying that she would be in touch on her return from abroad.

When she got back none of the planned activities had taken place. The personnel director had not conveyed his idea of separate consultancy for the union to the works manager who, when he heard about it, refused his consent.

> I could have insisted on keeping my promise to the convener but what would have been the consequences if I had deliberately undermined the works manager's authority in this way? It was hard to understand why none of the things we had arranged had taken place. It may be that I was being 'punished' for going away.

(She did not see the convener again until the official opening of the cannery, a year later. As a result of that meeting the convener said, 'All right – have another go and we'll co-operate.' But that time the management did not agree.)

The consultant thought that the project was dead and was surprised when at the end of the year the personnel director contacted her about continuing work. She said that, if work was to start again, a formal review should take place. This was done and considerable agreement reached about the nature of the issues. The review revealed that changes in the external economic climate had led to some shifts in priorities. Nevertheless, a plan of action was agreed consisting of eight items including, for example, dealing with 'unfinished business' at Y, reviewing what institutions the consultant should routinely take part in, planning training and development for in-house people, planning a continuous audit of the jobs as they developed when commissioning got under way, and so on.

None of these things happened. The main obstacle in this phase appears to have been the time pressures of the stage which the cannery development had reached (it was due to be commissioned within months) and the associated negotiations.

Reviewing the whole experience, the consultant reflected:

> There was an almost aesthetic quality about the industrial relations symmetry.
>
> Each side was able, always with good reason, to point to the intransigence of the other as a reason for not making any changes itself. What is particularly striking about this symmetry is the timing: those moments when one side was temporarily locked into the most negative aspects of its stance freed the other to express the most positive aspects of its own, without any real risk of change.
>
> Both sides did have a genuine wish for change but, when one considers the system as a whole, the need for equilibrium was clearly greater.
>
> I wrote this in a report to them. As an Appendix I wrote a little fable about industrial relations as Cinderella, caught between the two ugly sisters, Mangie Mingie Annie and Terrible Trudy, who are building themselves a new castle in a country called Northofwatfordgap.
>
> I said in my report that I thought the project had had very little effect, and that was the only part that made them angry. They say that the organisation of work in the cannery is very different from what it would have been without the project. I don't know, I can't judge.
>
> Oh, and they said that access for maintenance would have been designed better it we'd had a model!
>
> There's a kind of postscript. When I approached the company for agreement to publish an account, it turned out that all the members of management who had been involved had moved on, to other posts in the parent organisation. That might help to explain some of the things that were so puzzling: if a post of this kind is transitory, that would affect the amount of engagement one invests in the problems of a particular site.

G. Freight import and export: human sciences contribution to the development of a computer-based freightforwarding system

The client in this case was a freightforwarding company importing and exporting freight from branches in most large cities in the United Kingdom. It had successfully operated a computer system for accounting for many years and wished to extend computer use to the operations side of the business. As a result of previous work with social scientists, some members of the company recognised that major computer developments might have important human and organisational ramifications. They therefore sought the help of a university research group which specialised in research and application in the human implications of computer technology. The members of that group who became consultants in this project had backgrounds in occupational psychology and ergonomics.

An initial survey of the freightforwarding company

The consultants conducted a short 'getting to know you' survey at two branches and the headquarters. They concluded that there was immense potential for the application of computer technology in the branches. Typically a consignment involved the completion of many different complex forms (for the sender, the shipper, the customs, insurance, and the recipient as well as the freightforwarding company). In addition, individual consignments were usually consolidated with loads travelling to the same destination which led to further loading lists, and so on. Many of these forms contained identical information recreated each time by the freightforwarding clerk. One major possibility, therefore, was to hold all the information about a consignment on a computer file and use it to generate automatically the variety of paperwork.

There were also possibilities for using computers to support management decisions. One of the problems for the organisation was that the branches operated with little knowledge on one another, with the result that uneconomic part-loads were often sent to the same destination at the same time by different branches. A better flow of information between branches might make it possible for branches to cut costs by consolidating loads travelling to the same destination.

The initial survey suggested not only that the business could benefit from further use of computers, but also that it had a variety of human and organisational problems to overcome if such a venture was to be successful. Within the branches visited there were very different forms of work organisation. In one branch the staff were organised according to routes so that, for example, one clerk did all the Irish business, and another the Scandinavian business. In another branch the orientation was towards a functional form of organisation with some staff doing the typing, others receiving enquiries, others handling accounts, and so on. Computer systems tended to have implications for work organisation and might produce pressures for a standardisation of work organisation across branches. Another organisational implication was the effect which setting up systems to consolidate loads between branches would have on the autonomy of branches. Such systems tend to centralise decision-making. Underlying these examples was a general issue: computer systems tended to promote formalisation and standardisation in an organisation. This organisation appeared to be an 'organismic' one which grew, contracted and changed, involved considerable local autonomy and variability and, at any point of time, was likely to be characterised by overlapping and unclear roles for senior staff. It seemed quite likely that, without careful handling, the formality of a major computer system might clash with the fundamental character of the organisation.

These views were presented to the Board with the recommendation that a senior and broadly based computer steering committee (CSC) be established to ensure management control of the computer developments. This was accepted and the consultants were asked to join the CSC.

Systems development plans

A data processing (DP) manager was appointed from the parent company of the freightforwarding organisation and was asked to prepare plans for a computer system to support the operations of the branches. He presented his proposal to the CSC and it referred the proposal to the consultants, although they had not had the opportunity to meet the DP manager. The essence of the proposal was as follows: each branch would have a number of terminals connecting it on-line with the computer centre of the parent company, which would upgrade its computer equipment to cope with the new load. The operations to be performed by the systems were not specified, but the number of terminals per branch was calculated on the basis of the volume of transactions conducted by each branch. The proposal listed the equipment needed for the complete system and recommended purchase from a well-known manufacturer.

The consultants read the proposal with dismay. The document was a proposal for a specific technical system and there was no evidence that its organisational ramifications were understood. There was insufficient information about the functions of the system to be able to predict task consequences, but some consequences were evident. The specification of a limited number of terminals for each branch, for example, meant difficult job design decisions. Either the terminals would have to be shared between staff or, more likely, a functional form of work organisation would become standard across the branches with a small number of specialist terminal operators in each branch. The provision of equipment was based upon current volumes of work in the branches. The history of the company was of sudden expansions, contractions and changes in branch business and it was not clear how well the technical system could cope with these sudden changes.

The consultants' reaction was as follows:

> Underlying our concern was the proposed systems development strategy. This was an example of what we called 'technically driven, one-shot implementation'. It proposed as an initial step the purchase and installation of the computer hardware and a subsequent development of the software. It

was clear that any organisational issues would have to be resolved by accommodating the organisation to the technical system rather than by any modification in the technical system. In our view the proposal had all the hallmarks of the traditional systems design process which starts from the technology and works outwards. If system design proceeded in this way we would be left with the problem we normally encountered, of trying to help organisations cope with the consequences of a technological *fait accompli*. We had very little time to decide how to respond. The proposal was due to be discussed by the Board in a few days and we were invited to present our views to the meeting. Whilst we had no desire to begin the collaboration by precipitating a confrontation we felt we had no choice. One of us attended the meeting with the intention of challenging the assumptions underpinning the systems development strategy. We decided we must also be constructive so we also prepared an outline alternative approach.

The Board decided not to accept the DP manager's proposal but asked him to work with the consultants to formulate a proposal based upon an evolutionary strategy suggested by them. The DP manager accepted this brief. His views of proceedings were as follows:

> I was not happy with what happened at the time. I did not agree with a lot of comments that were made, mainly on the technical side: I felt they were not backed up by a detailed knowledge of the practical DP environment. Looking back on it now and knowing how the alternative plan worked, I thoroughly agree with the change of strategy. The change actually gave me an important opportunity. I had been brought up in a heavily disciplined mainframe environment and this was the first opportunity I had had to look across the whole DP market. I don't think I did it very thoroughly first time; I simply went back to what I knew. I knew the manufacturer I had in mind had a proven record and in a company that had very little experience of DP it seemed a safe course to go with them.

An alternative strategy

The DP manager worked with the consultants to develop an alternative strategy which was an evolutionary and learning strategy. The basic premise was that members of the organisation needed to decide for themselves what kind of system would suit their needs and that they needed time and opportunities to learn in order to take informed decisions. The strategy therefore had three strands which would be undertaken simultaneously:

(i) *Director seminars.* To initiate the learning process, a series of seminars was arranged for directors to examine possible computer developments and their organisational implications.

(ii)   *A pilot system.*   As a further learning opportunity, it was planned to introduce a small-scale pilot system into one branch which would give the company experience on which to base its main development decisions.

(iii) *The main development.*   While the company prepared itself to decide on the main systems development, a survey would be undertaken of potential suppliers.

It was planned that this strategy would be the responsibility of the CSC, consisting of two directors, the DP manager and the consultants and that the pilot development would have a local steering committee, with local users and the DP staff, reporting to the main one. At a later stage an additional user committee was formed to include users in other parts of the company. The company was partly unionised and regular consultations with union representatives were undertaken as the programme developed.

The company accepted and implemented this strategy. Apart from any other justification it meant that the purchase of a large system could be delayed for a considerable time. There was a query about the pilot system. Since this was not intended as a prototype system but would be phased out, one of the directors argued that they were being asked for 'throw-away money'. The concept was accepted on the grounds that it was actually 'learning money' that was being spent.

The director seminars proceeded through a series of evening meetings and ended with a weekend conference. The consultants arranged for a number of experts in different fields to present their various perspectives on organisational implications of technical change. One of the themes to emerge was that the company needed to take a collective view of its future business strategy because a major computer system might tend to tie the organisation to a particular way of working. The directors, who met rarely and were used to making short-term decisions and changing direction at short notice, found this difficult to do. The consultants therefore followed the seminars with a one-day meeting on management issues and a director interview programme. Each director was interviewed on future directions for the company and the results were compiled as an uninterpreted report for the directors to debate in closed session. This activity tended to develop a purpose of its own: it supported Board policy-making but its links to the computerisation programme became tenuous.

One of the consultants commented on this process:

> The overall strategy we had agreed with the company was that a consideration of business needs and organisation would precede decisions about the main computer system and this process certainly brought into focus the organisational issues. It was a very useful outcome to the director seminars programme. However, it developed a life of its own and I suspect in most

people's minds the connection with the computer development programme was lost. The greater clarity of organisational purpose which resulted certainly helped the process of determining the type of computer system required, but the main gains from this exercise were primarily in helping a Board more accustomed to resolving specific operational issues to stop and review its business strategy.

The pilot system was established in one branch and was used as the basis for preparing documentation for freight on many of the routes handled by the branch. The consultants worked together with the DP manager (who now had a staff of two) on the specification and implementation of the system but the programming was undertaken by the suppliers. There was some role confusion, and there were many people trying to work in a very small branch and this led to the DP manager asking the consultants to leave. In subsequent discussions the company suggested that the consultants should limit their work to contributions to the CSC set up to oversee the main development and should not become involved in detailed operational work. The consultants rejected these ideas and withdrew from the project because they felt that they could not assist the individual and organisational learning from this limited, strategic role.

The consultants' view of the situation at this stage was as follows:

In our view the next stage was to demonstrate the pilot system to the directors and the staff of the other branches and to share with them the lessons to be learned from experience with it. They would then be helped to relate this learning to their own activities within the organisation and come to conclusions about the kind of system they wanted. Our main anxiety was that the pilot system would settle into a steady state and would not be used as an experimental vehicle to test different ways of working, that the lessons would not be disseminated to the rest of the organisation and that the staff of other branches would not therefore be able to join in the debate about the new system. We saw our primary role as being to facilitate each of these processes. We did not welcome the idea that we restrict ourselves to membership of the CSC although that was a powerful position. We were afraid that we would be able to do very little from this role to maximise the use of the pilot system. We were also anxious that the organisation did not have the expertise to collect and disseminate the data, and to use it to full advantage in involving other members of staff in the systems specification. We saw ourselves sitting in on committee meetings without access to data about the branches and how they worked, and therefore unable to give informed advice. Finally we felt we would have great difficulty giving advice which the organisation would have the ability to carry through without help. In short we were afraid we would be cast in a critical and obstructive role when we wanted to play a constructive role. We decided to decline the offer and to withdraw from the consultancy arrangement and the formal funded collaboration ended at this point.

One of the consultants, however, proposed another way of continuing the collaboration:

> I proposed to the company that they collaborate with the university in a postgraduate student project by allowing a student to study the progress of the pilot study. This was viewed as a non-threatening opportunity and was accepted. The student worked in the branch for a year with me acting as academic supervisor.

The brief of the student was to describe the branch as a socio-technical system and to document and analyse the way the staff of the branch assimilated the new computer system. If deemed appropriate, she could also play a more interventionist role and help the organisation with any problem it encountered. Her work included the following.

1. *A socio-technical analysis of the branch* which showed it to be an organisation very open to an environment of customers, hauliers, shippers, overseas agents and Customs and Excise, and so on. One effect of this was that it was very difficult to detect a stable pattern in the way clerks undertook their tasks. One implication of this analysis was that any computer system that embodied within it assumptions about the sequence in which tasks would be performed would be difficult for clerks to operate. This was indeed found to be the case in the pilot study.

2. *A diary of system usage* was kept which produced a picture of an organisation slowly but progressively adjusting to the new potential it had available and changing its internal strategies and organisation to exploit the potential better.

3. *A study of changes in job structures.* The branch did not engage in formal experimentation with the system, but in practice it tried a number of alternatives at a number of levels which were logged as part of the evaluation. The clerks in one room, for example, experimented with the location of a shared terminal. They tried it on one of the clerks' desks but it was not easily accessible to others. They tried it on a spare desk but this involved carrying files and documents to the desk. Finally they tried mounting it on a tea trolley which could be moved from desk to desk, an arrangement which was more successful although the tea trolley had some deficiencies as a work station!

4. *An analysis of inter-branch co-operation.* The computer system was extended to provide a service to two neighbouring branches in order to test what degree of co-operation might result and to give other branches experience in using the system. The student was involved in the implementation of the system in these branches and recorded their experiences. The main problem was that the system could only provide a partial service and, once they became familiar with it, the branches wanted a full-scale service. The system permitted the branches to collaborate in consolidating loads,

but this did not occur to any greater extent than previously. The possibility of doing so did lead to a greater debate within the company about the effects of this kind of link on branch autonomy.

5.   Some direct contributions were also invited from the student. One request was to assess the degree of utilisation of terminals to help make judgements about the number of terminals required. This study showed a direct clash between task requirements, where an action with a deadline of a few minutes might be required, and the need to minimise the number of terminals by maximising their utilisation. In another example the student applied work-station design principles to help design work stations for the branches. She also began work on a user training manual.

The outputs from this work were regularly reviewed by the DP manager, the student and the consultant in the role of student supervisor. These sessions provided an opportunity to summarise what was being learned from the pilot study and also for the DP manager to discuss what was happening more broadly in the main systems development.

The DP manager commented about this phase of the work:

> I found the work of the student most helpful in showing what was happening in the branch and it was useful to have her undertake small-scale studies for me. The meetings were valuable because they gave me a chance to report what we had been doing and to discuss the issues that had come up with somebody independent of the company. I learned a lot in the process. All this of course went on, as far as most of the company was concerned, after the collaboration with the university had ended.

The main development occurred without much direct input from the consultants, although one of them continued to make help available in the role of student supervisor. Following the shortlisting of suppliers, the DP manager organised visits to see the pilot system and demonstrated the system via a portable terminal when visiting other branches. A user committee was established which used the experience of the pilot system to specify the main development (an 800-page document).

Conclusions and outcomes

The consultant evaluated the project as follows:

> I would see our main contribution as being to develop an understanding of the organisational implications of computer systems within the company and to change the system development methods from technology-oriented to user-oriented. Outcomes therefore would be expected not in the effects of the system but in the effects of the system design methods.
>
>   The system design method used changed substantially. It became a process in which the organisation tried something out and reviewed it before

going further. The DP manager started with one strategy, switched to a new and more exploratory one and was co-ordinating it himself without the aid of consultants by the time the supplier had been chosen. There was some evidence that some of the structures necessary to undertake systems design in this way, e.g. the computer steering committee and the computer users' committee, were becoming institutionalised.

At the level of knowledge gain there was widespread influence which is difficult to evaluate. The director seminars gave them new insights into the future with computing technology. They did not collectively use this to specify what kind of systems they wanted within their organisation: rather they allowed ideas for sophisticated co-ordinated systems which had profound organisational ramifications to drop by the wayside. The system chosen concentrated on providing procedurual support within branches rather than facilitating the consolidation of loads. It therefore allowed the company to adopt modern technology without putting the management style of the company at risk.

Conclusions: objectives and outcomes

In these cases, rather than attempting to create a climate for change the objectives of the social scientists were to influence the shape of a change that was already in train. Thus, the three cases all led to the implementation of new working systems: two new factories, for confectionery and for processed food products, and a computerised system for freight-forwarding. In all of these cases there were quite considerable changes but they were largely achieved because there was a strong economic and technical impetus for change.

The specific object of the social science intervention in each of these cases was to achieve socio-technical change in circumstances where, previously, design had been dominated by technical and economic imperatives. It is important to note that, in each situation, the social scientists did not presume to know the form the socio-technical system should take; they had no ready-made solutions. Although there were broad job design and organisational design criteria which they could employ, it was necessary for these to be interpreted according to the local needs of the organisation and its members. This implies diagnostic work and the participation of those who would be affected by the change or their representatives in addition to detailed design work with the design teams. There are then a series of outcomes one would hope to see:

(i) Did those who were going to be affected get involved in the design process and were they able to work on the socio-technical options that were available?

(ii) Did the design team embrace the socio-technical topics in general and the specific inputs of the employees in particular?

(iii) Did the system that was introduced embody social science principles?
(iv) Was the resulting work system effective in meeting organisational and individual needs?

Working backwards through these questions we are unable fully to address (iv), because it was beyond the time-scale of the studies. However, in case E an evaluation study by an independent research group suggests the answer is a fairly clear-cut 'yes', though the input to the work system evaluated came only partly from the consultant. There were indications in all cases that the work system that resulted embodied social science concepts. In case F the factory, for example, contained jobs with more autonomy, longer task cycles, more focussed on teams, than might have been. Since these are 'green-field' situations 'what might have been' if other design concepts had held sway is the only comparison. The confectionery factory was designed almost completely for the operation of autonomous work groups. There were no supervisors. In case G, the freightforwarding system was to be used in many different branches and was designed to allow for alternative forms of manning in order to give freedom to the operator to undertake tasks in a variety of ways. This was in contrast to an earlier pilot system which assumed a particular job structure and fixed the sequence of activities by which many tasks were undertaken. This pilot system was similar to the overall system originally intended which, if implemented, would not have permitted alternative forms of manning in different branches.

Despite these outcomes, the social science practitioners in each case felt that the systems designed were pale reflections of what could have been achieved. The job design solutions, for example, were often fragmentary and limited to particular jobs, leaving other jobs unconsidered in terms of job design criteria. The social scientists felt they had been unable to influence the design in any comprehensive or systematic way. Indeed, in case E the systematic achievement of the autonomous work-group structure in the confectionery factory was to some extent achieved despite the social scientist. There was a very strong desire among the management of the company to adopt this structure and this ensured its implementation, although the social scientist thought that it singled out one aspect of work, and one part of the system, in too ideological a way.

The reasons why there was only partial adoption may be traced to the answers to the first two outcome questions. In all cases there was some effort to involve those who would be influenced by the change. But in the 'green-field' situations the factories were being built a considerable distance from those they replaced and transfer of labour was unlikely. Therefore, those with knowledge to contribute might be losing their jobs and those who were to work in the new jobs had not been appointed. In the food processing case there was additionally a very new technology. In the absence of direct experience of it, and without a transitional system (a model) as the focus of job design work, preoccupations that were more familiar than job design continually pushed to fill the vacuum. In the confectionery case staff were recruited specifically on the basis that they were people who wanted to work in groups. In the freightforwarding case small groups of employees at head office and in one branch were involved but involvement did not extend to the other branches until considerably later in the design process.

Much of the time in these cases was devoted to working with members of the design or project teams and there were a number of instances of designers who declared they had made major changes in their approach to design and who were able to take into account a wider array of human and organisational issues. However, these designers were few in number, only found it possible to handle these issues in relation to some decisions, and in one case moved away.

This account leaves out an important kind of indirect outcome. As a result of being involved in this process the designers, managers and other members of staff were to varying degrees exposed to social science thinking. For some people, for example the chief designer in the freightforwarding case, this led to a major change in approach to design problems which had a pervasive effect on his subsequent design work. To some degree, though not in a major way, some of the processes involved in design became institutionalised in the organisation. For example, in the freightforwarding case, the concept of using a pilot system as a vehicle for learning what was needed from a computer system became an accepted part of design thinking.

In conclusion, these were cases where the initial objectives remained reasonably stable within the broader objective of making a major technical change. There was evidence of social science influence but it was less sharply defined and pervasive than the social scientists had anticipated. This was largely a result of other forces that influenced the outcome. The social scientists tended to be disappointed with the outcome to some degree but can take comfort in the evidence that a more lasting outcome may have been the effects of the process upon people in key roles and the possible institutionalisation of new design thinking.

8 Cases in behavioural change/problem-solving for specific groups

The common factor in the four cases presented in this chapter is that the social scientist was working in an organisation with a group of people who were grappling with a problem of great significance to them. In case H from the oil industry in the United Kingdom, in-house practitioners worked with the marketing department to help them redefine their marketing roles and their policies in the light of the redefined roles. The other three cases are all from the motor industry, although they involve very different groups and problems. Case I is from a UK motor components company which was in severe financial difficulties. In this case the social scientists worked with groups of staff, who initially saw themselves in conflict, to determine and agree new organisational structures and policies which might enable the organisation to survive. Case J reflects the use of 'guest workers' in the West German motor industry and describes the development of 'learning shops' to enable them to learn the language and practices of the industry. Case K starts with the shock of a strike in a West German motor manufacturing firm and describes the development of workshops for supervisors in leadership and interpersonal behaviour.

In the oil example and the two West German cases the practitioners were internal OD specialists. In case I, a firm of commercial consultants provided an OD specialist to support the motor components company.

H. Oil: the organisation of marketing

Background to the project

This project arose within the corporate marketing department of a large multinational organisation. The marketing department provided a co-ordination centre for world-wide marketing in the thousand companies that comprised the multinational. A central team of staff liaised with five regional marketing groups whose briefs took in world sectors and who, in turn, liaised with the operating companies in their sectors.

The manager of the central team, the marketing head, had undertaken a review of the future role of marketing. This had, in part, been triggered off by a manpower-planning exercise which had shown a concentration of staff who would be retiring in the next decade. This led to questions about whether their replacements should be staff of similar or different skills and thence to questions about whether their roles would change. Initially the marketing head asked his subordinates to prepare papers on the future of marketing, but he found that each person adopted a different view based upon his specialist function. Realising that he needed assistance, the marketing head consulted his personnel manager who consulted the headquarters OD team.

The multinational had a history of using OD specialists. For many years it had run courses on OD for managers and each of the major operating companies had an OD team. The climate for OD work within the company was therefore based on considerable, widespread exposure to it and may therefore have been more favourable than in most large organisations.

Initial involvement of the OD team

The standard approach of the OD team was to 'get on the bus where the client is', i.e. to understand the client's perception of the problem and related issues, before offering any proposals. To this end the team made a content analysis of the review papers provided by the marketing head's subordinates. They concluded that each person was writing from the partial perspective of his own specialism and had a tendency to jump rapidly to organisational solutions before engaging in a thorough diagnosis.

Another standard feature of the team's approach was to reflect back to the client the conclusions they reached. When this was done, two major conclusions were drawn. One was that there was a need for a data collection exercise which would make a more thorough diagnosis of the present situation and would be undertaken by the OD team. The other was that the marketing staff did not operate much as a team and had little understanding of one another. To this end the marketing head established another goal for the project, which was to develop teamwork and to create some 'synergy' in the group.

The OD team interviewed the marketing head's immediate staff. It emerged that morale in the organisation was fairly low and in the view of many there was a history of poor management. There was also consider-able scepticism about the OD enquiry.

The results were fed back to the marketing head and his immediate subordinates and the OD team proposed that the marketing staff should be involved in the establishment of the new role. The debate that followed was difficult because many issues had been brought out into the open which had hitherto been hidden.

The proposal put forward a model for obtaining consensus within marketing for a role and organisation suitable for a period roughly ten years hence. It envisaged group planning exercises involving marketing staff, the first two of which would occur in parallel. One of these was to examine the current organisation, its roles, and the tasks it undertook. The other was to examine relevant trends and events, in order to establish future scenarios which would indicate the roles required in the future. Out of this would come the information to enable further group discussions to formulate the strategies and specific roles required to fulfil the overall future role. Subsequently these conclusions would need checking out with a wider range of marketing staff before the specific mechanisms for moving from the current organisation to the future organisation could be established and implemented. The OD team envisaged this as a process to determine the future role and organisation but they did not see it as a one-off procedure. They recognised that there would be a continual need for the marketing team to review and revise their role as the years passed, and their overall objective was to see this kind of process established as a regular part of the management.

After considerable debate the marketing staff accepted the proposal and the implications for their own time in being involved in it. It was accepted on the basis that the OD team felt it would work and, given the failure of other approaches, it was worth a try. The OD staff were therefore under pressure to show that it could work. There was a strong element of scepticism, which persisted for a long time.

As the senior OD adviser recalled:

> We would walk into meetings, as I have never done before, without the slightest idea of what the outcomes would be. We were being challenged the whole way along. It did improve generally but there were always one or two critical people. But all of it was stressful – how much should we defend what we were doing? We had to believe in it and keep it in sight the whole time and stick with it. Once it was launched, they said, 'We are taking you on trust, we will try it and see whether it works.' It was really quite frightening because we invented the process; it wasn't tried and trusted.

The role definition exercise

The exercise involved twenty-three staff from the central and regional marketing groups. For the initial activities two groups were formed with representatives from each part of marketing. The group studying the current role devised a questionnaire with the help of the OD team. It went to nearly everyone in marketing and asked about major tasks and roles. As a result it identified twenty-six main tasks and eight major roles. The second group operated by holding brainstorming sessions in which they identified likely trends and events. They engaged in a massive information search, consulted external bodies and produced comprehensive data sheets. At the end of these exercises the two groups met together in a whole-day meeting in which they presented conclusions to one another. This was to ensure that the whole group felt that they owned both sets of conclusions. They then divided into three sub-groups, each with the same task: to examine each of the eight roles (and twenty-six tasks) identified by Group 1 against the implications of the most likely future identified by Group 2, and to identify how these roles might need to change. The work was undertaken during a two-day event and ended with a meeting at which all conclusions were presented. A high level of agreement was found.

The OD staff acted as process consultants throughout these group exercises and concentrated upon the process by which the task was being carried out. The overall model for the role definition exercise was used as the central plan, and one necessary role throughout the group work was to remind members where they were in the task. There was a continual tendency to move beyond the brief of the particular group and enter the next stage. After a while group members recognised this tendency and specifically asked the process consultants to remind them when they stepped out of line. Another way of leaving the brief in the first round of group work was a tendency to move into the territory of the other group. The process consultants also worked on the 'task process' within each group, drawing attention to the task plan adopted by each group and progress made towards it. There was also some work to be done on the interpersonal dynamics within each group but the emphasis was upon the task.

The senior OD adviser recalled:

> Everyone was going through a great learning process. I'm not saying there wasn't a lot of scepticism from some of the people as the process went on; certainly there was a lot of debate at the beginning. They kept saying, 'There are specialists on the future, they are experts, let them tell us.' But our thesis was that they were the managers of the future and they needed to go through the learning process. By the end they felt it was very useful and they learned a lot.

The process remained a tense, anxiety-provoking one for the OD staff, since they were always uncertain of how each phase would go and always felt 'on trial' as the custodians of the model about which there was still scepticism.

'Testing out' and management change

The next stage was to test the conclusions in relevant parts of the organisation and there was a lengthy period in which marketing staff used opportunities in regular meetings and conferences to make presentations and collect feedback. The OD staff did not have a specific role to play in this diffuse activity and the momentum towards change was to some extent lost. During this period another event occurred which threatened the momentum of the project. The marketing head was promoted to another role but, on advice from the OD adviser, the managing director took a personal interest in the project until a new marketing head was in a position, following detailed briefing, to assume control of it.

Once the checking-out process had been completed, the question of how to move to the new organisation could be tackled. The full team met in a residential setting and divided into three groups, each with the same task, to define what was needed for the new role and how to get there. After presentation and discussion of group conclusions there remained two alternatives and these were developed and tested by the staff in their central marketing roles. Subsequently there was a gradual move in the direction of the new role with management operating more as a team. The OD contribution continued in the design of information systems to support the new structure, but there was little direct involvement in the main implementation. In the perception of the senior OD adviser this stage of the process was tenser than other stages. One of the reasons was that they were no longer dealing with future abstractions but were dealing with what would become of their own jobs, their own interests and their own ambitions. It became more apparent at this stage that the central and regional staff had different roles which gave them different perspectives. Whereas the previous exercises enabled them to work jointly on a common problem, this one was in the 'here and now' and had to be approached from the existing role of each participant. Fortunately, the experience of working together through the previous phases meant they had developed an ability to see issues from the other's point of view, which served them in the work. In particular, the insights the central staff had obtained into the point of view from the regions and vice versa had been a valuable investment.

Outcomes

The outcomes from this project were at many levels and some were more direct than others. In listing them we begin with those that were about central and explicit objectives and then move to the more implicit and indirect 'spin-offs'.

1.   The widely shared objective for this project within the client group was to achieve a redefinition of the central marketing role and to plan steps towards its achievement. The model provided by the OD staff was followed throughout the eighteen months of the project and, as a result, a new form of organisation was adopted. At this level the project achieved what it set out to achieve.

2.   While the role redefinition exercise had a ten-year horizon, it was widely recognised that in a rapidly changing world there would be a continuing need to review periodically the conclusions reached and perhaps change the role again. One of the ambitions of the OD team was that the process by which the management team deliberated the need for a role change should become an integral part of the management process in marketing. This ambition was shared by the original marketing head.

In practice this did not occur. The marketing management, while they worked much more as a team, saw the role-redefinition exercise as a one-off activity and concentrated subsequently upon specific implementation activities. In the view of the senior OD adviser this was at least partially due to the change in marketing heads. The new marketing head had a very different style from the previous one, and to operate an open-ended exercise of this kind would have been unnatural to him. The senior OD adviser felt that the new marketing head was particularly suited to the final phase of the project, the determination of the new form of organisation, but he would have been unhappy with the earlier phases. Indeed, she wondered if the project would have taken place at all if the complete cycle had been under the control of the new marketing head.

3.   An explicit aim of the project was to undertake team-building in an environment in which management did not operate as a team. The team exercises certainly acted to build teamwork which subsequently carried over into normal management practice. The whole process not only assisted the central marketing staff to operate as a team but also fostered a better understanding between central and regional staff.

4.   An important and explicit aim was that managers should be able to consider future events and trends, learn from this experience and identify the implications for their personal futures as managers in marketing. It was a rich learning experience at the time and provided a valuable investment for the future.

5.   The review of the existing organisation conducted in the first phase proved useful in its own right. It was the first time the organisation had attempted a systematic self-analysis and the summary of roles and tasks was used on a number of occasions later as a database about the department.

6.   Engagement in the exercise had a material effect on the development of staff. One example concerned a member of the marketing staff who the marketing head felt had potential but who lacked experience of the management of people. The marketing head discussed this problem with the senior OD adviser who suggested giving him a leading role to play in part of the role-definition exercise. The manager subsequently became a major force in the exercise and, in time, joined one of the operating companies in a senior position. He also became a major source of strength to the OD team in the operating company.

7. The 'role for marketing' study provided the marketing head with data he could bring to the attention of senior management, with the result that marketing moved into a more influential position. Consequently support was gained for further studies in the marketing department, for example about their relationship with an advertising agency, an examination of their business information needs, and a further exercise on their management process.

8. While the process of role review which had been developed in this work was not directly or immediately institutionalised in marketing, there were later movements towards it in other parts of the company. The OD team made some presentations of the process in an effort to make it more visible. One of the senior OD advisers thought the process could be valuable for building a proper bridge between planning staff and various management teams. OD made some presentations to very senior managers in the organisation, to business planning, personnel planning and organisational planning. Two of the managers who had been through the exercises took part in the presentations. The new marketing head came to the senior management presentation and was very supportive.

The meeting was a success, and there were subsequent developments, but the senior OD adviser found it difficult to draw a direct link:

> I hoped it might stimulate one or two people and get them to think about going that way. It certainly made them think: in fact some things are happening now. I'm sure they are not attributable to our meetings but a guide has been written on the integration of business planning and resource planning and I played a part in the description of the process element in it. The people in planning were a bit threatened by this and one of them said to me, 'You are doing the job we should be doing, building the bridge.' But I am now engaged in a separate exercise with planning. The whole planning cycle is also being reviewed by the company and they are bringing in some of the things I have diagnosed many times as gaps in our system. I'm working on this exericse. Basically I've used the learning from the marketing study whenever the opportunity presented itself.

This case exemplifies the advantage of an in-house resource being in place when the need arises. It also demonstrates the processes of internalising and converting into use rather than the direct application of findings. The strategy was not so much the adaptation of a general approach to a particular situation as one of asking what a particular situation needed in the framework of the general approach. The uncertainty and creativity associated with this approach had a cost in the anxiety it generated for the practitioners.

I. Motor components: payment systems as a factor in modifying organisation structure

Background to the project

The client in this case was a large organisation on one site which supplied components to the motor trade. At its peak in 1977 it employed 2,500 staff, organised into three production units engaged in light engineering work, typically small-batch production but with some assembly-line operations. The basic system of pay was individual piecework but the system had developed many anomalies, creating friction between employees on similar grades. During the 1970s the industrial relations climate had deteriorated until in 1977 there were fifty official strikes as well as many unofficial stoppages. This, together with the recession in the car industry during the 1970s, began to affect demand for the company's products. Management had made various efforts to modify the payment system but recommendations could not be implemented as disorder had spread throughout the whole organisation.

The parent company of this organisation decided to engage as consultants a large commercial management consultancy firm. This consultancy had a behavioural science unit, manned by senior social scientists, most of whom had a wide range of industrial experience. After some years of practical experience in applying social science they had reached a conclusion about the kind of application which could be undertaken with some chance of success. The main requirement was that it should be large scale, in the sense that the change should pervade a large social system. The reason for this requirement was that projects undertaken on a small scale are often thwarted or limited by the action of related parts of the social system and there are severe limitations to the degree of generalisation of results in the parent organisation. Therefore, wherever possible, the behavioural science unit preferred to start with the larger social system as its client, and to work towards change in the whole system.

Although aiming for large-scale change, the unit did not expect an initial contract which specified a large-scale project in terms of resources or time-scale. Rather, they established with the client a regular review (for example three-monthly) which established the budget and plan for the next phase. While working in detail from phase to phase, the unit sought recognition on the part of the client that the commitment to the project was long term and expensive in terms both of consultant fees and the resources required within the client organisation.

The unit also had a specific way in which it liked to work with clients. It provided one consultant who would have the client as his main responsibility, and who would spend a considerable part of each working week on the client's premises. The consultant would aim to remain with the client throughout the life of the project and would get the client to provide most of the resources internally to do the work. Where this was not possible, other consultants would be commissioned to do specific pieces of work. Not using the prime consultants for other work ensured that there was no confusion about the role of the consultant. The main consultant was supported by one of his colleagues in the back-home organisation, who was available for a small amount of time to advise and support the consultant as well as some members of the client organisation.

The preliminaries

The consultants were first invited to make a brief overall study, in the course of which the plight of the site became obvious. When the consultants talked to the shop stewards on the site the stewards made an interesting offer. They said that if the management wished to discuss wages they should do this in the normal way; put it on the table and negotiate. However, if management were willing to engage in a full study of the problems of the whole site, the unions would be willing to co-operate for as long as it took. It had become obvious that, if radical steps were not taken, the run-down of the site would continue and all the jobs there would be in jeopardy.

As a result of this initiative by the trade unions, the management engaged the consultants with the broad aim of trying to find a new way forward for the site. The consultants began to work on the basis of the following framework:

(i) They had to look for a strategy by which the staff on the site could collectively begin to plan a change. The consultants were therefore not seeking a particular organisational solution, but acting as catalysts in the process of change. All employees would need to play a part.

(ii) The consultants' procedures would have to be participative and open to all parties. As a result of the poor industrial relations climate the site consisted of many different groups with entrenched, hostile attitudes towards one another. In an atmosphere of mistrust there was very little communication. The consultants had to find ways of bringing these groups into a common, problem-solving endeavour.

(iii) While the payment system was obviously a major source of problems, there were many others and it was important that the process should take these on board.

An initial attitude survey

The resident consultant began by conducting an attitude survey which focussed on the pay system but took account of other issues people wished to report. The survey involved interviewing about 20 per cent of the workforce. Its aims were twofold: to allow all the interested groups to express their views and problems, and to get the consultant known and accepted on the site. The data from the survey were not reported formally, but fed back through a series of meetings in which the consultant presented his findings tabulated by rank and grade across the site to show the distinctive viewpoints of each group. The consultant concentrated on simply feeding the problems back and did not attempt to make interpetations or seek solutions. At the end of each presentation he offered a way forward, which was to convene a number of groups, based on grades, to consider the problems in much greater detail. The employees gave their support to this approach and, as a result, management was prepared to fund the next stage.

The consultant's comments about this stage were:

> It was a very significant step. I would certainly follow a similar strategic approach in a similar situation. It was vital that we get from them a commitment to proceed. The intention was to say, 'These are the problems; they are not management's or mine, they are everyone's; what shall we do about them?' They could have said, 'Thank you very much, that's nice but we don't wish to continue' and the study would have ended there, but they showed the commitment to form the groups and continue the work.

The consultant's team leader commented about the contractual aspects of seeking commitment in this way:

> After the initial sell, rather than persuading the client that there is something to be done and costing it, we have been in the position of working there on site on their problem and at each stage it has really been the workforce saying, 'It's a good idea, let's go ahead.' It's only with that backing that management have been prepared to pay some more. This was not articulated as a formal policy but it has been the strength of the project.

The first group sessions

The groups met about once a fortnight and initially were always convened and led by the consultant. The commitment of staff time to this endeavour was not questioned, except by a few managers who complained about losing their staff. The consultant's aim was to get each group to talk openly about core problems and, when it became apparent that different groups had similar problems, to bring the groups together. In this way he hoped to move away from a group perspective towards a perspective in which people were working on shared site problems.

At the end of this period he held another round of feedback meetings in which the core problems were identified, and suggested moving from grade-oriented groups to problem-centred groups. Again there was a commitment to proceed and the process began to develop its own momentum, allowing the consultant to move away from the leadership 'driving' role and into a facilitating role.

The consultant's team leader commented about this phase that:

> It was dominated by discussions about pay although the earlier interviews had revealed many other problems. But pay and pay differentials were where the head was and what the fighting was about. It would not have been possible to get them onto broader issues until they got the pay problems out into the open. Basically this period was beginning to draw the fire from the pay issue.

The second group sessions

In the next phase five working parties were established to look at the main problems of the site. For example, groups were set up to examine piece-work, timework, and clerical staff/management payment systems. This time the groups were deliberately mixed: staff, pieceworkers, timeworkers and management. The shop stewards decided that the union representatives would be a different set of people from those normally involved in pay negotiations and management reciprocated by not sending their negotiators.

As the process moved nearer to the proposing of solutions, the consultants became concerned about the possibility of leading group members into a 'blind alley' in which their recommendations were not acceptable to management. To lessen this danger, a number of management planning groups were also established, again led by the consultant and composed of the various staff and management experts on the topics being considered by the work groups. The management planning groups met and worked one step ahead of the working groups.

Some of the groups made rapid progress with their topics, while others found them fairly intractable. The consultant did not adopt a pure facilitating role; where he felt that there was a technical input he could make, he did so. As a result the working groups began to converge on some recommendations for solving some of the central problems of the site.

This point was reached about eighteen months after the consultant had started work, and his team leader felt considerable progress was being made in changing the climate at the site:

> There were some real glimmers that something was beginning to happen; a change of attitude was occurring. One illustration was the attitude of the stewards to the working groups. It had become almost a tradition that there is a strike when the annual pay rise is being negotiated; you could almost book your holiday for strike week. This year, too, there was a ritual strike but

the stewards in the working groups were told to continue attending meetings during this period.

He also commented on a more general change:

> The level of strikes had dropped by about 50 per cent after eighteen months and has continued to fall. It is difficult to claim that the programme is causing this improvement in industrial relations, but the two processes have certainly occurred in parallel.

The recommendations booklet

At this stage, while the consultants were pleased with the progress within the groups, they were concerned about a number of broader issues on the site at large.

The consultant explained:

> We (and others on the site) began to think we were not making much impact on the people outside the groups. The stewards tended not to report back to the others anything that was progress or good because, over the years, the only thing that you involved anybody in was problems. There were no mechanisms for communicating anything positive and we were never really successful in solving this problem. We put out regular consultant progress bulletins but that was really only scratching the surface.

There were also signs of greater hostility and opposition among those who did know what was going on. The consultant again:

> Some members of management were getting quite nervous at this stage because major things on the site that they had developed and managed were now being questioned. Similarly, there was a small minority in the unions who were beginning to mount a vigorous opposition.   They were mainly the people who had been involved in the major strikes of the 1970s, who suddenly saw a threat to the system with which they were comfortable and which they were able to manipulate.

As the recommendations began to take shape, therefore, the consultants found that management were not immediately prepared to commit themselves to the proposals. Although they were prepared to accept them in principle, they wanted to be sure that they were acceptable to the work-force as a whole. It was felt necessary to present them to the workforce, not as management's proposals, but as the recommendations of the programme.

To answer these needs the recommendations were sent to the entire work-force at the site in a specially prepared brochure which made clear that the proposals came from the consultant's programme and not from the management. The aim was to explain the recommendations and to ask the workforce to give their backing in principle (though not in detail) in a special vote organised within a few days of the distribution of the booklet.

The proposals included a new organisation structure in which the site would become six semi-autonomous manufacturing units served by a central services unit. The pay system would be changed in line with the organisational structure, so that an overall output bonus for each unit would be paid. The pieceworkers would be paid a much higher base rate to give higher guaranteed earnings and timeworkers would be paid, as a result of a job-evaluation exercise, on 7 grades instead of 123.

The recommendations presented in the booklet had emerged from the discussion groups but there is the question of what role the consultant had played in their development:

> I would say the basic recommendation about units came from us but it was so readily accepted that it got adopted very quickly and taken from us and developed. The seed came from us and I would not want to pretend otherwise.

His senior colleague elaborated on this point:

> Because of the nature of the working groups and the position of some of them in a lot of areas, the one thing we have not done is to take the pure facilitator role. Where technical inputs are obviously sensible we had no reluctance whatsoever to put them into the group. They had the option of either running with them or rejecting them.

Employees had a fortnight to consider the recommendations, during which time there developed a major recession in the motor trade. The vote, however, gave overwhelming support (95 per cent) to the proposals and management agreed to fund further work on the proposals.

The implementation phase

The implementation process involved detailed working on the new organisation and the introduction of the unit structure, changes in the pay systems and physical workplace changes. The aim was to establish local participative action groups based on the unit structure to decide the local form the implementation would take.

The consultant was attempting to achieve three broad aims through these activities:

(i)   To move the process so that it was management-led with the consultants as less of a driving force.
(ii) To play less of a leadership role himself in the groups and to move into a process consultant/facilitator role.
(iii) To ensure that, along with the specific changes recommended in the

booklet, the new structures would also embody as normal working practice the participative process which had generated the proposals. However, as the consultant noted, other forces intervened:

> At this stage events did rather overtake us and, although the process continued, it was slower than anticipated and the way it was accomplished was not quite as intended.

A major recession hit the motor trade at about the same time as the vote was being taken. It led to short-time working and a major shift in the industrial relations climate. A more militant convener replaced one who had been sympathetic to the change process; discussion groups were difficult to arrange and some of the topics, notably the pay system, came to be dealt with in negotiations rather than in problem-solving groups. The consultant could play no direct part in this.

Also, because of the cut-back in work volume, management sought to implement the unit structure and physical layout changes as a matter of urgency. This again cut across the change process the consultant had envisaged. He commented:

> The recommendations were picked up and led by management, as we had hoped. What was implemented was close to the original proposals. But the process was not participative. It was management saying, 'This is the way it's going to be'; but it did not seem to be a problem. It was what people had already agreed to and, on this site, there has never been any trouble about reorganisation anyway. For most people this is regarded as management's prerogative.

The consultant, however, found an important role in organising team-building exercises as the unit structure put members of staff into new and unfamiliar role relations. These exercises consisted of taking groups of employees who would be working together away from the site for a weekend session in which they were asked to look at their goals in the new structure, to identify their 'core mission' and then to work on agreeing the roles each of them would play, as well as the procedures that would operate in the new structure. The consultant ran the first few sessions and then helped to train the personnel manager who took the work over.

This case was put in the category concerned with behavioural change and problem-solving for specific groups, because the history of conflict in the organisation meant the consultant had to devote a great deal of attention to specific group work. However, the broad base on which the project was created, including the nature of the funding, meant the infrastructure was in place when findings had to be disseminated and the whole site engaged in the process. It is noteworthy also that, despite the intensive attempt to create a culture change at the site, the implementation phase showed signs of the re-emergence of the adversarial style of management/union relations. It is a project undertaken from a commercial base but does not appear to demonstrate great intrinsic differences from the way the work might have been carried out from any other kind of base, except that there was a clear expectation on the part of the client that it would take substantial resources.

J. Motor industry (guest workers): the 'learning shop' model

Background to the project

The project took place in a company manufacturing motor cars. During the boom years of 1968–73 the proportion of foreign workers employed on car assembly had risen to about 90 per cent. This led to severe problems of communication and, because of this, to problems of product quality: there had developed a sharp rise in labour turnover and absenteeism rates; supervisors were overloaded and under stress; the training and induction of the operators were poor; and consequently reject and re-work rates were going up. Moreover, a growing emotional and social distance between German supervisors and their foreign subordinates, as well as between different groups of foreign workers, became apparent.

It was decided that the key to solving these problems had to lie in improving the language skills of the foreign operators. Visiting general language courses had turned out to be costly and unsuccessful: most of the students failed in language laboratories, and the foreign workers found institutions like polytechnics or language schools too strange. The drop-out rate from outside courses was up to 80 per cent.

So, the idea of an in-house educational process was born which, in addition to teaching the language, should convey the necessary technical terms and also contribute to the social integration of the staff. This teaching should take place as near as possible to the workplace, so that the links between what was being learned and the practical aspects of its use in the work would become clear. Thus the model of a 'learning shop', situated near the workplace, quickly developed into a more comprehensive aid to working and to the integration of the various groups on the factory floor.

The initiator of the new training method was a member of the central personnel department who had a background of industrial and commercial training, but who had been given responsibility for the general integration of foreign employees in the company. He had come across the model of the so-called learning shop at a conference and had asked the designer of this method, who ran an independent consultancy institute, to introduce the concept to the senior management of the company.

The programme

Management decided to apply the model in the company. The man who had introduced the idea was to work together with the external consultants who had developed it. The initial task of the learning shop was the creation of learning materials specific to the needs of foreign workers in car plants. The language taught was therefore dominated by the vocabulary used on the shop-floor and the means of making requests, giving and receiving orders, and so on, needed for day-to-day work. Learning materials were created in concrete and practical forms which did not rely on language, for example large drawings were used of the objects found in the factory. An important part of the model was that the leaders of the learning shops, the 'language masters' were to be the foremen, chargehands and colleagues of the foreign workers. These were trained to prepare the learning materials and to run the workshop. The intention was that the learning shop would not just be a language-skills-development opportunity but a means for developing shared understanding, team-work and co-operation amongst all the workers in the car plant.

This approach to language learning proved very effective in speeding the integration of foreign workers into car plants. Within a few years the model had spread through the company and had become a central instrument for integrating new workers at shopfloor level. As the model spread it was also developed further. It was used, for example, not only to help foreign workers with immediate work problems but also to help them cope with other day-to-day difficulties of living in another country, such as completing income-tax forms, dealing with the foreign departments of the police force, and acquiring somewhere to live.

The broadening of the learning shop concept also led away from language teaching. German production workers frequently complained that, while foreign workers were being helped, little was being done to help them with solving their problems. Moves were therefore made to make the learning shops a general service to the shopfloor. The concept was that workers of all kinds should be able to gather together to share common problems and experiences and to find better ways of coping with the problems. The ethos was one of self-learning rather than referring all problems up the hierarchy to management. As the concept spread it became quite normal for learning shops to be formed spontaneously, with minimal notification of management or the office of the learning shop programme.

After a period of successful work, the man who had initiated the learning shop concept moved to a different plant in the company, in order to undertake the introduction of the learning shop model there. This new location was in a rural area, and the workers there were mostly German, so that language teaching moved more and more into the background. In this case the learning groups in the learning shop developed into teams which worked on organisational problems and conflicts under the professional guidance of 'communication aides' (moderators or facilitators).

The introduction of the learning shop model in the new plant was preceded by a comprehensive diagnosis of the current situation using qualitative interviews with individuals and groups. As a result the learning shops were able to work on the problems and difficulties specific to the plant which, set in a rural area, had many German workers with a farming background and no experience of working in an industrial plant.

Although after a period learning shops did become established in the new plant, implementation proved much more difficult than in the original plant. Part of the difficulty lay with the blue-collar workers who did not find it easy to express their personal problems in the public arena of a learning shop. Another difficulty lay with management, especially junior levels of management, who found it difficult to accept the way the learning shop focussed on the self-organisation of workers at the lowest level of the hierarchy. Not all managers became convinced about the learning shop concept and, making a virtue of necessity, the introduction of the concept was restricted to areas which were the responsibility of more open managers.

When the initiator of the learning shop concept at the central plant moved to the rural plant, a new manager took over the programme. Conditions in the industry had changed and stronger forms of managerial control were being advocated. In the face of criticism of the *ad-hoc* and unconventional ways in which learning shops were often run, the new manager did not succeed in sustaining the programme and after one year it faded and the manager was moved to new work. However, a year later the company was again confronted with the problem of integrating foreign workers into its central location and the sub-division of personnel responsible for 'Projects and special events' was successful in reviving the learning shop concept.

Principal problems in the introduction of the model

The learning shop concept was very successful in the initial phase in the central location but ran into difficulties when attempts were made to transfer it elsewhere. The initial impetus at the central location was also lost when its chief advocator moved elsewhere.

The main difficulties in both situations were that some influential members of supervision and management had reservations about the unconventional method of work in the learning shops. It did not fit into the general hierarchy that education activities were being provided for those at the lowest level of the organisation. Moreover, the staff who were carrying out the training did not always 'go through channels', i.e., they sometimes made decisions in an *ad-hoc* way without getting agreement, and in general had a more unconventional way of going about things than was the custom in the organisation. The movement of the learning shop concept away from its language-teaching origins also served to dilute the strong and agreed purpose, so that managers exposed to the later forms of learning shop saw it more as an alternative and rival way of managing.

K. Motor industry (supervision): a programme of organisational and personal development

Historical background

This case concerns a company in the German motor industry. It employed about 31,000 people, of whom 24,000 were blue-collar workers, about two-thirds of them foreign. The proportion of foreign workers was greatest at the most junior, unskilled levels. Works committee representatives, on the other hand, were mostly German, drawn from the ranks of skilled workers.

In the summer of 1973 there was a series of unofficial strikes about wage levels in the metalworking industries in Germany. In this company a strike of any kind was a very rare event; but this 'wildcat' one was additionally fuelled by the fact that 500 Turkish workers had been dismissed for overstaying their summer leave. There were demonstrations by strikers and counterdemonstrations by non-strikers, including supervisors, and a fight in which the police were drawn in.

The role and position of supervisors

Events during and after the strike led to the position of supervisors being considerably discredited among the workforce, especially among the foreign workers. Quite apart from this, the role of supervision was in a state of crisis.

The motor industry has always been open to, and often in the vanguard of, technical developments. During the 1950s assembly lines were being superseded by transfer lines as the central technology, accompanied by electronic data processing throughout all functions. In the 1970s, moves towards total automation were being made. Before discussing the effect of this on supervisors, some theoretical categories need to be put forward.

The logic of the production process requires a great deal of planning, and the more rigid production facilities are, and the more costly it is to improvise and make changes, the more urgent is the requirement to behave according to the plans. On the other hand, the logic of satisfying the market requires flexibility. High-cost automated technology would require ever-longer production runs and more homogeneous production models, and this negates the logic of the market. Computer-based methods of production planning can compensate for this. But, while they lead to a better overview of the situation, they at the same time lead to increasingly centralised production management and reduce the freedom to initiate adjustments at local level.

Thus production management means organising production in a way which harmonises the logic of production and the logic of the market. But there is also a third element, related to discipline, i.e., to defining the norms of human behaviour and ensuring that they are kept. Norms of this kind, however, are necessary but not sufficient conditions. They need to be supplemented by willing and autonomous collaboration, i.e., by conscious, constructive co-operation. Thus there is a norm principle and a co-operation principle. In modern industrial organisations there seems to be a division of labour in the hierarchy, whereby some functions tend to represent the one and some the other.

In a rationalised undertaking with functional organisation the role of the supervisor is very limited. He is at the receiving end of preordained plans and standards from both line and staff functions, with very limited autonomy. He has to think up further improvements, i.e., extend rationalisation ever further. In relation to the discipline function, he used to represent both the norm principle and the co-operation principle and could decide the relations between them in particular circumstances. In modern industry with functional organisation, he has a very limited role in setting norms; he merely communicates them to his subordinates. Staff departments decide about recruitment and dismissals, about the level at which someone fits into pay grades, and about work study. Although he still plays a part in these functions, it is with less power than before. In addition, where there is a high level of automation he has less of a technical expert role than before.

On the other hand, where there is conflict between the demands of norms and of co-operation, there are new tasks for the supervisor in obtaining co-operation, both among his subordinates and between them and others in the organisation. He is responsible for smooth everyday running in terms of relations on the shopfloor and has a key role in seeing that work is fairly distributed, so that people can 'make their money' and get all-round experience, and in facilitating the introduction of new technical developments. Research has shown that supervisors relate to these changes in a pragmatic way gradually, and item by item, and do not make theoretical connections or see them in a wider frame of reference. Both they and their superiors rely on supervisors' experience, with little or no psychological training for leadership. With its reference to the past, the emphasis on experience is likely to lead to rigidity. This can only be counteracted by a problem-orientation, i.e. the orientation to analyse a situation critically and systematically and test it for improvement potential. Research shows such problem-orientation to be missing.

OD activities in the company

The plant under discussion was headed up by a management team of ten, one of whom was responsible for industrial relations. The industrial relations function included a number of departments, one of which was responsible for training and one for quality circles. The head of the training department had been in the company's personnel department for some years. 'Training' was intended to provide seminars and project activities about behavioural change; its previous head had mainly provided theoretical seminars in the behavioural sciences for middle and senior management.

The present incumbent had, since 1972, begun to introduce OD activities. His aim was to work towards change indirectly, by helping people to achieve greater insight and understanding. He rejected techniques which put people under emotional pressure, such as TCI (Theme-Centred Interaction), sensitivity training and transactional analysis, and preferred cognitive methods such as feedback, as well as support for learning from the environment.

The OD activities began with development seminars for senior management, which were designed in collaboration with an outside institute. The conclusion was that, while the technical and economic systems in the company were functioning well, the social system was creating a bottleneck. At all levels there was a need for more serious attention to leadership.

The next phase was to organise so-called 'family-training-seminars' among engineers, but this series was felt to be unsuccessful. Then, in 1976, work began to focus on the problems of supervisors, which were well known. A series of aims was formulated, which were intended to enhance the role of supervisors, increase their competence in technical and social leadership, and improve their relationships with subordinates; supervisors were to be involved themselves in devising the project. After these aims had been agreed by top management a project group, including the consultant from the outside institute, took on the task of translating them into practice.

The first task was a diagnostic one of exploring the learning needs, motivation and existing skill of supervisors and senior supervisors. It was decided not to do this via a questionnaire but in a five-day 'analysis workshop'. Sixteen representatives of middle and junior management took part in this workshop in March 1978. The aim was for the project group to be able to learn about the capacities and motivation of likely future participants through observing and taking part in a range of discussions, case studies and exercises.

The workshop yielded a mass of information about the needs of supervisors, from language difficulties with foreign workers to problems about the product mix and inadequate equipment. Overwhelmingly, however, the needs expressed concerned human and social topics such as relations between people, culture, language and behaviour of foreign workers, human types and phases of human development, teamwork and conflict, problem-solving skills, company organisation and how to tackle one's own development.

The results of the analysis seminar were presented to top management with a recommendation that seminars should be held with all supervisors and senior supervisors in line and staff, combined with follow-up sessions in which concrete work problems could be discussed. An internal training staff was proposed, to include some supervisors and middle managers. Seven training teams were envisaged, each to consist of a professional trainer and a middle manager or senior supervisor. All these proposals were accepted.

Most of the professional trainers came from the original project group; junior management members were selected from recommendations made by department heads (several members of the original analysis seminar re-appeared at this stage). A training handbook was prepared, describing in detail the eighteen proposed learning units, which were based on the findings of the analysis workshop. Briefing sessions and residential training workshops for the training teams were organised.

The emphasis was to be on learning from experience: the learning units consisted of exercises, role play and case studies, with some short theoretical inputs, occasionally supplied by outside experts. The content was designed to achieve a higher level of insight into the role and function of leadership in the firm; understanding of the factors that influence personal style and behaviour; experience of the different effects of different leadership styles; and practice in co-operative leadership and problem-solving.

In the course of eighteen months, 27 one-week supervisor seminars took place. Although participation was voluntary, all the 450 supervisors in the larger of the two plants took part. It is said that they were really experiencing a need for such development.

Although at the time of writing this series had not long been completed, some positive indicators of its success were:

although there was a crisis in the motor industry, management was
maintaining the OD activity;
the follow-up sessions were going well;
follow-up activities were being strongly supported by the supervisors'
own bosses.

A second series of seminars was being planned, with the aim of training
supervisors in the skills of coaching and training their own subordinates.
Also, the outcomes of the original training were to be turned into material
for management training. As a first step, the results of the seminars had
been presented to top management.

Other OD activities

1.   A different section of the industrial relations department had initiated
the creation of 'quality circles'. With the agreement of the works council,
seven quality circles were running at the time of this study.
2.   A second major project in which the training section took part was in
the staff department for material planning. This was a central department
at the European level of the company. The work had been requested by a
new head of department, and a needs analysis had been carried out.
However, turning this analysis into project activities, at the time of writing,
was running into cross-cultural and political difficulties due to the multinational nature of the company.

Conclusions: objectives and outcomes

The objectives in this group of cases were to use social science concepts
and methods to deal, in each case, with a relatively specific problem which
was widely accepted as a problem within the organisation. There were four
cases of this type. In the UK oil marketing case (H) a department of a
multinational organisation recognised that its role was changing because
market forces were changing dramatically and it wanted to reconsider its
role, particularly to feed the requirements for staff skills and characteristics
into its long-term manpower planning policy. In the second UK case (I) a
motor components factory had experienced major downturns in its
business with the local contraction of the motor manufacturing industry.
Over a very long period there had developed a poor industrial relations
climate which made the organisational changes necessary for survival
very difficult to implement. The two German cases were also in the motor
industry. There was no connection between them, except that the changes
taking place in the industry triggered the problems that each programme
addressed. In one company (case J) the influx of guest workers, mostly

from Greece, Yugoslavia and Turkey, to take many of the shopfloor jobs, was causing problems because it was difficult to assimilate workers who did not share the language or culture of the organisation. In the other company (case K) a rapid deterioration in industrial relations had led to strike actions which had come as a great shock to management and one of the conclusions was that supervisory staff needed help with man-management skills.

In each of these cases there was an identifiable group of employees who needed to take stock of their position and develop new ways of working. Social scientists were commissioned to design and run training courses or other types of 'event' which would help these employees analyse their circumstances and develop ways of coping with them. The nature of the problems meant that the 'events' and the issues considered were very different. In the case of marketing the employees analysed the future of their industry, and in the case of the guest workers 'language shops' were organised where a special version of German was taught which covered the technical language needed for the shopfloor. In the case of the motor components factory, in order to break down the barriers of mistrust between different groups of employees, events were organised which enabled staff to share matters of common concern.

The first level of evaluation must be whether these programmes were actually instituted and run. In all cases this occurred, courses and events were organised and participants attended them, often with considerable enthusiasm. In case K, for example, 27 one-week courses were held. The second level of evaluation is the impact of these events on participants. The programmes themselves, while there is little formal evaluative evidence, did appear to have the planned effects on their participants: there was a widespread increase in understanding of the relevant issues and development of appropriate attitudes, expertise and skills. In some cases, as with the guest workers, this was a tangible gain in knowledge, such as an increased German vocabulary, whereas in other cases, as in the motor components factory, it was a change in attitude, such as an increased recognition of the viewpoints of fellow workers and a willingness to work with them to solve the problems faced by the organisation.

A third level of evaluation has to be whether this changed awareness level was translated into changed behaviour which contributed to the resolution of the organisation problems the learning programmes were established to tackle. It is difficult to be sure of the effects at this level, both because formal evaluations were not undertaken and because many other factors than the learning programmes started to have an influence on events. In the guest workers case there are reports of much better inter-worker relations on the shopfloor, not just because the foreign workers could communicate more effectively but also because, in helping to plan and run the workshops, the German workers achieved a better appreciation of the problems of their new colleagues. The company that instituted the supervisory training experienced no further strike action, but in general the wider consequences of the supervisor training are not known to us. In the motor-components factory there is strong evidence that the new climate created a situation in which policies for organisational restructuring and changes in the reward system could be discussed and agreed. Similarly, in the oil marketing case, the new awareness of marketing staff meant that they could go on to look at organisational issues consequent upon the new role they had identified, for example, how marketing should be organised across the world, the kind of human resources it would need and the information systems that would be necessary to support them.

This set of cases seems to show a clearer and fuller achievement of initial objectives than some of the other types of case and this may be, in some measure, because they start from a specific problem which the participants agree is a problem and which, in some cases, has reached the status of a crisis demanding action. These circumstances give both direction and impetus to the work of the social scientists.

It would be wrong, however, to convey an unqualified view of success. As these cases move outwards from the focus on specific events for a defined set of participants, so there is greater evidence of the same problems that beset, for example, the structure/policy cases. As the motor components factory considered its plan for organisation change, so forces not involved in creating the plan began to reassert the conflicts that had previously dominated relations. When there were attempts to transfer the learning shop idea to another factory and to generalise it beyond language learning, it did not work. As marketing staff started to work on the consequences of their role examination, their plans were upset by promotions and transfers which destroyed the continuity of development and brought in new people with different ideas. The social scientists worked, with some success, to mitigate the effects of these changes but in all cases felt that the programme was losing its impetus and coherence.

As these prgrammes matured they tended to move in two directions. Firstly, they involved more people in the type of event which started the programme but often these people had less commitment to the events (the 'not invented here' syndrome). Secondly, they moved the initial participants from awareness into the more difficult area of action. In all cases this was widening the boundary of the activity; it had the effect of bringing outside forces to bear and left the social scientists with the experience of losing control of the process, or at any rate losing a sense of effectiveness.

9 Cases in behavioural change/development for management

The three cases in this chapter are from West Germany. They are all concerned with programmes of management training which seek to help managers review their management style and offer opportunities to develop other styles. The overall aims were to introduce a new management climate throughout the organisations.

Case L is a large distribution company in which a senior OD practitioner was empowered to implement a large programme of management training with humanistic objectives, for example to 'do away with hierarchies and specialisation'. Case M is a company manufacturing telecommunications equipment which, finding itself having to cope with very rapid changes in its market, asked its management training and OD section to set up a leadership programme. This programme was derived from humanistic psychology and group dynamics and provided a structured programme through which managers could review their problems, establish alternatives and develop detailed plans for their implementation. The final case (N) is in the rubber industry. In this case the OD practitioners had been using management training methods since the 1960s and, over the years, had explored many different alternatives leading to a form of transactional analysis which provided a comprehensive method for implementing change across the organisation. In each case the practitioners were working from an in-house base within the training and/or personnel functions.

L. Distribution: strategy and legitimation of a broadly based OD programme

Background: the organisation and the personnel development department

The firm in this case was a distribution company which had been founded in Germany after the war. It had grown rapidly and was at the time of the study structured in the form of a number of independent profit centres.

There was a Board member responsible for organisation and personnel.

The departments for which he was responsible were organisation, recruitment, personnel administration and social affairs. As well as this he had, in 1973, recruited an OD practitioner, Mr Y, to head a separate personnel development department (PDD).

Having been recruited because he was personally known to the Board member, and because they shared a humanistic orientation, Mr Y was in a position to shape the organisation and work of the PDD. He saw it as his task to improve the living and working conditions of the people who worked in the organisation, and the Board member deliberately set out to create opportunities for the introduction of OD activities for him.

The PDD had its own budget which was administered autonomously; there was an annual review with the Board, both in terms of accounting and content. However, the budget did not include resources for carrying out personnel-oriented activities such as OD activities, training, and so on. The different profit centres had budgets for these areas and made their own decisions as to how to spend them. The PDD therefore only had an advisory relationship with other parts of the organisation, which meant that the different departments or profit centres had to be convinced each time an application was made. This created the need for a great deal of persuasion among the responsible people in these areas in order to win them over for the work of the PDD.

Relations with the works council seemed to be unproblematic, and several members of the works council took part in OD activities, without negative reactions. The level of trade union membership in the firm was very low.

There was recognition within the company of the basic conflict between the aims of the organisation and the aims of the workers. The need to make a realistic assessment of the tension between the goals of the organisation and those of the workers was seen as a specific task of company policy, and especially of personnel policy, the aim of which was to bring the two areas as closely as possible into accord with each other. The staff of the PDD considered that an organisation was only capable of development if it accepted, and knew how to hold in dynamic balance, the conflicting interests in the thoughts/feelings and needs/wishes of its members. The goal of 'harmony' was seen not only as an illusion but itself as an expression of power-seeking and conflict-avoidance.

The basic philosophy of the PDD was seen as a need to do away with hierarchies and specialisation. In this framework, the department considered that it had a dual task:

on the one hand, to aid the critical adjustment of workers to increasingly demanding circumstances;
and, on the other, to enable workers to exert an active influence on changing working conditions.

It therefore pursued interdependent organisation-related and person-related goals. Thus removal of conventional hierarchical structures was not to detract from the responsibility and authority of certain individuals, but rather to develop transparent, creativity-furthering structures and to remove the individual and departmental egotism which can hinder efficiency. Secondly, there was a need for lifelong continuing learning, since increasing changes in the economy and in society made ever greater demands on flexibility and mobility.

Methodologically, the OD work was very strongly oriented to the concepts of TCI (theme-centred interaction). This was demonstrated by the fact that all the external moderators who were brought in were TCI trained. This emphasis on TCI methods meant that seminar moderators had to work in a non-directive way. However, the moderating strategy appeared to be dialectic: on the one hand, the moderators appeared to accept the behaviour of seminar members as they were, but on the other hand, they picked out aspects of behaviour verbally and made them into the theme of the interaction. Thus a certain indirect pressure was in fact exerted on the members and the internal moderators accepted this.

Objectives and activities of OD

The 'problem' was defined as how to penetrate a normally functioning undertaking with OD. Successes in this area can be attributed in some great measure to the personality of Mr Y.

In pursuit of the person-related and organisation-related goals, there were three OD activities in use in the company:

the personnel development programme;
technical training;
departmental seminars.

1. Changing persons

The PDD saw the *personnel development programme* as coexistent with general education and training programmes, and as the more strongly person-oriented side of OD. They did not equate personnel development with career planning. The aim of the programme was (a) to enable people to become clear about their own goals and skills, and how they related to their present and future tasks, and (b) to enhance flexibility and adaptiveness, and enable people to cope with the increasing complexity and instability of the organisation's work and decision processes. In terms of content, the emphasis was on dealing with conflict, improving communications, the ability to assess oneself and others, and working on case study examples of situations taken from organisational life. The design of the personnel development programme was based on the belief that such programmes must be concerned with the structures and working conditions affecting workers, as well as with purely factual and personal contents. This applied especially to the use of new knowledge and experiences. But members of the PDD realised that there would only be a genuine diffusion of such programmes if the people responsible at the local level were themselves prepared to take part in an active way; not only giving verbal support to workers who wanted to do something for themselves, but also time.

Thus an effective personnel development programme would presuppose the change in climate which can abandon linear thinking about promotion and hierarchies. The programme was intended to stimulate further development in cognitive, emotional and behavioural learning, both in its content and through its methods, which can happen through the transmission of information, behavioural training and personal experience.

The programme consisted of three two-day seminar sessions and four afternoon sessions, spread over five or six weeks. It was staffed by two people from inside, and one from outside the organisation. About half the content of the programme was suggested by the staff, and half by the members. At the end of the third seminar there were development consultations with each person taking part. The managers or supervisors of those who applied to take part were informed, but could not prevent attendance. No reports were made about a member's performance, and all records were destroyed after two years.

The personnel development programme was supplemented by *task-oriented training* such as shorthand, languages, supervision, and so on. This was planned by the PDD, who also designed its institutions. However, it was not normally carried out by members of the department, but rather by relevant others, either from inside or from outside the organisation.

2. Changing structures

Probably the most important instrument of OD in the company were the *departmental seminars*. These consisted of about twenty members of a department meeting with their managers for two to four days of joint work on technical and personal issues connected with the job. The initiative was taken by the particular area, i.e. profit centre, and the PDD then issued the invitations.

Departmental seminars were designed on the following principles:

they had to take several days in order to get the participants used to a new atmosphere of interaction;

they had to take place outside the firm, in pleasant surroundings: great
importance was put on the design of the informal part of the activity on
free evenings;

at least three levels of the hierarchy of the department had to be represented;

staffing had to consist of an internal and an external moderator. A single
moderator could not handle the multiplicity of tasks, the nature of
which required two people. The internal moderator not only provided
specific knowledge about the situation in the company but also
ensured a person-related continuity for future contacts. The external
moderator contributed his independence; being unaffected by organisational politics, he could break taboos concerning particular topics
and bring a wider experience. The external moderators all had TCI
training;

the work had to be exclusively about specific problems of the participants;
one of the tasks of the moderators was to ensure a balanced mix of the
problems that were presented, between those which were task-
oriented and those which were person-oriented (a principle of TCI).

At the end of a seminar the members produced action plans. The PDD
admitted that carrying out such plans could be difficult once the pace of
normal work took over again. There were follow-up activities, including
further seminars. In the purchasing department a six-month seminar cycle
had developed.

Since 1973 about 50 per cent of the relevant areas or departments of the
organisation had been included in these departmental seminars. However,
this did not mean that 50 per cent of the positions in the organisation had
been included. There were still sections within the organisation which
explicitly rejected these area seminars. There were also parts of the organisation which had not yet been included because of a lack of resources.

This last fact was seen as something very positive, since it meant that the
demand for departmental seminars had become so great in some areas
that, with the limited capacity of the PDD, it had not been possible to meet
it and they were therefore booked up for a long time ahead.

Some time previously the departmental seminars had ventured on to
new ground when, out of the about 2,000 employees, 120 junior supervisors were included in the seminar. These were mostly people with
low-level qualifications, occupying positions like leading hand, group
leader, foreman, and so on. To be able to work with people from these
areas it was necessary not only to change the language of the seminars,
but also to use new kinds of media techniques. Methods such as role
playing, drawing, and working with puppets were used to replace the
usual verbal and written expressions of abstract themes.

It was significant that the PDD carried out departmental seminars for itself. All the members of the department took part, including technical staff and secretaries. This work required a highly qualified moderator. The verdict of the members of the department was 'not too bad'. When questioned about the problem of very different levels of competence in verbal communication, members answered that naturally the professionals dominated. To counteract this, the departmental seminars of this department were generally led by a moderator who had training in therapy.

The stress and strain of those working on OD was seen as a major problem, particularly for the internal agents. It was said that, for the first generation of members of the department, OD work was not a job but a 'mission'. Many of these people worked too hard, to their own detriment. This was said to be particularly true of those who came from the humanistic side. On the other hand, it was also said that there had been some misuse of power. The connection between power and responsibility among people working in OD was seen to be very strong.

Because of this, a form of supervision had recently been instituted for the internal OD agents. Every two weeks there was a case consultation in which opinions were exchanged about one or other activity, and the activity was critically evaluated. This supervision was developed because it was recognised that it was impossible to give too much attention to the training of the moderators. For this reason particular care was taken when taking on new moderators, who usually had to undergo a long period of induction before they could work independently. There were therefore perceptible difficulties in recruiting new internal moderators.

Evaluation of OD activities

Two years before this study an attempt began to be made to evaluate systematically the effectiveness of the OD activities. This evaluation was concerned with the following questions:

How can individuals' views of change be described or demonstrated?
How can one prove or demonstrate the effect of the seminars on the participants?
How can the participants be helped towards insight about the actually achieved development of personality?
What cost-related successes can be demonstrated?

Members of the PDD said that the evaluation was not mainly to legitimate OD *vis-à-vis* the company, but for their own control purposes. They therefore did not find it necessary to use so-called hard methods of evaluation, and in any case found these inadequate. They preferred to collect information through unstructured interviews, which could take several hours. A code for interpreting data, based on a computerised system of analysis from linguistics, was being tried. This was going to take many more months. The data which had been collected from supervisors in the area of skilled trades was regarded as particularly interesting. The evaluation project was being carried out together with the firm's subsidiary in the USA and the analysis by external scientists. Analysis by people outside the organisation was a deliberate decision, since the members of the PDD were thought unsuitable, having become so familiar with the situation over the years.

Future plans

The main difficulties in establishing OD in the company, both in the past and in the present, were seen at two levels:

there were strong reservations against the new form of learning, mainly because of its TCI orientation. The principle 'You don't only learn with your head' met with particular resistance – although this was decreasing;

there were also said to be big problems for OD arising from the German view of economic behaviour. Ideas in the Federal Republic about work and career, about decision-making and teamwork, and so on, were said to be in the opposite direction to OD. It was often accused of 'strengthening the people at the bottom'. OD questioned conventional roles and possibly threatened positions in the hierarchy.

These were the problems around which the department saw the main area of work for the next phase. Management was not qualified to create new work structures on the basis of OD; the departments or areas were 'growing' faster than their managers. Therefore, for the next period the development of managers was to play an important part in the work of the PDD. If this did not happen, there was the danger of OD being blocked by these managers, who could then block all further developments because of their fear for their own positions.

A second important task was the creation of work structures with more emphasis on the quality of working life. In parallel, new 'life-phase-themes' were to be incorporated into the work. Both career and personal perspectives were to be drawn to the attention of the participants. However, the members of the department said that they were still coming up against brick walls of resistance in this area.

Since it was thought that in future there would not be much growth in the resources of internal agents for OD work, a clear trend towards withdrawing from the role of change agent to that of adviser or consultant was recognised. This was seen to require training a large number of moderators, who were to be recruited from among managers.

(We understand that, not long after the end of the study, OD in the company was abandoned and Mr Y left. Given the very positive phase described above this is unexpected but we have no further data to explain it.)

M. News technology: management training and OD

Background

The company in this case was a subsidiary of an American conglomerate. It manufactured products concerned with news technology: communications/telephone systems and consumer electronics. Although strong in the early 1970s, this company had experienced difficulties since then, because of increased competition and some strategic mistakes in technology development policy. It therefore had to cope with the challenge of quickly finding new markets in glassfibre technology and office communications. Facing this challenge was made more difficult by the rigid control systems of the parent company and its short-term orientation.

Management training and OD was one of five sections forming the training department within the personnel department. The orientation of its staff was affective and towards group dynamics. They divided their activities into three areas:

(i)   Leadership (such things as management information programmes, motivation, counselling and appraisal, supervisor seminars, selection interviews).

(ii) Techniques of work (for example, time management, memory, concentration, reading and relaxation training, creativity, problem and decision-making analysis, training in negotiation, sensitivity and behaviour training, moderator-presentation training).

(iii) OD (for example, moderating and consulting, problem-solving workshops, team development, co-operation).

The leadership seminars had priority; the others were arranged on demand.

When concrete problems or conflicts appeared, the department offered workshops involving techniques for working on these. If changes were being introduced in whole departments or units, the department offered help or advice on how to initiate, support and evaluate such processes.

In helping people meet the challenge of change, the role of the management trainer was seen as 'communication helper', and the development seminars were offered under the heading 'help towards self-help'. Personnel staff in the various areas discussed training needs with the line management, and the task of the management training department was to turn these into a seminar programme.

Orientation

The trainers saw the rationale for this programme in the comprehensive changes going on in the company. Mainly as a result of their own personal histories, the members of the department had moved away from the cognitively oriented teaching strategy being used in the firm before they arrived, to one based on humanistic psychology and group dynamics. Affective and social goals were in the foreground and their aim was 'to remove the sand in the organisational engine'. Dissatisfaction, poor performance, waste of energy, sickness and psychological malaise were seen, on the one hand, as factors of an inhumane work situation and, at the same time, as cost factors which could be countered by focussed behavioural change, attitude change and change in the organisational climate. In parallel with such changes in organisational life, measures that increased skills should enable people to deal with organisational change more easily.

The programme

The overall programme was conceived as a three-phase cycle: problem-analysis, problem-solving and decisions and implementation.

(i) During the analysis phase, interviews would be carried out with staff at all levels and staff brought together in problem-analysis workshops. In parallel, the training staff would evaluate the data produced.

(ii) The problems listed as a result of the analysis would be discussed with relevant functional units and with management. Management would then develop various alternative solutions and decide between them.

(iii) These broad decisions would be turned into detailed planning by the functional units concerned. Training activities would accompany the implementation and ensure that there were no dysfunctional effects.

Within this broad framework the various measures listed earlier could be carried out, for example moderator and consultation training, information and communication 'markets', measures to improve work techniques, seminars in team development and co-operation, leadership and motivation, leadership in special situations, counselling and appraisal,

supervisor training, simulations and role play, training for selection interviewing (only for those involved in selecting 'important' or 'expensive'
staff).

Problems of implementation

The training department was given a detailed budget for its various
activities. This was to be explained by the concentration on management
and on strategies for ruling. The works council had views on these
measures, but did not take much interest until its own 'clientele' was going
to be affected, i.e. until a seminar for secretaries was being planned.

But mainly the training department's activities were concerned with
management. For instance, people interested in promotion were sent to
leadership seminars. Although it was said officially that no information
about the behaviour of members in such events was passed on, there were
nevertheless channels for being selectively indiscreet.

The management training department was therefore very dependent
on the organisation's management and this, together with the distanced
role taken by the works council, gave them the reputation of being
management's 'handmaidens', and created resistance among members of
the organisation. On the one hand, people who wanted promotion could
not avoid taking part, on the other hand, the group dynamics events were
experienced as stressful, with attacks on and discrediting of personal
behaviour.

The reputation of being the servants of top management was not
compensated for by any special protection for the management training
department. On the contrary, attitudes towards them of management as
well as of ordinary members of the organisation were rather negative. The
view of them as marginal and rather exotic was underlined by their
organisational and physical situation: they had no chances of promotion,
their qualifications being seen as having no function for the organisation;
they had no say in assessing training needs and personnel development
planning, which was done outside their department; and they were located
in a house outside the main site of the company.

The consequences for members of the department showed, on the one
hand, in the fact that the trainers were thinking of career moves outside
the organisation. On the other hand, they appeared to avenge themselves
within the training for the status discrepancies they were experiencing: by
group pressure, making people appear ridiculous, and other psychological
strategies of an almost sadistic kind, they attempted to undermine the
security particularly of those people whose initial attitude was confident or
especially ambitious. Participants in training events were seen either as
accomplices or to be attacked.

Discussion

This case shows the problems that develop when members of a training department attempt to initiate strategies of organisation development which are not anchored in the institutional and organisational framework of the undertaking. Another important observation is that the outsider-role of the members of the training department led to problems of status and of implementation which in turn prevented a functional adaptation of the programme to the opportunities in the company, as well as its innovative development. There was therefore a vicious circle, from which the members of the department could only think of escaping by seeking other careers. A conclusion would be that their strategy and procedures had not been task-centred and had a life of their own, separate from the processes of the organisation.

N. Rubber: change of topic and method in an OD programme

Background

This case concerns an organisation in the rubber industry, which had been American-owned. The parent company prescribed the organisation structure and only permitted deviations where local laws or hard economic grounds required it. The organisation was sold to a German firm, but the development of OD activities can only be understood by reference to the original US parentage.

The first OD method, introduced in the 1960s, was the Managerial Grid concept by Blake and Mouton (1964). In preparation for this, managers had been sent to a course on Management by Objectives (MbO), and there were separate seminars for different levels of management on problem-analysis and decision-making.

The whole Managerial Grid programme is an ambitious one consisting of six phases, but in the parent company only the first two had been carried out. After this, OD had been abandoned. In the European division, however, because of the personal motivation of some individual trainers, OD became an important part of the company's reorganisation. A contributing factor was that the organisation was not yet settled and was being challenged by expansion of activities, diversification and market developments. In this relatively open situation the trainers began to develop a management and personnel development programme, the first element of which was sales training.

OD philosophy and target group

The trainers owed their philosophy to the Human Relations Movement in the USA. They defined the aims of their work like this:

that people in the enterprise should accept and understand each other better;

that teams should put their energies into co-operative efforts so that conflict and competitiveness should be reduced and creativity maintained;

that teams and domains in the organisation should accept and support each other in order to reach the goals of the organisation together.

There was a positive response to this philosophy, and they developed a training and Organisation Development system, with a number of assumptions: changes in technology and production should be included in the training; economic and market considerations, issues of economic survival, should play a part; social science knowledge should be used to work on problems of organisation and personality structure.

The training department saw as their clients, on the one hand, the organisation as a whole and, on the other hand, individuals. The senior management of the organisation sometimes seemed to show some reservations towards OD methods, especially where these seemed to the trainers most necessary. Thus the target group was all the employees of the European division, i.e., 2,200 people. However, only a small proportion of these were served intensively with training measures: about 180 people in senior and middle management, 130 people in junior management, and 80 salesmen.

From Managerial Grid to comprehensive OD strategies

Management training was to cover:

personal development and career position via contact groups of trainees;

OD through seminars for middle management (supervisors and leading hands) and office staff;

improvements in quality and in the achievement of objectives through leadership training, sales training, and contact seminars;

training of service personnel.

As already stated, the first attempt had been to achieve these objectives by introducing the Managerial Grid. But already in the second phase of the Grid programme some resistance was shown by the participants. In an attempt to rescue the programme, all those who had taken part were offered insight into various group phenomena in additional three-day seminars. The training manager chose Transactional Analysis as the

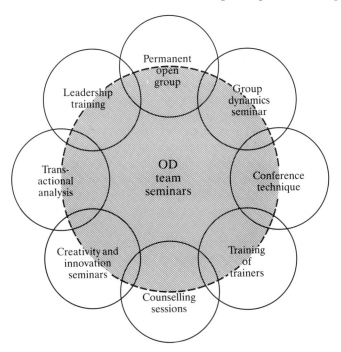

Figure 5   *Methods and strategies supporting OD team seminars*

accompanying strategy. The reason was that interaction and communication within the groups had already led to conflicts. A better understanding of one's own and others' behaviour in relation to communication and motivation should lead to changes in behaviour.

In shifting from the Managerial Grid method to Transactional Analysis, the training manager named growth of independence and autonomy of individuals as the main goal. A number of other methods were also taken up, which together acted as support measures to the central OD team seminars. They are shown in figure 5, which shows the workplan of the training department.

The *Transactional Analysis seminars* were received positively, since most teams had experienced difficulties with the second phase of the Grid method. The training department therefore began to carry out a needs analysis before planning other new methods, carrying out forty interviews with groups of staff. The results were discussed with section heads and their closest colleagues, and this led to a trusting relationship between line departments and the training department.

An important outcome was the introduction of the *TCI (Theme-Centred Interaction) method*, a seminar form which occupies one evening and three days. This was introduced first at middle management level and then spread upwards and downwards, upwards as far as the top management, and into production departments as far as leading hands and shift-leaders. A particular characteristic was that at the end of each seminar action plans were formulated in writing, and became the responsibility of the most senior and influential members of the team; these were therefore more or less forced to take action as a result of the work of the groups. The work was thus prevented from being 'merely therapeutic'.

The TCI method was felt to be so successful that after a time the training department used it in the design of '*team training*' for junior management. It had been felt that absenteeism, labour turnover and the frequency of accidents pointed to weaknesses at junior management level. Therefore, three-day behavioural seminars were organised for all supervisors, inspectors, and so on, at this level.

Another institution, perforce arising from the growing demands on the training department, was the *training of further trainers* from within the organisation.

The multiplicity of different kinds of people working in the firm led to the idea of creating '*contact groups*'. Each contact group was led by a leading hand, and it was said that these peoples' own leadership style was influenced by the experience. The contact group model was to some extent based on learning shops (see case J). The first topic introduced to the contact groups was an offer to help Turkish workers with their income-tax forms. Other subjects worked on were the use of strong language at work, and the induction of new people. Training for contact group leaders was developed, and the contact groups could then be given considerable freedom in developing the subjects they worked on.

After the contact groups had been proving themselves for some time, the training department felt able to risk moving into administrative departments. A team seminar with typists was developed, on similar behavioural lines as earlier ones. This was a startling innovation for the firm, partly because it went down to the base of the hierarchy but especially because it involved indirect workers.

Embeddedness of training activities in the organisation

Only the salaries of trainers were centrally funded. Other costs of training and OD activities had to be met out of the training budgets of the client departments. This ensured that the training department oriented itself carefully to the interests of client departments, and also that it offered high-quality products. However, the training manager felt that such a market orientation was only possible once social science activities had achieved a solid standing in the organisation. To begin with, they needed some protection to help them get established. At the time of writing, demand was often greater than supply.

The training manager had originally been head of one of the firm's sales branches. There he had developed a method of sales training, and later became head of sales training for the country. A new European personnel manager had the idea of expanding this to a more general OD programme. The sales training manager got himself some training in group dynamics and OD, and was appointed to the post of training manager for the company. His strategy was to explore techniques being developed outside the company and adapt them, for instance modifying Transactional Analysis and TCI in the direction of taking account of organisational constraints. Outside experts were only very seldom drawn into these activities. They would generally be colleagues whom the training manager had met in the course of his own self-development activities. Mostly, however, trainers were recruited and developed from inside the organisation.

Conclusions: objectives and outcomes

These three German cases are all programmes in which there were attempts to provide managerial staff with experiential events which would heighten their awareness of their behaviour in interpersonal situations so that they could, individually and collectively, become more effective in management. Occasionally the programmes were beginning to extend to non-managerial staff.

The sought outcomes in the case of these programmes are usually described as humanistic in character. They attempt to help people know themselves better in order that they can manage their relations with others more effectively, can lead and motivate others, cope with conflicts openly, recognise and work with other values and interpretations, and so on. In each case the aspirations are not just to change individual behaviour but, by this route, to change the nature of the management process. In case L, the distribution company, the aim was to 'de-hierarchise' management structure so that power and influence could be diffused more widely. In case M, the news technology industry, the aim was 'flexible managers for flexible organisations'. In the third organisation (case N), the rubber industry, management training had been attempted but the form was being questioned so the objective was to find a form of training which had a real impact upon the interpersonal skills of the management.

In each of these organisations an extensive programme of management development was undertaken. The methods were experiential and, while they differed considerably, they all included feedback to individuals in group situations to help them perceive group dynamics and their own contributions to them. The programmes were directed at all levels of management and were usually run by training departments.

In two of the cases, at any rate, there is ample evidence of the courses proving popular. In case L (distribution), they spread over a period of years to include delegates from over half of the sections and departments of the organisation. At one time the shortage of skilled trainers meant that the OD department could not keep pace with demand. In case N (rubber), after initial subvention, the courses became self-financing, and demand was also said to be greater than supply.

In the view of the respondents, both the trainers and the course attendees, the courses served the purpose of increasing awareness and helping individuals develop their capacities in interpersonal situations. Examples were given of people feeling better able to cope with conflict, listen to subordinates, work with uncertainty, and so on.

At the higher level, where the effects should be seen in terms of a changed managerial culture, there is less evidence of change. Indeed, one of the reasons for trying a different style of training in the rubber industry was to try to obtain changes in managerial practice. There are signs in this case of the phenomenon found in others, that of the clients beginning to exert their own control over the learning process. They tended to mould the lessons they had learned in the courses to fit the company culture and practices rather than using the lessons to change the culture.

While we only have the self-report of interested parties as evidence in these cases, a pattern does seem to emerge which fits the pattern of the other cases. These cases appear to achieve their initial objectives, where OD practitioners help people obtain a new level of self-awareness. However, once away from the training environment the effects are not easily translated into practice. Some of the OD practitioners had aspirations of revolutionary changes in managerial practice but these did not appear. Indeed, it is possible to hypothesise that the stronger the forces they were able to muster for change, the more likely they were to meet strong opposing forces. At the same time, activities which appear to have had quite a lot in common in terms of content seem to have had quite different outcomes, depending on how they were grounded in the organisations.

10 The content and process of social science utilisation

The fourteen case studies in organisations provide examples of a variety of approaches to social science practice. Outcomes have been discussed. The purpose of this chapter is to explore what was being used and how it was being used. Our aim is to explore the processes of engagement between the social scientists and the clients, the roles that were adopted by each and the methods used in the engagement. One aim is to examine whether anything systematic is emerging about the practice of social science. The analysis of the cases is informed by the distinction we made in chapter 2 between two frames of reference, that of knowledge-into-use and that of the dynamics of action. We ask what concepts, methods and findings were being used, how they were used, and what roles were adopted by social scientists and clients in these processes. Similarly, we examine the dynamics of action in the cases, the methods adopted in the change process and the roles adopted by the participants.

Organisational structure and policy cases

There were four cases, two UK and two German, where the primary target was to bring about major policy changes or changes in organisational structure. In each case there were attempts to make use of substantive knowledge, although the strategies employed showed considerable variation. The concepts, methods and findings being employed covered a wide range including theories of organisation, socio-technical systems concepts, job design methods, role theory and ergonomics, as well as theoretical perspectives on conflict and negotiation.

In case C (electrical products) the knowledge-into-use framework was very explicit. The social scientists were asked to review the social science literature for relevant theories, approaches and findings which would be of use to the company. They found this very difficult and concluded that the literature had nothing to offer which exactly fitted the requirement. This was an attempt to locate 'off the shelf' social science findings which could be directly applied, and made little allowance for the complex process of internalising the knowledge and converting it into a form applicable in a particular situation.

Case A (transport) and case B (banking) both began with diagnostic investigations. In the transport case the emphasis was on using survey techniques to gather data about the attitudes and problems surrounding the supervisory role. The researcher had conducted similar studies in other industries and could use them as a reference point. In the banking case the social scientists adopted a more general exploratory, diagnostic frame of reference using a battery of unstructured and semi-structured interview techniques, tracer techniques and observation methods. The reference point was the conceptual one of trying to understand branch banking as a socio-technical system. Both studies undertook in-depth investigation of only a small sub-set of the relevant organisational units (two depots and four branches) in order to generate hypotheses about critical issues rather than to test well-formed hypotheses. These investigations were therefore not hypothesis-testing research studies, but were ways of uncovering issues to be explored further in the action phase.

The studies enabled the social scientists to relate general theoretical orientations to the specific contexts of the client organisations: to the interplay between policy, customer needs, technology and work organisation in a branch of a bank and the conflicts of the supervisor occupying a role between management and workforce in the transport industry. At later stages in both projects, further diagnostic studies were commissioned from the social scientists, of the international division in banking and a different kind of supervision in transport.

The studies enabled the social scientists to convert social science concepts into a form which could be used in these organisations and to generate empirical findings the organisation could review. The next necessary step was that the client organisation should process these findings and convert them into action. In some senses the process had already begun in the way client staff were involved in the investigations.

In the bank branches and the transport depots the staff were subjects in an investigation conducted by social scientists. The collaboration of staff and access to their data was always a matter of negotiation, with arrangements for confidentiality and feedback being agreed. Feedback of data to its originators served the purposes of validation and also provided the originators with a potentially useful output from the investigation.

In the transport case two of the client staff took part in the data gathering and learned the survey techniques from the social scientist. In this way the organisation developed its own resources for this kind of work. At a later phase in the banking work the social scientists taught interview techniques to the staff of a subsidiary bank so that these could undertake their own diagnostic study and, in an exercise unsupported by the consultants, members of the O and M department undertook a branch survey of their own using some similar methods.

In both cases reports were prepared of the investigations conducted by the social scientists which were thoroughly debated with the client staff. The form of these reports bears on the question of how 'knowledge' is translated into action. In the banking case the client first asked for recommendations which, despite some misgivings, the consultants provided. They were then asked to remove the recommendations before the report was circulated, and actions resulting from the findings of the study were developed as a result of meetings between the consultants and groups of client staff or by the client staff themselves. In the transport case the findings from the survey were transformed into a set of recommendations for supervisory staff training and management practice by the director in the client organisation who had sponsored the study. Thereafter the director piloted the recommendations through the relevant senior committees until they were implemented. In a subsequent investigation, of a different type of supervisor, the social scientist and director played similar roles, although the social scientist played a fuller role in the development of recommendations and their presentation within the client organisation. The process of working through the findings from investigations with client staff was in large measure the principal way the social scientists became involved in the action and implementation aspects of the process.

In the banking study the consultants worked through the reports of their investigations with separate groups of staff including managers, staff in the branches where the study had taken place, personnel officers, trainers and O and M specialists, and each group took from the report what they considered relevant and could act upon. Working with these groups took the consultants into the dynamics of action, finding ways of working with individuals and groups upon change processes. The consultants, for example, developed and ran a series of experiential training courses for the sub-managers of branches because the investigations revealed that this category of staff received no help with management practice, although they were the chief organisers of branch work. The action aspects of the banking study became fragmented as different groups examined the implications of the reports, whereas in the transport case the action strategy was focussed at a senior level by the director who had sponsored the project and who used the findings to develop and implement major policy changes.

One feature of these cases was that the consultants felt they were not wholly part of the process by which client staff internalised findings and converted them into practice. Indeed, in evaluating the outcomes of these projects, the consultants felt unable to give a definitive view, because many action phases may have been undertaken without their knowledge. In one phase of the banking project one of the consultants contributed to the action debate as a 'ghost'. A network of committees named after the consultant was established to work on the findings of a survey, but conducted its work without the consultant being present. In these cases, therefore, the consultants played major roles in the translating of social science into a form for potential use in the client organisations, and thereafter played more facilitating roles in the dynamics of action as client staff internalised the findings for their own purposes. In this process, client staff tended to take findings and to interpret and use them independently of the consultants.

On the other hand, research in these cases was itself also an action strategy. For instance, the exploratory study of branch banking served to create a base of understanding the system, and a relationship, which led to the consultants being called upon directly in many small ways not immediately connected with the findings; and, indeed, being called upon again several years after the end of the assignment.

The process of using social science without using social scientists is even more pronounced in the case of precision engineering (case D). In this case there was wide recognition of the need to change the working culture from that appropriate to products and production methods based on mechanical engineering to a form suitable for electronics. The staff of this organisation employed the concepts and findings of job enrichment and ergonomics to provide staff with greater autonomy and control over their work. They did this with the help of a method for evaluating alternatives obtained from another German company, i.e. by making use of the experience of others. By using this and their general knowledge they were able to convert knowledge into action programmes to their own expressed satisfaction, without recourse to professional social scientists. The level of evaluation it was possible to undertake in this case was not sufficient for an assessment to be made of how far professional social scientists would have identified with the content of what happened.

In the other three cases, A, B and C (as, of course, in all the cases except D) what was being used was also the previous experience of the professionals. In the electrical products case this experience was of academic research, and the most active and clear-cut contribution the social scientists made to the overall project was evaluation research. In the transport case the professional's previous experience was also of research, and this was the form the first study took. By the second study she had developed interest in and some experience of implementation and sought – and obtained – a more active part in it; she would, however, have liked it to be more active still. In the banking case the professionals had considerable experience of action and implementation. They were able to move directly into designing a training course, or proposing development strategies, that would integrate findings. This, however, brought them up against already-existing institutions concerned with such things.

Systems development cases

In three of the UK cases the target was a social science contribution to the design of a major technical system. Again, in each case, the social scientists were external to the organisation. The aim in all these cases was to bring a consideration of human and organisational issues to a technical design process, in two cases the design of a new factory and in the third the introduction of a computer system into a freightforwarding organisation.

In each of these cases the social scientists were working simultaneously in the knowledge-into-use and the dynamics of action frameworks. The basis of the former was the rich literature that exists demonstrating that technical design usually proceeds without adequate attention being paid to the human and organisational changes attendant upon it. In effect there is a tradition of splitting, in which technical design is performed by technologists employing methods which emphasise rational and logical application of physical laws. Subsequently, at implementation, management and workforce have to cope with organisational changes in ways which then often have more to do with resistance to change and the management of conflict. Socio-technical approaches provide a range of concepts and methods which offer ways of avoiding this splitting and informed the work of the consultants in these cases.

From the point of view of action, there was in each case a complex process for technical systems design institutionalised and underway, independently of the social science consultants. In all of them there was also a policy-level wish to take care of human and organisational aspects, with different degrees of strength and different views of what this would mean. The consultants then had to develop ways of helping the staff already involved in technical design to embrace human and organisational issues. They also had to find ways of bringing other interested parties (managers, current workers, future workers, and trade unions) into the development process.

In all of the cases the achievement of these purposes meant changing the way the technical design was being undertaken and the consultants were to varying degrees successful in influencing the re-shaping of the design process. In food processing (case F) a job design committee, for example, was established within which representatives of future operating staff could consider the job implications of technical plans for the new factory. However, many other aspects of the planning were not reviewed in this way and a complex industrial relations climate made full representation at the right time difficult to achieve. In the confectionary case (E) management was highly committed to a social and organisational perspective and instituted design structures which enabled it to address these issues. This was an unusual case because the consultant did not have to argue for a socio-technical framework but had to find ways of turning an ideal into practice. In the freightforwarding case (G) the social scientists reviewed the planned technical design process at an early stage and because of its technologically deterministic nature reported that they could not work within it. The directors of the company thereafter adopted an alternative systems design process proposed by the consultants which incorporated management and user involvement.

The overall structure of the interventions of the consultants was dictated by these design processes and did not, for example, exhibit the overall problem-solving cycle shown in the structural change cases, i.e., diagnosis/report/action. Within these processes the social scientists took a number of roles. Investigative activities tended to be small scale, were undertaken on different occasions during the design process and were undertaken for different purposes. Initially, the consultants undertook small exploratory activities partly to develop some understanding of confectionery manufacture, food processing and freightforwarding and partly as a 'getting to know you' exercise for both parties. Subsequently other explorations were undertaken to establish the requirements and concerns of different work roles to be affected by the technical design. In the freightforwarding case, for example, forms of task analysis were undertaken to determine the user requirements from the computer system. In the confectionery case there were various forms of exploratory role playing, and the involvement of the operators of the factory that was to be closed. In the food processing case there were exercises in establishing priorities among design criteria.

A major way in which the consultants worked with the companies was, however, concerned with the processes involved. The consultants identified, for example, a continuing need to facilitate the process whereby technical design decisions were reviewed for their social system implications. One way of doing this was to get people to make their values and priorities explicit, to make explicit the values that were implicit in the technical designs, and to try to arrive at a match. Another way was to make evaluations of technical proposals from a human and organisational perspective. In the confectionery case, for example, the consultant was asked to evaluate two different shapes for the building and layouts within it. In the food processing case, some work was done to evaluate competing layouts for their impact on job structures, and the final plant layout was examined with the job design committee from the point of view of machine pacing. In the freightforwarding case the consequences of three different ways of allocating computer terminals were evaluated for their impact upon branch organisation.

To help them in this process the consultants were using the substantive research findings available about the impact of technology upon jobs, about the way in which machine pacing and very short task cycle times can erode autonomy, physical layouts can disrupt team working, and so on. These findings provided a basis for criteria by which technical proposals could be evaluated. However, in most circumstances the consultants did not make direct evaluations themselves. They felt they had insufficient knowledge of the reality of the relevant work processes and that it was important for the client staff to express their own requirements and values in making these choices.

The consultants therefore sought opportunities to bring management and staff into roles where they could evaluate the technical options with technical specialists and evaluate organisational options in the resultant socio-technical system. The techniques used to facilitate these judgements involved the creation of transitional systems which were themselves temporary socio-technical systems. Firstly, organisational structures such as the local CSC in freightforwarding and the job design committee in food processing were formed in which technical staff, management and staff representatives could consider the design proposals. Secondly, physical manifestations of the technical alternatives were often constructed to help participants understand the proposals and their implications. In the confectionery case a Lego model of the factory layout, developed by company staff, was used in this way. In the freightforwarding case a fully functioning but 'off the shelf' computer-based system was implemented in one branch and provided a basis for the client organisation to explore what it really wanted from such a system. In the food processing case it was considered too expensive to build a model of the factory; for the evaluation the participants worked from the technical drawings prepared by the designers.

In working with these transitional systems, the consultants were to a large extent acting as detailed process designers and facilitators. In working with technical designers they were encouraging them to offer alternatives and keep options open. In working with management and staff they were seeking ways to help them express and prioritise their requirements and values and to use these as criteria to judge technical options. However, they also made substantive contributions, for example by listing criteria arrived at elsewhere, running workshops or seminars where the experience of others was introduced and arranging direct exposure to the experience of others through visits and tape-recordings. In designing and running these exercises the consultants used a variety of frames of reference and findings, from socio-technical systems concepts, job satisfaction and job design research, and so on. This knowledge was not used directly, but was employed to explore alternative technical opportunities, for example when a machine had too short a cycle time. The physical manifestation appeared to be particularly important in helping client staff assess the significance of an issue. In the freightforwarding case, for example, the consultants offered management the research finding that computer systems could influence the degree to which decision-making was centralised in the organisation, but management could not see how this abstract finding applied in their organisation. Once the pilot system was connected to two branches and these tried to co-ordinate their work, the loss of local autonomy became evident, the implications of the research were understood and this feature of the planned computer system was discontinued.

The roles adopted by members of the client organisation were transitional ones in respect of the design processes. The technical designers (including mechanical, production and electrical engineers, architects, DP staff, and so on) occupied their usual roles but were encouraged to take a broader view of their role so that it expanded beyond technical and economic considerations to encompass human and organisational variables. In the food processing case, for example, the project engineer began to write job specifications which were quite different from the conventional ones. For instance, he specified the task of a (vegetable) soak-tank operator in terms of opening a valve on the tank instead of pushing a button in the control room, so that (a) he could experience the connection between his actions and their consequences, and (b) he had an opportunity to move out from the isolation of the control room. In some instances the designers were also asked to operate with design processes which were not familiar to them and at times this caused difficulty. In the freightforwarding case, for example, the consultants undertook a task analysis and the technical staff found that it did not provide the kind of systems specification data that they required.

Management and staff found themselves in unfamiliar roles in this process. For the most part they seem to have found it possible to make constructive contributions to their own futures. However, in the view of the consultants this was not achieved on the widespread front required so that, while some elements of the system showed signs of integrated socio-technical planning, elsewhere the normal splitting occurred: technical design decisions were taken in a technical forum while elsewhere in time and place management decisions were taken about organisational issues or negotiations conducted about conditions of work.

In general, the action-oriented nature of these cases shows a complex interplay of the knowledge-into-use and dynamics of action paradigms. The mechanisms set up to facilitate the change process created the opportunities to convert findings into a usable form and clients internalised these concepts and developed their own interpretations and action strategies.

Cases involving specific groups

The four cases in this category, two UK and two German, focussed upon the specific issues and problems of particular groups of employees. The process of engagement, initially at least, consisted of the social scientists working closely with these members of staff. One characteristic of these cases is that the consultants appear to have played major roles in the formulation of the process by which the issues were tackled. This may, in part, have been because the target was relatively bounded and because other approaches had been tried and had failed. For example, in the motor components case (I) traditional negotiation approaches were not helping to stop the slide into insolvency. Another factor may have been that in three of these cases the consultants were internal to the organisations concerned and so had more time to work intensively with the relevant staff.

The character of the process by which the consultants chose to work with these groups of employees showed some similarities. In none of them did the consultants investigate the issue, formulate social science-based recommendations and offer them to the client groups, nor did they include substantive suggestions based on experience, either their own or that of others. Substantive inputs came later. The approach adopted was more immediately in an action framework, i.e., the consultants joined with the clients in an evaluation of the problem and acted in a facilitator role whilst client staff underwent the learning experiences associated with developing a solution and implementing it. There were also differences in approach. In the motor components case the consultant constructed a process whereby groups of employees who were previously hostile to one another could gradually come together to consider matters of common concern. Once joint problem-solving had become possible, formulating and implementing solutions could be undertaken. In the oil marketing case (H) the process provided marketers with the opportunity to examine current and future roles before designing a future role for themselves and a way of getting from the present to the future. Both of these cases involved a participatory diagnostic process followed by a participatory design process. By contrast the two German cases involved a participatory diagnostic process followed by the design and operation of training schemes. In the motor industry guest-workers example (J) the German nationals and their guest workers designed and then ran learning shops for new guest workers. In the supervision case from the German motor industry (K), a participative diagnosis of the problems led to the design of leadership training courses for the supervisors. In both these cases the work of in-house professionals was supported by the experience of external ones.

There were investigative phases in these projects, but the roles adopted by the social scientists in them were primarily to facilitate the work of client staff. In both the motor components and oil marketing cases the social scientists undertook relatively unstructured interview programmes themselves to learn the issues, get to know the relevant employees and be able to formulate an appropriate process for tackling the issues. Thereafter they created transitional systems for studying the issues and deciding what action to take and they acted as facilitators to these systems. In both cases this involved creating specific roles for people, with limited agendas, and when these were complete reformulating the groups to tackle the next stage of the process. In the motor components case the initial groups consisted of the same grade or type of staff, and it was only when problems common across such categories had been revealed that mixed groups tackling specific problems could be formed. In the oil marketing case the two initial groups worked separately on different questions before coming together to be re-formed into groups working on the same question.

The role of the social scientists in these cases was both process designer and facilitator, seeking ways of supporting group process so that all participants could share in the ownership of the issue and the group learning that took place. The social science skill that was being employed in these cases relates to the design and management of group events and, in the two German cases, the design of learning experiences. Although their early explorations yielded findings which might be applied, the consultants did not initially contribute such findings to the search for solutions. They concentrated upon facilitating an open and committed attack on the problem by the client staff. Later, when there was a collective search for, and evaluation of, options, the consultants in the motor components case contributed input on reward systems and work structures. In the oil marketing case the social scientists subsequently made a substantive contribution to the design of the socio-technical system to support the new marketing role. In the other two cases they acted as trainers.

The role of the employees in these cases was of participants in diagnostic studies and then in policy-making, design and implementation. In the motor-supervision case (K) the diagnosis was not done through a study, but through an analysis workshop. In this case and the learning-shop example, some participants also became trainers. This 'do-it-yourself' approach brought commitment to the chosen solution but came as a surprise to participants in the oil marketing example, who were used to external experts doing the research and offering considered recommendations.

In several of these examples the transitional systems functioned effectively for the people directly concerned but, in time, the process had also to be related to a larger population. In some cases attempts were made to take the learning from the place of origin to other parts of the organisation, without going through the whole process of helping new participants internalise the rationale and experience the learning. In the case of the learning shops the training programme was not so successful when transferred to another plant. In the oil marketing case the plan was to transfer the process as a role-review procedure to other departments and some interest was being shown in this type of transfer. In the motor components case there was a need to gain the support of the entire workforce for the changes proposed by the staff engaged in the transitional system. To accomplish this a different process was designed: a booklet describing the recommendations was developed and a vote was organised, preceded by a period in which staff could consult the consultants about the recommendations. There was a resounding vote of support, which paved the way for the recommendations to be implemented. In the final part of the process the consultants played other roles, including designing and facilitating team-building exercises as groups of staff prepared to take on new roles in the new work organisation.

These cases are, by and large, successful examples of consultants concentrating on the dynamics of action to work with a bounded part of the client organisation; playing the roles of process designers and facilitators in situations where a limited group of employees could be helped to work on the problems and issues that were of concern to them. Knowledge-into-use was only occasionally a feature of these cases, in circumstances where the consultants felt the group process could receive some research findings and use them effectively.

Cases in behavioural change/development for management

In three of the German cases the target was management development across the hierarchy of large organisations. In each case the aim was to change the management culture of the organisation. The work was undertaken by OD consultants operating from inside the organisations in the framework of the dynamics of action. The design of the process was controlled by the consultants and consisted principally of the planning and running of experiential events. In these, managers could examine their own styles of leadership and the management of interpersonal behaviour, and could explore other approaches, usually of a more participative character, and begin to understand their effects. These programmes were undertaken in the distribution case (L), the case from news technology (M) and the case from the rubber industry (N). In these organisations, some of which were subsidiaries of American companies, the major theme was the use of management development approaches that had originated in the

USA. This included using the documentation associated with the courses involved in these approaches.

The roles of the OD staff in these programmes was to plan the process in the sense of establishing which approach to use for which managers, the sequence of course delivery, the follow-up, and so on. There is no evidence that either the consultants or the client staff adopted any kind of investigative role of organisation problems in these cases, although in the rubber case a training needs analysis was carried out. The training programmes in these cases were not developed locally but were imported from elsewhere and tailored to fit local needs. The search for types of training which were effective under local conditions was in some cases quite extensive. In the rubber industry the consultants tested four different approaches to management training. The only other investigative procedures were the self-explorations made by trainees on the courses and, in the distribution case, evaluation studies. The OD staff acted as trainers on the courses, which meant primarily facilitating the experiential learning of the participants. The main difficulty encountered once these courses became popular, as they did, for example, in the distribution case, was the shortage of skilled staff able to act as trainers. The OD staff across the three cases had access to a wide range of techniques for personal development, revealing management style, managing group process, and so on; they were not aiming to work in a knowledge-into-use framework.

The role of the client staff in these programmes was that of trainees using the experience to review personal and managerial development and test out new possibilities. There can be little doubt that these courses became very popular in some of the cases and that the trainees felt them to be worthwhile. It seems unlikely that some of the broader aims of the consultants in these cases to transform the nature of management, to 'de-hierarchise' the structure, and so on, were as successful. The cases differed substantially from each other in the degree to which the work grew out of and was rooted in the organisations or was grafted on. It may also be that other contributions from social science, for example those concerned with task and organisation, would have been necessary to establish relevance.

Conclusions: knowledge and action

The fourteen cases provide a very wide array of examples of what can be applied from social science and the means by which it can be applied. One way of characterising the strategies used is to analyse the cases for the extent to which they represent a knowledge-into-use or a dynamics of action framework. The data implied by the phrase 'knowledge-into-use' are of two kinds: on the one hand, ideas, concepts and findings that originate

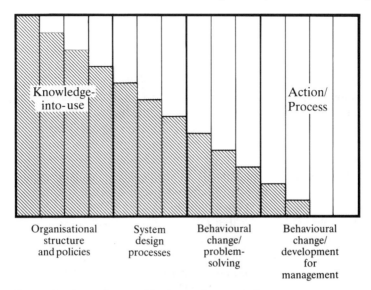

Figure 6   *Approaches to utilisation in the case studies*

within the social science world, and, on the other, data about the particular situation that has been gathered in some systematic way that includes social phenomena. A representation of the results of this analysis is given in figure 6. The figure is clearly not intended as an accurate representation, only a broad schematic one.

Most of the cases show a combination of the two frameworks, but there are relatively 'pure' forms. The cases in the structural- and policy-change category are predominantly knowledge-into-use. In the transport and electrical products cases (A and C) the contribution of the practitioners was almost completely within the knowledge-into-use framework, the dynamics of action being the province of senior client staff. In case A this was by agreement, in case C it was not. In the cases of general management change, a concern with process was the almost exclusive strategy; the objective was to apply behavioural change techniques and there are few examples of the application of particular themes or findings, or of internal investigations to generate context-specific findings. The specific group category is dominated by the dynamics-of-action framework but contains a number of examples of knowledge-into-use applied to the problems that the group identified; for example, in motor components (I) the practitioner brought to bear findings relating to payment systems and job design. These cases are also, by definition, characterised by knowledge of the particular situation informing what happened, sometimes supplemented by local investigations to test or extend that knowledge. The technical design cases involve hybrid strategies, the action element taking the form of teaching, advising, making judgements about when not to advise, introducing additional methods, all as vehicles for conveying the concepts and findings involved. These vehicles then also had other functions, for example of unfreezing a traditional way of thinking about a production process (E) or of bringing several trade union groups onto the same committee (F). A conclusion one might reach from this analysis is that, unless the objective is to use universally applicable behaviour change techniques, the successful intervention must be able to manage both frameworks. In the hybrid cases some episodes can be seen as the triumph of pragmatism over dogma: in some instances practitioners were, for example, uneasy about the implications of intervention, but saw a real need which they could meet directly.

We said in chapter 2 that the practitioner needs somehow to integrate these two frameworks. It turns out that the level of integration is indeed one of the keys to effective application. Those projects or phases where integration was low or non-existent were also those which generated most problems: in case C (electrical products) the social scientists entered the project as academics only; the organisation's expectation was that they would be consultants and they were not given the opportunity to do local diagnosis, which would have demonstrated a professional use of methods and provided some data. In the event 'the mutual learning process between social scientists and industrial practitioners turned out to be so complex' that the actual content of the project faded into the background by comparison. In case B (banking), contact was lost during a research phase with the steering institution that had commissioned the study, and this institution was disbanded. As a result, subsequent work was less effective than it could have been.

On the OD side, the least problematic cases were those which were based on knowledge of the situation or problem (H, I, the first phase of J, and K), or where a needs analysis was eventually undertaken (N). In cases H (oil marketing) and I (motor components), although it was part of the strategy not to offer substantive contributions, the sense that the practitioners were nevertheless knowledgeable must have contributed to the impact of professionalism. The diagnostic studies undertaken to generate data in the specific group cases were undertaken by the client staff (for example, oil marketing (H) and motor industry guest workers (J)). In this case, the do-it-yourself approach ensured the internalisation of the results and smoothed the path to action. Where diagnostic studies were undertaken by the social scientists, this gave them an opportunity to understand the situation, perhaps to map onto it a variety of frameworks and levels of explanation (as described in chapter 3) and so be in a position to offer context-specific help to the client. The two approaches to diagnostic activities provide very different opportunities.

In the cases where the knowledge-into-use strategy was dominant, it was the client staff who almost invariably took the lead in the action phase of the work. While there are some exceptions, it is this aspect which was the most disappointing to the social scientists. Having generated relevant data, most of them had the experience of taking a back seat whilst others made partial or inadequate use of the potential for useful action. In some cases, having done some research, they appeared to get stereotyped into a research role; there was almost an expectation that the social scientists' role was to engage in further investigative studies, leaving the translation into action to the client. The danger, from the point of view of the practitioner, was that client staff might not have internalised or worked through the concepts and findings enough to do them justice.

It is striking that, across many of the cases, a similar kind of solution was developed to deal with the hiatus between both the phases and the roles of research and action. This was to create some kind of 'transitional system'. Transitional systems took many forms: working parties and conferences to receive and debate the findings of studies, training events and exercises to work through possible courses of action, or scenarios and simulations of the future which offered new visions to be analysed. Whatever the form taken, it provided an 'off-line' opportunity for relevant client staff to review where they were and the alternatives for the future. One of the skills of the practitioner appears to be the design of opportunities of this kind.

Transitional systems of this kind appear to serve several purposes. Firstly, they provide the room and the time to consider issues of long-term significance away from normal day-to-day business. Secondly, they may provide the authority and legitimacy for later actions. In the transport case (A) the senior manager regarded the 24-hour event he organised at the beginning of the project as the critical activity because it was attended by very senior staff, and this gave legitimacy for the programme of work that flowed from it. Another objective is that the transitional system should provide a supportive environment in which new concepts can be under-stood and explored, risks taken and mistakes made. The process-oriented strategy in some of the cases displays examples of training events in which people could explore interpersonal behaviour. The technical change examples (E, F and G) display another kind of vehicle to support this process, the development of a physical manifestation of the future, for example the Lego version of factory layouts in case (E). In the same case, even hypothetically role-playing the raw material (a piece of sugar) and the transformations it had to go through, provided such an opportunity. One of the present authors (Eason, 1988) has explored the role of computer prototypes as a means by which prospective users can explore the implications of information technology systems which they might implement, as is seen in the freightforwarding case (G). These physical manifestations of the future serve a very useful purpose if they are able to translate abstract concepts into practical examples which support the internalisation process and allow people to explore and evaluate future possibilities. A great deal depends, however, on how such transitional systems are designed and handled. They can create situations where people can take on board the options that may be available, become aware of the issues that might arise, and find their own best fit; or they can be used to try and 'do something to' the people that attend.

While there are many differences between the cases in the way in which social science was utilised, a very common feature is the concern of the social scientists for the design of the processes by which they engaged with client staff. In the general management cases (L, M and N) these were largely standardised imported procedures, while the major characteristic of the OD strategies used for specific groups (H, I, J and K) was the design of unique processes geared to the particular issues and problems of the relevant groups, for example, learning shops for guest workers (J) or role-review processes for oil marketing (H). Similarly, in the technical change cases (E, F and G) the processes by which managers, designers, future users and their trade union representatives were engaged in the change process were of dominant concern to the social scientists. Some elements were imported (for instance, a list of design criteria) while others were invented. It must be noted that the effectiveness of 'participative' methods was restricted where the different parties to the process had not had the same preparation and access to the necessary knowledge.

In the processes whereby groups of people with specific issues engage with social scientists, the intervention seems to be most confident. Once there is a need to engage with more diffuse issues or with wider numbers for broader dissemination, the success rate declines.

11 What supports and hinders social science utilisation

One hypothesis we might advance about social science practice is that, no matter how good the quality of the input, it can only be effective if a framework exists in which it can be used. This framework has to facilitate the initiation of work, support it when it is underway and enable its lessons to be appropriately diffused. The fourteen cases provide many examples of factors which facilitated the use of social science and factors which impeded it. This chapter reviews the cases in a search for a strategy which optimises the chances of successful outcomes. The four categories of cases used in the previous chapters are again used for the review.

Organisational structure and policy cases

In reviewing these cases we broadly consider the factors at work in project initiation, during the project and when outcomes were more widely disseminated.

In all four cases where the aspirations were structural or policy change there was senior commitment to undertaking the work. In the banking case (B) the personnel director commissioned the work and the committee charged with a campaign for better customer services became the client for the initial work. A director with personnel responsibilities was directly responsible for commissioning the work in the transport case (A) and remained the principal client. The electrical products case (C) was a major project initiated when senior management decided to take part in the West German Humanisation of Life at Work programme, and the precision engineering case (D) was agreed by both management and the works council as a necessary programme of adjustment from outmoded mechanical skills and work practices to the new ones required in the electronic age. There are two specific features which single out the latter case from the others. Firstly, the project was initiated and driven from much closer to the target for change than the others and secondly, it was a joint management and worker representatives venture. The other three cases were all in large organisations and the senior support gained was at the expense of a lot of subsequent effort to get clearance and commitment from other levels of staff.

The reason for the initiation of the project also had a bearing on the strength with which effort was sustained and the degree to which it could spread through the organisation. The precision engineering case (D) was born of a recognition of the need to make organisational changes to cope with the impact of technical changes that were occurring. This was a clear-cut problem, was widely recognised and gave sanction to the work throughout the organisation. The transport case (A) arose from the need to see whether social science could offer insights into the longstanding problem of supervisory practice in the organisation. Again, this was a specific problem which sustained the work. In the other two cases the initiative was not related to a specific problem, but was based on a broader vision of organisational needs and took advantage of an opportunity to attempt some more general development work in the organisation. In the case of the bank (B) the personnel director used the customer services campaign as an opportunity to test what social science could offer the organisation. In the electrical products company (C) the Government programme provided a similar developmental opportunity. It provided a contract and a subsidy that sustained the work, even though its objectives were not shared by some influential groups in the organisation or were not objectives to which they attached priority.

The importance of these factors became apparent as the work progressed. The seniority of the support made it possible to undertake much work but, at each stage, there were new people to consult, to gain agreement from, to whom the rationale of the work had to be explained, and so on. Each new group had new needs that could equally have formed the basis for the study. In the banking and transport cases the first phase was diagnostic and investigative so that the clearance process was essentially a matter of gaining access to people as suppliers of information and of agreeing the conditions upon which information could be obtained. Once the investigative phase was over, many more groups were involved because of the policy implications of the findings and, since many of the groups were new to the study, more effort was expended in bringing these groups into the picture. A characteristic of this process was that it carried the study beyond the functional territory of the initiating department. In the banking study what began as an initiative by personnel had consequences for line management and such specialist departments as management services. It led to a study in the international division, which was commissioned by that division's own chief executive. Implementation of findings resulted from his renewed intervention. The electrical products case led to the involvement of many client departments and had the additional problem that several research teams were contributing, each with its own technical specialisms and values.

The problem with this process of spreading was that more and more people became involved who did not share in the initiation and perhaps did not share the goals or value of the work. At best the new people to be involved may have a 'not invented here' experience and reject outside influences in favour of developments that they initiate themselves. At worst they may experience the developments as threatening to their own aspirations and seek to limit the impact.

The process of receiving and using the findings of the work was at its most effective when the initiating group – the primary client – remained in place, retained its energy and commitment and was sufficiently powerful or broadly based to engage in constructive debate with those coming new to the programme. This was the case in the transport industry where the director was willing and able to carry the findings through all the relevant committees in order to bring policy changes to fruition. It was also the case in precision engineering, where the relevant management and works council staff were able to carry the programme to the various departments of the organisation. It was more problematic in the other two cases. In the bank, the intention to feed the results back to the committee responsible for improving customer services was frustrated because the committee had been disbanded. The personnel director who had commissioned the study was not in a direct line position and in any case did not want to use centralised authority. In the absence of the original initiators, the social scientists sought other interested parties to receive findings. In the electrical products case there was little attempt initially to create a framework within which the work of the project could be received and it was received with some doubt and scepticism by the managers of client departments.

The contractual base from which the resources operated also had a significant effect upon the nature of the work undertaken. In the banking and transport cases the client organisation paid for the time of the practitioners for each phase of the work although, in the banking case, an overall yearly budget permitted activities to be pursued outside the framework of a particular work package. Such contractual arrangements turn out to be more influential than the actual institutional base from which the social scientists came, and which formed the basis of our sampling. While the agreed programme approach to funding was a tidy mechanism for bounded pieces of work, it was a constraint when it came to 'getting to know you' activities and other work necessary to maintain the institutional base of the work which was not part of the immediate, agreed task. In the electrical products case the funding for the social scientists was from state resources and was much greater than in the other cases. This appears to have encouraged the social scientists, who came from a university, to maintain a research perspective and client departments to adopt a cavalier attitude to the academic input. In the precision engineering case there were no external consultants with whom to agree contractual and funding issues and this freed the individuals concerned to provide time as was necessary.

Systems development cases

The three UK cases of technical systems design were initiated as a result of senior management recognising that technical design had human and organisational implications. In the case of the confectionery factory (E) there was a vision at Board level that the new factory provided the ideal opportunity to improve the nature of industrial life by using concepts like autonomous working groups. The vision of food processing (F) was rather less grand but this company also saw the new factory as an opportunity to improve industrial relations by improving job satisfaction. The freightforwarding Board (case G) was more concerned with avoiding likely problems than with positive aspirations; computerisation was an unknown venture for them, but they knew of disasters and they hoped that social science would help them achieve the benefits rather than the disasters of computerisation.

In all three cases the social scientists were external to the client organisation and the financial basis was that a succession of periods of work was funded by the client organisation. In freightforwarding (G) the funding was for specific pieces of work, and in confectionery (E) it was for actual days spent; but in the case of food processing an arrangement of a number of days per six-month period enabled the consultant to spend days at her discretion and this proved very useful in building relationships, getting to understand the organisation and other aspects of work not directly related to 'deliverables'.

The sponsors of the social science contribution were in powerful positions but by no means controlled the resources necessary for the contribution to be successful. In food processing the practitioner was introduced by the parent company. In all cases the practitioners had to attempt to build relations with a much wider clientele to facilitate their work. In each case there were, for example, technical systems developers with whom the social scientists had to work to influence the design. In the confectionery (E) and food processing (F) cases the technical designers included control and production engineers, internal design teams and external contractors. In the food processing and the freightforwarding (G) cases there were design teams in the company and in its parent company. In the freightforwarding case the technical designers were DP and management services staff. Since the technical design teams did not initiate the involvement of social scientists and, in many cases, this involvement had elements of uncertainty and threat, the building of constructive relations was often a major feature of the work. The start of the freightforwarding case was, for example, marked by a direct criticism by the social scientists of the system development plans presented by the DP staff.

Another set of relations to be developed was with local management who were to run the new systems. They sometimes did not share the visions of their superiors and, whether they did or not, were generally not in post during the initial work. Understanding and valuing the work of the social scientists therefore also required attention at appropriate points in the project work.

The final set of relationships to be developed was with the work people and their representatives. In the freightforwarding case this did not present a major problem because computers were to be introduced into existing offices and the existing staff could be engaged in debate about the future system. There were no major threats to existing jobs and their trade unions were able to co-operate. In the confectionery case the issue was more complex because the knowledge of existing work people served the quality of working life of new staff at the new location, but the development was a threat to their own livelihood. The confectionery factory was not unionised. The unions at the existing site in the food processing case were preoccupied with matters outside the topic for intervention and the engagement had an on/off quality. The technology in the new foods factory was so different from that of the existing factory that the work experiences of staff in this factory were barely relevant to the new one.

All three cases were characterised, therefore, by the need to work in parallel with different groups of staff and to build relations with new people at all stages of the work. The work was heavily influenced by the time-span and timetable for the technical developments. The work of the social science practitioners could only be relevant if it was undertaken in the period prior to appropriate decisions about the technology. The need to respond in this timetable could conflict with the need to take time and trouble in building relations with work people and their unions. In the food processing case, for example, a decision not to engage directly with technical designers on job design issues until the unions felt able to join in the debate meant that many job design options were closed by technical decisions before a contribution was possible. The difficulties of parallel activities occurring in relation to the development in different places also became a major problem for practitioners who had limited resources to deploy. The pattern of technical development started small and central but spread into many parallel activities as implementation drew nearer so that the problem for practitioners became greater as time passed. The practitioner was absent for one month in the food processing case, for example, and this contributed to the premature ending of the work of the steering group. It was a disadvantage not to have a team deployed that could cover for the absence of one person and institutionalise the activity.

The other major issue to arise in relation to the technical system development was the congruity of the goals of technical designers and management and the original goals of the social science contribution. As the need for decisions became pressing and the choices harder, so the commitment to some of the original goals became more difficult. In confectionery a goal of leaving options open got lost with time in this way. In the food processing case, where the economic climate changed, the requirement to limit manning numbers took precedence over job satisfaction requirements. In the freightforwarding case, in some circumstances manning structures were selected for economic reasons which reduced job satisfaction. Minimising the number of visual display terminals meant that each had to be heavily utilised, which led to repetitive work for full-time terminal operators. The confectionery case was different in that the management held to their concept of autonomous working groups which were supported by previously institutionalised OD practices. Other aspects of job design were not similarly institutionalised.

The outcome of the influence of these factors was that the nature of the change was most heavily influenced by the values and ideas behind the technical change which were in place before the social science contribution. In the food processing case the management felt that this was not so; the impact of the social science contribution in all instances was in any case more piecemeal or fragmentary than had originally been envisaged.

Cases involving specific groups

The common feature of these cases is a target population which was going to undergo change or was felt to need to change for the collective good of the enterprise. The aim of the project was therefore bounded: in the oil case study (H) it was confined to the future role of marketing, in the motor components case (I) it was the conflicts between the hourly and day-rated workers in the factory, in the motor industry learning shops (J) it was the learning needs of guest workers and in the motor supervision case (K) it was the man-management skills of supervisors. In the motor components and motor supervision cases the initiative was, to some extent, born out of crisis. Industrial relations and conflicts between different groups of staff were so bad in the motor components factory that they threatened the ability of the factory to adjust to changes in the industry. The German motor factory had suffered its first wave of wildcat strikes and saw increasing the interpersonal skills of supervisors as a major way of correcting the decline in relations between management and workers. The oil marketing and guest-workers cases were stimulated by longer-term but nonetheless equally specific issues which had to be tackled. In all these cases other remedies had been tried without success and a social science approach offered another avenue. The work was supported in each case by the management directly responsible for the target group and also, in all the cases except oil, by more senior, central management.

In three of these cases the social scientists who acted as primary resources were part of well-established OD teams, where initial funding to work on problems was part of the normal budgets. In these cases requests for additional funds could be made from central sources or from the client departments when the nature of the work became clear and in the motor industry, guest workers and supervision cases it was used in part to fund external specialists and in part to pay for the time of the people to be trained. In the motor components case the practitioner was external but was funded, in several separately financed phases, to work full-time in the factory over a period of years. In general, therefore, the resource provision in these cases as compared with many of the others was considerable.

The combination of resources and specific, bounded objectives supported by relevant staff in significant roles appears to have created the time and space in which useful work could be undertaken. As time passed, however, most of the cases experienced problems in maintaining the support they needed to do the work, in part because of changes in the organisation and in part because of shifts in the work plan.

One of the problems was continuity of staff in key roles. In the guest workers programme (J) the person responsible for introducing the concept left the central location to develop the programme at another site. Although learning shops had been thriving under his direction they petered out at the central location when he left, only to be revived several years later by people who saw it as a 'new beginning' rather than a development of the earlier scheme. In the motor components case (I) the programme progressed a long way, with the trade union representatives giving their support both to the change programme and to a joint problem-solving style of working with management. In a local union election, however, the 'moderate' convener was replaced by a 'radical' steward who went back to an adversarial style which made implementation of the plans more problematic. In the oil marketing case (H) the senior manager who had been the main client and sponsor of the work on the marketing role was promoted at a critical point. However, in this case the practitioners took some explicit steps to deal with the situation. They asked the superior of the person who was leaving to provide continuity support for the project until they were able to work with the new person in the role and enable that person to form an informed judgement of the value of the work. As a result, the work continued without interruption or change of direction. In the motor industry supervision case (K) the training programme was carried out by seven training teams, so the movement of any particular individual would have less impact on the programme as a whole. (However, we have no data on whether individuals in fact moved.)

The other problems arose when practitioners sought to move the work from its originally agreed bounded origins and at the same time to institutionalise it more widely. This was particularly noticeable in the case of the guest workers' learning shops. Originally these were devised as participative ways of teaching guest workers the limited and necessary language skills to cope with shop-floor conditions. When this worked well it was expanded, successfully, to include participative work on whatever problems were being experienced at shopfloor level. The attempt was then made to transplant this approach to another factory where management was suspicious of the participative style that was being adopted and the need for the programme. This resistance was eventually overcome but much work with the management of the site was necessary first. In the supervision case problems were encountered when work with a central staff department had implications for other European units of the organisation.

In the motor components case (I) there was a point at which the plans for change were well developed and enthusiastically endorsed by the staff of all types who had worked on them but the attitudes of the remainder of the staff were unknown. The problem was the common one of broadening the base to bring in a different population. This was done by publishing the recommendations and organising a mass vote on them with opportunities for people to consult before voting. This appears to have been an important focal event in the factory, bringing the attention of everybody to the work that had been undertaken.

In general, within their boundaries, these projects were relatively successful. The more successful ones were, on the one hand, oil marketing and motor components, where methods were explicitly devised to handle the transition from one client or client population to another, and on the other hand, motor supervision where there was less reliance on key individuals, since the supervisor training activity was broadly institutionalised.

Cases of behavioural change/development for management

In the three German cases which were undertaking broad OD programmes the initiating agent was a senior manager responsible for training or personnel development. The motivation for the programme was slightly different in each case. In the distribution case (L) there was a commitment shared by the head of personnel development and a longstanding member of the Board (who had hired him) that humanistic values were needed in the organisation and attempts should be made to 'de-hierarchise' the structure so that more staff had the opportunity to pursue both organisation- and person-related goals. In the rubber case (N) a senior training manager had been receiving ideas about OD methods from the American parent company and elsewhere in Germany, and was interested in adding them to the repertoire of his department. In the news technology case (M) the organisation had been performing badly in a rapidly changing market and the OD programme was introduced in an attempt to create a flexible and adaptive management.

In all three cases the main resources used for the design of training and for the training itself were internal staff. There was the occasional use of external staff for specific purposes. Funding normally came from central training budgets but, once a particular course was out of its experimental phase and in some demand, there was usually a move to ask client departments to pay for it. This form of self-financing was widely regarded as a sign that the course had been institutionalised.

In all three cases the problem for the initiators was essentially that of selling their OD 'product' to the user departments of the organisation. In one of the cases (news technology) the programme was just beginning and the main problem was to convince sceptical user management that a programme of interpersonal skills and personal development training was of value when they expected a training department to provide practical and cognitive skills training.

The rubber case (N) provides an illustration of several years of effort trying a variety of OD techniques. The philosophy was initially one of identifying a method that was successful elsewhere and trying it. This was attempted with one well-known management style training approach and it was not well received; there were no repeat orders. The strategy was then amended and the method selected modified in the light of presumed organisational needs before trial courses were offered. Another technique offered in this way was of only moderate success. The strategy was again modified, this time to begin with a needs analysis survey in an attempt to learn what kind of training was deemed to be appropriate. As a result, a further technique was identified as appropriate, and successful implementation followed. This confirms the commonly held view that understanding the market helps sell the product, but it also demonstrates that people who have played a part in selecting a course are more likely to attend it.

The widest dissemination of courses was achieved in the distribution industry case (L) where the practitioner became very well known for the work he did. It was estimated that 50 per cent of management attended one of the courses on offer. It is notable, however, that some departments

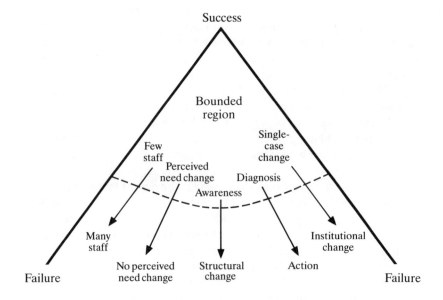

Figure 7   *Factors contributing to successful outcomes*

refused to take part and could not accept the ideology behind the courses. While the courses were still being widely applied, the chief practitioner's role ended and the OD activity was run down.

Conclusions: success or failure?

Having analysed the cases from a number of perspectives we can now return to the question of what characterises a successful utilisation of social science. Do the outcomes of these cases show that the social science interventions have been a success or a failure? The results seem to show that they have been both. The optimist will find many examples of useful contributions. The pessimist may conclude, along with many of the practitioners, that the contributions fall considerably short of what is possible. Despite the fact that the evaluation methods are neither sufficiently longitudinal nor sufficiently exhaustive to give a full picture, and the fact that there is a high variety of method and content in the sample, there do appear to be some common patterns that relate to the degree to which sought outcomes were achieved.

From the point of view of the intervention itself, some of the major dimensions which seem to distinguish between success and failure are identified in figure 7. If all the success poles of these dimensions are gathered together it can be seen that they share a common property. They refer to a situation which is in some way *bounded*, while the pole that relates to failure refers to an unbounded, large or diffuse situation. Much of these two chapters has been concerned with the difficulties that ensue when the project moves beyond its 'bounded' origins. Social science interventions worked best within a limited and manageable domain. The nature of the 'bounding' varies enormously across the dimensions listed in figure 7.

An obvious route to 'success', therefore, would seem to be to limit the intervention to a small number of people who can be studied and worked with in an intensive way. The help that can then be given to understand oneself, change one's strategy, internalise substantive findings, evaluate alternative organisational structures and policies, and so on, can be considerable. Once the numbers become large, it becomes impracticable to provide on-going and intensive contact between the client staff and the practitioners unless it takes the form of standardised training, and other more indirect techniques have to be employed. They are less successful. A related factor is the extent to which client staff share a perceived need or are engaged upon an agreed change process. The cases seem to be most successful where the starting-point is a limited group who accept that they have a need: marketers who need to re-define their role (case H) or foreign workers who need to adapt to a new culture (case J) and so on. The intervention of social science practitioners was much harder where this was not the case. In banking (case B), for example, there was no small group with an agreed need and there was no ready-made client for the findings of studies made in the branches.

In most cases, as the work progressed, so more and more people became involved. Even when it started with a bounded group, the action process tended to bring in more people. These were often people who did not share the perceived need and had not worked with the social scientists on it. Typically this lessened the chances of 'successful' outcomes. New people who became involved could not easily identify with the work already undertaken. The 'not invented here' syndrome seems to be a major obstacle to the spread of outcomes from one part of an organisation to the rest. Social science practitioners continually face the problem that the late entrants in a project need as much work done with them as the initial clients, or more.

The chances of success were also high if the initial target was training, i.e. improving the awareness of people about themselves, their dealings with others, or about substantive social science theories and findings, or about the problems facing their organisation, and so on. Some of the most developed techniques in social science appear to be those that design events by which small groups of people can attain significant gains in these forms of awareness. In many of the cases there are examples of events which appear to have had significant impact upon their participants.

While greater awareness is a worthwhile goal in itself, it becomes of direct benefit to the organisation if the person and institution concerned are able to translate it into changed behaviour patterns which improve organisational effectiveness. In many cases the improvement in awareness was seen as a prelude to such behavioural changes, for example a different style of management. While the evidence we have is not suitable for detecting behavioural changes of this kind, indications are that in a number of cases the transition from awareness to practice proved difficult. It is a common finding that managers returning from management development courses find it difficult to adopt new strategies in circumstances where everyone else continues as before.

The next factor which appears to be associated with successful outcomes is the dimension which leads from diagnosis to action. The social scientists were often directly instrumental in undertaking, or causing client staff to undertake, investigations within organisations which led to new evidence or new perspectives on the problems to be tackled. Many of the social scientists expected to be able to pursue these findings into an action mode and to play a part in helping with appropriate structural or policy changes. One striking result of this study is that, in most cases where this was the hope, the client staff took over the process of managing the action part of the process and the social scientists felt that they made little contribution. It could be argued that the end result was influenced by social science thinking because the staff concerned had in some way internalised the concepts and results provided by the resource. However, many of the practitioners saw the changes actually made as a pale reflection of what could have been done or heavily influenced by forces other than those with which they had been working.

It needs to be said that we are here referring to perceptible change. Mainly, the social scientists simply do not know what, if anything, happened outside the bounded area. Sometimes they referred to incidents where they had unexpectedly come across evidence of impact. Whether this is 'grasping at straws', or whether there really were some more diffuse effects, neither they nor we are able to say.

The final variable in figure 7 is the form of mechanism that carries the change. In these cases, temporary institutions were created for the special purpose of implementation. The interventions began as a single case for a specific purpose. These arrangements, be they training events, diagnostic studies, or design procedures, were the means by which client staff made their own selections from and internalised what was offered. If the learning associated with the project was to be maintained and developed in the organisation after the association with the social science resource was over, some of these arrangements would need to be institutionalised: made a normal part of the culture and practice of the organisation. There are, however, few examples of institutionalised practices of this kind in these cases. However, while a social science practitioner may not feel that the processes introduced have become embedded, the staff themselves may feel that what they have derived from them does indeed constitute an institutionalised form of social science. As an example, in the freightforwarding case (G) the chief designer practised a form of user participation after the relation with the social science practitioner had ended. It was not a form of user participation the practitioner would have recommended, but it was a practice that would not have happened were it not for the project and it became a normal part of that designer's work.

The designer, in fact, reported some years later that he was working for a different company and was implementing some of the ideas he had derived from the project. In the banking case (B) the opportunity to return after nine years demonstrated that many staff, now more senior, had internalised much from the earlier project and had used this as part of their normal work in many different projects. In the foods processing case (F) the practitioner could not trace any links between project activities and the new plant, but the people in the company were quite sure that working arrangements were very different from what they would have been.

In summary, a scenario for the bounded circumstances where a social science intervention would be most likely to lead to a successful outcome would be as follows: the organisation would have an agreed problem or change plan which would have associated with it a limited number of people with whom the practitioner could work. For the purposes of the work it would be possible for the practitioner to introduce special methods and procedures. The required outcome would have to be in the form of a diagnosis only, and/or a new level of awareness among the staff involved in the work.

However, while this analysis shows that it is easier to operate within bounded circumstances, we clearly do not conclude that social science efforts should be limited to projects of this type. There are a number of reasons for this. Firstly, a bounded project from which diffusion does not take place may be of marginal value. A bounded project with these characteristics may constitute a lot of effort for limited return for the client and the practitioner. It is necessary to find ways of being effective in unbounded conditions. Secondly, a major initiative which only has partial or unclear success may nevertheless be judged more worthwhile than a bounded one which is wholly successful. Thirdly, while there is little evidence of widespread effects in the unbounded areas of these cases, there is evidence of some areas of success in different cases. An analysis of the methods and processes which have shown some signs of success may indicate how this kind of problem could be tackled. Fourthly, the fact that we have little evidence of widespread effects in the more diffuse cases may not mean they did not occur. There are two methodological considerations which may mean that the case studies undervalue the impact of the intervention. The evaluations ended not long after the formal completion of these cases, but the diffusion process may have taken much longer. Also, the nature of diffusion means the effects become mixed with other influences and it becomes progressively more difficult to discern the causal link with the case study. This seems particularly to be a factor in the way client staff internalise the lessons of the case. From a number of cases it seems that staff need time and distance from the practitioner in order to make the lessons their own and use what they have learned in their way. In two of the 'diffuse' cases (B and C) effects were experienced outside the scope of the projects described. In B, this was nine years later in time. The opportunity to return to the bank, after nine years, demonstrated in particular the way staff still referred to the earlier study as influential in their development and were engaged in projects which could be related to the earlier work. In C it concerned diffusion of the learning about how social scientists may work in applied mode within the wider Humanisation of Life at Work programme, as well as diffusion of the work structuring experience outside it.

The above discussion is based on analysis of the type of activity which tended to be more, or more clearly and perceptibly, successful. However, the theme that recurs is that success is dependent on the context within which the work takes place. There is therefore a second set of dimensions about the conditions under which such work is more, or less, likely to succeed. Some of these are listed in figure 8. Many of these variables apply to the institutions from which social science is practised at least as much as to those at the receiving end. Discontinuity between those who contract for a piece of work and those who carry it out, for example, is a powerful signal of danger.

While the nature of the institution from which the social science activity was carried out appears not to be as influential as we thought when we based our sampling frame on it, the funding structure does appear to be crucial. The social scientists in case C were legitimated by a public programme and could survive setbacks, as could in-house practitioners. In many other kinds of framework legitimacy has to be earned, and worth demonstrated, again and again.

There are therefore two conclusions to be drawn from the outcomes of these cases. Firstly, there is a body of practice that can cope quite well with projects which have bounded characteristics. Secondly, to extend effectiveness, there is a need to establish and sustain an infrastructure base for an initiative which can support the work as it becomes progressively

Conditions tending to *support* success	Conditions tending to *hinder* success
* Sponsor and client are the same, i.e. do something with *us*'	* Sponsor and client are different, i.e. do something with/to *them*
* Sponsor has line authority	* Sponsor has staff authority
* Key people stay in post through to implementation	* Key people move away
* Coherent strategy for consultancy	* Competing consultants engaged on same problem situation
* Funding structure permits work on contextual issues	* Funding structure does not permit contextual work
* Institutions available for implementation	* Institutions for implementation not available

Figure 8   *Contextual variables supporting and hindering success*

diffused in the organisation. Infrastructure support is necessary in all cases, but becomes more critical, and the appropriate infrastructure more difficult to attain, outside the bounded area.

It may be necessary to translate diagnosis into action, turn awareness into behaviour and structural change, involve many more people and to replicate the single-case procedures for subsequent use. It appears that it is these processes (that often follow a start characterised by the above factors) which are difficult to manage.

It needs a base within the organisation which initiates it, provides the necessary time, space and resources, champions its work and creates the framework for diffusion within the organisation. The cases show three ways in which the nature of the base may be problematic.

(i) *The base may be unstable.* Organisations are dynamic entities and the person or persons who initiate activities may not stay in post or even with the company. Parallel activities in the organisation, such as the progress of technical change, or outside it, such as change in the market-place, may cause dramatic changes in the base. The practitioners may find therefore that their support has disappeared or that the demands on them are different from those originally agreed. Whatever the starting-point for the case, it seemed to suffer from these problems. There is need for a framework for continuing review and adaptation.

(ii) *The base may prove too bounded for the work.* The base which initiated work was usually responsible for a specific aspect of the work of the organisation. Yet as work progressed it was very common to find it crossing boundaries in the organisation. It was often necessary, if the original objectives were to be pursued, to recruit the support and resources of parts of the organisation well away from the base which initiated the work.

In the systems design cases, for example, the movement was between technical designers, management and potential users. In the general OD programmes participants had to be recruited through the training organisation. Whenever this kind of 'client drift' occurred there was a heavy premium to pay, in engaging with the new people to be involved and those to whom they reported to gain support and commitment. Needless to say, in a participative programme, this often led to a redefinition of priorities. It may be thought that if the initiator is sufficiently senior, for example, the whole Board, these problems will not be found. It is certainly true that this gives broad sanction to the work but sooner or later, and especially if the organisation is in any way practising devolved power, it will be necessary for practitioners to gain local acceptance, and 'earn the right' to work with all who become involved.

(iii) *The base may limit dissemination.* We saw earlier that the projects that came nearest to meeting their objectives were those with bounded ambitions, devoted to certain changes amongst target groups of staff. Such projects tend to meet difficulties if attempts are made to disseminate outcomes beyond the original boundaries or to institutionalise the developments for subsequent use. This is again a case of stepping outside the base which shares the values and objectives and has internalised the outcomes, into unprepared territory which is not ready to receive and use the lessons that have been learned.

Since all cases experience these problems to some extent what can be done about them? Some cases seem to manage these issues well and three levels of effort contribute to the success:

(i) *The organisational base must not leave it to the practitioners.* The successful cases are those in which the people who have initiated the activity have supported and championed it with their colleagues throughout the work programme. Ideally they have broadened the base by creating a client grouping which provides champions in the different parts of the organisation and protection against the disappearance of a specific champion. The most difficult circumstances for the practitioners are those where the initiator takes no further interest when the work begins. This almost seems a guarantee of failure by the organisation to make use of any work done.

(ii) *Practitioners must devote time to their base.* It is tempting for practitioners to work directly with the people they have been commissioned to work with. The danger is that they will be continually surprised by changes in the base or the lack of understanding and support when their work carries them beyond the initial territory. There is a considerable 'overhead' associated with practice, which is the time and effort needed to understand new people, explain the rationale of the project, review it in light of their situation, check the understanding of the initiators, prepare the ground, understand and work with the political realities of organisational factions, and so on. The need to give priority to these kinds of activity if the long-term aims are to be achieved is demonstrated many times by the cases and it is important that a proportion of the funded resource be devoted to this activity to ensure it receives the priority it needs.

(iii) *There should be joint search for ways of hanging on to gains.* Here there are lessons to be learned from the systems design cases. A structural change does not depend on a particular kind of behaviour or sustained enthusiasm for its continuing effect. The omission of a layer of supervision, the shape and layout of a building, the size of a buffer zone in a production process, are relatively robust kinds of institutionalised remnants that have fairly long-term effects.

12 Five practitioners

As we said in the introduction, in the course of collecting case material and in the course of our general movement within this field, we have come across many examples relevant to the general topic but which do not fit neatly into the pattern of case studies of projects in organisations. In this chapter we present five such examples, all from the United Kingdom. They are individuals, coming from different discipline backgrounds, who in conversation have described their approach and strategy rather than a particular case experience. They illustrate the importance of the practitioner's own background and his or her route into the work. They provide a feel for the realities of the individual practitioner in the field and the more pragmatic approach that circumstances sometimes demand. In particular, the importance of gaining acceptance in an evolutionary way is highlighted in some of these examples. Three of the five are in-house consultants or researchers, while two work from outside. Of these, one is in a university and the other in an independent research institute.

The reader is once again asked to remember that these are fragments.

An ergonomist in a trade union research department

A research assistant for technology

This union represents the employees in a major technologically based industry and established one of the first research departments in UK trade unions. In 1980 the industry within which its members worked was going through a major organisational change and many technological changes were imminent. The union decided to appoint a research assistant to deal with the significant issues of technical change. They did not merely want someone who could understand the technology (principally electronic or information technology) but someone who could understand its human implications and explain them to the officials of the union.

They appointed Mrs A. She was a graduate in ergonomics with three years' experience in research on the human and organisational implications of technical change. She was also a local councillor on behalf of the

Labour Party. From the perspective of the union, Mrs A had the right technological background, had already gained some union expèrience and was a member of the Labour Party.

The job

Entering the job from a post within a university, Mrs A found that what she said now mattered because, as the only expert, people listened to her views. Conversely, she had to cope with a very wide array of issues and had very little time to master them. At first she found the job rather reactive: she responded to requests and usually had, at most, two days to formulate a very practical and specific answer. The union officials had no time for abstract arguments or for statements about the need for more research, she had to arrive at recommendations.

After some months she began to find ways of being more proactive. She began to put summaries of publications pertinent to technical change into a technology bulletin. In time, the circulation of this grew to include not only union officials, but the sponsored Members of Parliament of the union and the research staff of other unions.

She also began to find ways of using her training in ergonomics more effectively. She found that it was possible to follow up a topic and do more work on it when a section of the union felt strongly about it and made the necessary request for the work. She could therefore approach officials who had expressed concern about an issue and ask them to make a request if they wanted it taken further. In one instance, for example, the introduction of microfiche into a specialist kind of office had gone badly. As the result of a request from the official responsible for these offices, Mrs A undertook a survey of the problem. She visited the offices, discussed the problem with the members of the union and wrote a lengthy report on her conclusions. This was immediately adopted by the union officials, who rarely obtained such a detailed, well-documented case, and it was sent to the employers. These refuted many of the findings but implemented many of the recommendations. The report was subsequently reproduced in the union's annual report and drew a big response.

Relations with the discipline

Mrs A does not mind that she cannot publish her work or undertake other activities that would enhance her academic reputation. But she does find that she needs contact with her academic base. She needs to get authoritative and up-to-date information on a wide range of issues quickly. She makes use of her wide circle of academic contacts in order to obtain leads on where to obtain information, which the union's libraries can then follow up. She also sees a need to develop a bibliographic search system for the considerable information available in trade union documents, which can help someone in her position, faced with a specific request and a need to make a specific response in a short time.

Future developments

In addition to her work within the union, Mrs A is beginning to find that her services are being sought by her colleagues in other unions. She sees hope in this response to her role that similar posts may soon develop in other unions.

An internal OD adviser

Mr B is someone who has grown into the role of OD adviser rather than obtaining formal qualifications and seeking a post. He works within one division of a large multinational chemicals manufacturing company.

History of the role

Mr B was trained as a chemist and, for fifteen years, followed a conventional career pattern within the company to become plant manager, plant superintendent and then area manager. In the process he developed interests in management and personnel issues. In 1967–8 the company applied MbO (management by objectives) as a technique throughout the division and when the MbO adviser was promoted, Mr B was offered a secondment from his line role to this work. He did not return to his former role. When the training officer left, he took on training as well. Gradually Mr B realised that he was filling an OD function for his works.

Having got into this role without formal training, Mr B began to develop his knowledge by attending short courses about change agents and OD. These were followed by a one-month course and then an advanced course, 'Organisation Development for Advanced Practitioners', run at Columbia, USA, which involved four separate short courses at two-monthly intervals. He continued to develop his own skills and capabilities in this evolutionary way. He had recently attended a course on business studies because he felt that by concentrating on psychological and systems perspectives, he was losing touch with business issues.

OD in the company

Mr B has become part of a loose network of OD staff within the company. These roles can be traced back to a company initiative begun in 1966, to move away from paying workers via bonuses and towards creating a staff role for everyone with weekly pay, sickness pay and so on, with the aim of helping everyone to feel a full part of the company. In order to achieve this 'New Deal', the jobs in the factories were restructured to create job enrichment. To accomplish this, teams were formed consisting of management, unions and specialists from methods study and elsewhere, to devise new job descriptions. At the same time, managers attended courses on management development to learn about the Managerial Grid (Blake and Mouton, 1964) and some of the well-known theories of motivation.

At the centre of this massive change programme was a small group of corporate OD advisers and at divisional level other OD advisers were appointed. The OD adviser for the division in which Mr B worked was an outsider who, for example, ran a Managerial Grid programme in which B became involved. To assist the full-time adviser, a number of people who already held internal appointments were given part-time area responsibilities for the programme. Mr B became the responsible person for the very large works where he operates.

He remains a solo operator, although the other advisers, both in the division and at corporate level, form a loose network which provides mutual support. The reporting structure is, however, internal; there is no responsibility to the corporate OD staff.

The process by which OD has developed in the company, and the development of Mr B's own role, has essentially been pragmatic. He describes it as follows:

> What has often bothered me is that whenever I have searched for a grand design I always failed. I've said to myself there ought to be a strategy and I've made some pretty sophisticated attempts to get one, but without success. As long as I work in a pragmatic way and work on whatever opportunities there are around I survive, do a job and do very nicely. But it has always bothered me that there is no grand strategy.

The nature of the work

In part the work consists of playing a facilitating role in large-scale change processes, for example the MbO programme, the closure of a large plant and a training programme to develop OD skills among management. However, much of the work is short episodes conducted to help individuals or groups cope with changes or problems.

An example is typical of the pattern: the chairman of the division says he is not satisfied with the link between the research laboratories and the production facilities and asks B to talk to each of the directors and senior managers involved and see what action may result. Following the discussions, a meeting is held and a high-powered technical committee is created, of which B is asked to be secretary.

No specific charge is made for B's time and expenses in engaging in these exercises. A central budget covers these costs. He considers that many of these activities, which are usually initiated before the problem has become clear, would not start if the customer was expected to pay.

The future of OD and of OD advisers

Mr B works alone and anticipates continuing in this way. He does not plan to build up a team. He can only operate as he does because he is widely known and his contribution is valued and respected. There is no question of a formal evaluation of the value of his role:

> There is no answer to the evaluation question. I've not found anybody who can show me a successful way of doing it that was cost-effective. One of my bosses always said that if he did not get any bad news about me, he knew I was doing a good job.

The value of the role was indirectly acknowledged when the personnel function was cut and many jobs lost. There was no suggestion that the role of OD adviser be removed.

In terms of developing OD within the division, Mr B and his colleagues are working to add OD skills to the abilities of the people who have to spend most of their time as change resources (management services staff, personnel staff, training staff) and line managers who may also need these skills to act as change agents for their colleagues.

When it comes to his own successor, he considers the sensible choice would be one of the internal staff who is already developing into an OD role:

> If you ask me why we would not look outside, it's probably because we are not perfect!

An organisation theorist

Professor C has carried out major, long-term, research programmes in organisation theory. The work is best known for its measures of organisational structure and organisational climate and for the systematic analysis of how these variables affect organisational behaviour. However, the framework adopted for these studies is essentially interdisciplinary and not wholly industrial sociology. Professor C describes himself as 'de-disciplined':

> My first degree was in psychology, then I went to work on inspection and I had to learn some sociology fast. Since then, I've been sitting on the fence so long, I can do hand-stands on it. I believe, in the end, that disciplines are

simply the restrictive practices of academics. I don't mind that, we have to put the boundaries somewhere, but they have no sense in my view except as that. I don't wish to know about boundaries between psychology and sociology; I want to draw the boundary somewhere else.

Professor C's main interest has been teaching and the execution of long-term research programmes. Consultancy activities play a lesser part in his work; his views and activities concerning consultancy relate to his interests in research and theory.

The boundary between consultancy and research in field investigations is not clear-cut. In his experience, organisations that grant access for research usually get some benefit, but because it is research it is rarely possible to say what will happen, and such benefits cannot therefore be guaranteed:

> I have heard research described as 'smash and grab', but my experience contradicts that. You can knock on the door and say, 'Excuse me, can I look at your appendix', and they say, 'Come in, I've a very interesting appendix.' People usually enjoy research interviews; they find them helpful and they don't get many such opportunities to talk.

They also get a feedback report on what the researches have revealed. In Professor C's studies, the research findings provided a basis for the organisation to compare itself with other organisations which was of considerable interest and provided a valued return for the research access.

Beyond the incidental consultancy benefits of research, Professor C considers that there are two important ways in which researchers can and should engage in consultancy. The first concerns the use of research tools as tools of value to the practitioner.

An example of this was an organisation which had hired a consultant to give their managers leadership training. At the prompting of the consultant, the organisation decided to evaluate the training. They decided to appoint independent consultants to undertake the evaluation and the project was conducted by two members of Professor C's research team. They used a method to evaluate the impact of the training which had been developed as part of the research programme to assess organisational climates:

> This is appropriate consultancy for researchers to do. First, it was a research survey they did and secondly, they were testing whether concepts and methods designed for research could be usefully developed and used for applied purposes.

The second reason for researchers to engage in consultancy is to provide help or advice in return for research access. In a recent research study, Professor C has been examining the behaviour of the Boards of three companies. The study was longitudinal in order to rectify the limitations of earlier cross-sectional studies. (As a method, cross-sectional analysis makes it difficult to make causal inferences.) However, the longitudinal study required a commitment from Board members to let themselves be interviewed for one hour every two weeks for nine months. This, in his view, meant that a tangible return had to be offered:

> This was a reasonable investment of their time and although it was likely they would enjoy it and find it helpful, we felt we should offer a pretty general consultancy service in return. I would not ask for this degree of access without it.

The consultancy offered was an examination of Board communications. This used established techniques, the measures of organisational structure developed in the research studies (which are quick to apply), communication nets and sociograms. In one case the report was rejected because it was too tough and challenging. Professor C comments:

> I left it to a younger colleague to write the first draft and the younger you are the more forthright you are. I toned it down, but the person who writes it first sets the tone. Shortly afterwards, the chief executive was promoted and left. The new man read it and said, 'That's right', but he did not feel he could use it because he was new.

In another of the firms, the consultancy showed that the Board was very rational in decision-making, but left members with 'bottled-up' anxieties and feelings that the right decisions had not necessarily been taken. As a result of the report, they asked for some training and a one-day event was organised in which Board members engaged in exercises to stimulate openness in interpersonal relations.

In the third firm, the consultancy input raised issues about organisational structure, but the firm at the time had no way of tackling these issues and the report was shelved. The consultancy style adopted by Professor C is not to provide recommendations, but to try to focus on a series of questions and issues which the organisation has to take seriously. For interpersonal reasons, the company could not face some of the questions posed, but later there was a major change in personnel and some of the staff believe the consultancy input indirectly hastened this change.

Professor C does use the results of his own research when he takes a consultancy role, but as the examples show, he believes in applying whatever is appropriate from the 'OD consultant's bag of tricks'. In general, he prefers consultancy methods which have been well established and are backed by established research findings on organisational behaviour to those in which the consultant uses his own response to events as data.

A psychoanalytically oriented consultant to organisations

Mr D has moved through the disciplines of mathematics and psycho-analysis to working with organisations. His methodology is to collaborate with them in exploring and rethinking issues and problems of practice. In doing this, he uses himself as a sounding board, noting and reviewing the information, situations and the responses which are triggered off in him by what is going on. This would include aspects of his own behaviour or reactions to it during the conduct of the joint activities.

A central feature of this approach is the learning and development that goes on in the client group or organisation and how to continue and pass on the learning deriving from the collaboration.

Mr D puts this way the relevance of psychoanalysis and psychoanalytic concepts for work with organisations:

> I happen to be a psychoanalyst working with organisations, but what I practise is not psychoanalysis. To talk of 'psychoanalysing an organisation' is not only inappropriate but off-putting. The question that I have sought to answer is, to what extent and in what ways the psychodynamics inherent in individual development processes apply to group and organisational life – and if they do, in what ways can they be recognised.

He sees two parallels that can be drawn: one is the relevance of looking at the unconscious processes that occur and the way they are affecting the tasks in hand – long-term and short-term. The other is the use that the consultant can make of the way in which the client organisation makes use of him or her. On unconscious forces, he notes the following dynamic in organisation:

> Over time, a group or organisation develops a culture of its own and that development will have been affected by the different historical, economic and other contexts through which it has passed ... the sub-groups of functions, geographic areas, technological or divisional activities will also have cultures based on discipline, speciality, values, norms, locality, etc. which will have to be reconciled with that of the wider organisation to which they belong. In addition, the objectives or tasks which these different kinds of component groups attempt to achieve have also to be reconciled with the balance of objectives, strategy, and policy set – or felt policy set – for the overall organisation.

It is in attempting to bring these aspects together operationally that D thinks defences and structures get created to guard against anxieties about survival, loss of power or self-esteem. Being unaware of these anxieties can lead to poor decisions, misjudgement or inadequate organisational design.

The second parallel with psychoanalysis is in making use of what psychoanalysts call the 'transference'. In organisational work this means being aware of how the client is using the consultant and thinking about whether this could be highly indicative of ways in which the organisation works. However, D warns that the dynamic in this is often very complex. For example, clients presenting their situation might give the consultant an overwhelming amount of material, flooding him with information and superficial problems but little or no indication of the basic issues involved. Among the various possibilities which could be assumed, the consultant might recognise that he or she is being tested out to see how far he or she is really concerned to help and/or competent enough to know that more serious issues needed to be explored. At such times, too, the client may also convey to the consultant the feeling of what it is like to be in the client's shoes! – inducing in him the frustration felt by the client by depriving the consultant of the relevant data to do his job. Such feelings and impressions would need to be judged against the 'certainty' with which the 'music behind the words', as D describes it, is conveyed. Any consequent choice of selected communication would also need to be made against D's 'counter-transference' i.e., the awareness of his own tendencies and reactions in corresponding circumstances and situations. It is here that D's own psychoanalytic training and experience provides him with the capacity to make such choices.

This way of working can be seen therefore to entail tolerating much complexity and uncertainty. D describes it as being able to 'stay lost', putting up with not knowing or having to reach solutions or conclusions. He traces back this quality of 'active quietness' to when he was teaching as well as to its development through psychoanalytic training:

> It is not infrequent or unusual to find oneself entertaining different kinds of turmoil or crisis in school life. Reactive teachers tended either to assert themselves strongly or be overwhelmed. Its equivalent in analytic situations occurs when the patient may emotionally, actively or verbally, tend to produce a form of panic or sense of crisis without an indication of rationale or meaning. It is helpful to be able to 'stay lost' with everything milling around and has much to contribute to the timing of appropriate interventions. This is not therefore to be regarded as a passive position, or a 'blank wall' response or even an indecisive approach. It certainly should not be practised as a technique. I have then nearly always found it possible to draw attention to some aspect or feature which can begin or develop the *process* of finding out what is happening or of reaching understanding without needing to solve the matter at once. Not least, it helps to bring the individual and/or the group in on the search.

Mr D also describes this aspect as following an 'unfolding model' rather than the classic sequence of diagnosis, acceptance, application, in letting understanding, choices and resolution occur in a more organic fashion.

Another concept that he uses in this process and which is important to the kind of self-reviewing process he endeavours to facilitate with his clients is the notion of creating the right kind of climate. Here D draws on the work of Winnicott (1971), a child psychoanalyst who developed the concept of the 'transitional object' in relation to early child development. A transitional object as used by Winnicott was some object, often a teddy bear or special blanket, which the child could use to work out certain early conflicts, especially the 'me/not me' aspects of identity. D describes how this concept can be adapted, and its relevance to the development of organisations, as follows:

> For the young infant the transitional object provides not only an acceptable 'cover' as an overt play companion but a medium and mode through which an 'area of illusion' [Winnicott] can be explored and the issues involved worked through to a 'good enough' [Winnicott] position or stage of the solution. [There are] many examples of the importance of such transitional dynamics in later phases of life ... to give some examples initiated by me before ever learning of the psychoanalytic approach ... developing a 'stock exchange' in the school at which I was teaching mathematics as a means not only of learning about percentages, profit and loss, etc. but mainly to overcome anxieties about the subject of mathematics itself.

What one often needs then to prompt this kind of exploration that will reveal new understanding is what D calls the 'empty space'; a gap or even 'no man's land' in social, organisational or role/person affairs which will offer, in conjunction with a relevant, acceptable purpose, the degree of mental/emotional challenge within which this kind of exploratory testing-out activity can take place. He elaborates it like this:

> In the large majority of cases, I have found ... that a 'growing point' of some kind already exists ... By picking up the 'weak' as well as the 'strong' signals from different sections of the wider as well as immediate environment, it is possible to ensure continuous learning and development of the 'growing-point site'.

What is important, then, is that the 'growing-point' is picked up by someone who has the authority and is ready to do something about it; as D puts it, someone who is truly 'bothered'. What D is talking about, therefore, is the importance in his approach to consultancy of creating a climate, a space, in which there is safety of expression while allowing for the appropriate degree of challenge:

> This enables the organic 'live entity' to form, test itself out in a variety of ways, and begin its building. Developing and maintaining that building needs to be accompanied by the relinquishing of earlier established positions. The equivalence in organisational and community terms must be to create appropriate 'institutions' or 'covered bridges' of valid kinds where the real underlying work of dealing with anxieties and raising the level of conscious-

ness can go on without blurring issues, while avoiding crunches or 'cutting people down to size'. Of course, there will be times when the soil for creative expression may not be as friendly or as devoid of human frailty as we would like in dealing with differing outlooks and ideas. Teddy bears may be treated in such a way that they cannot be used as transitional objects! e.g., where they have to be kept clean and mended and treated kindly at all times. In the same way, conferences, workshops, courses, meetings, work patterns and structures and many other recognised forms of enquiry, mutual communication and decision-making, etc., can be so designed and operated as to invalidate all I have said of their potential.

If this setting (the climate) is right, then the results are that this sort of deeper review of why certain decisions are happening can take place or as D again puts it 'understanding the learning to be gained from the music behind the words of the working relationship'.

So far, consideration was of the work of 'setting the scene' in which these sorts of things can emerge. What does the consultant then do with it, how does he communicate it, and how does he disseminate this learning? D warns of many hazards here, the dangers of simplistic 'clever clever' interpretations or simply quoting an authority. Again he stresses that it is important to check that one is perceiving the reality and not just responding to some need in oneself to see the situation in a certain way. Also, it is important to recognise and communicate the complexity. The tendency of some practitioners to idealise leaders in the field is one which D thinks can lead the consultant not to use his own thinking and experience but simply to quote an authority. This D sees as often constituting a 'cop-out'. Why does this happen? He sees the tendency to idealise certain figures in the analytic or social science field (or any field) in these terms:

> What we are talking about is the anxiety and uncertainty of people about their own professional and technical outlook, about their own quality of work or their own experience.

At the same time, he believes that such figures may act in a way which invites others to make them into an institutional godhead. Pronouncing in theoretical language is not an intervention, says D; yet all too often this becomes the front as a protection against experiencing any possible differentiation within the colleague group. As an example, D referred to Golding's *Lord of the Flies*, where the conch shell becomes institutionalised and revered in this way and for similar purposes.

The issue here is the need to avoid the fashionable guru image which then inhibits thinking and real learning in the group. The problem of how to pass on one's own understanding is very crucial in his approach and it can create dilemmas and stresses for the consultant as follows:

> One of the precepts I've always adopted and which again goes back to my teaching days, is to pass across both the knowledge and the way of thinking

about things so that the individuals can begin to do it themselves ... Winnicott really stands out for me in this respect; not as someone whom one reveres in the kind of terms we were describing before, but to whom one acknowledges a debt and who has given me something which I can then build on myself. But, unlike the guru approach, one must not expect, in working my way, that individuals, groups or organisations should express gratitude for what they have been able to achieve. Certainly one may feel one's part has now been completely forgotten and left out. The gratitude may be implicit in the awareness of a joint activity well fulfilled. Of course, there is also the possible unsatisfactory ending, because there are failed projects as well as successful ones – for whatever reason. But, in either case, a way of working and learning has been evolved which can be evaluated and worked through.

While the approach derives much from the use of self in the process of learning, there is the rapidly growing awareness of its value in building such learning into groups and systems. D, however, does not see the issue as 'institutions versus individuals'. What is important is the willingness continuously to review what is happening, including institutions, beliefs and objectives; and this reviewing process is even more important today, he emphasises, in our increasingly turbulent and open-system world, where there are ever greater degrees of interdependence.

Ultimately D then would see the success of his approach in the group/ organisation taking over the process role from the consultant and being what he describes as 'more itself', with the individual members becoming able to be 'more themselves' in their contributions.

Psychological services in a public service organisation

Structure and function

Mr E is manager of a large unit with a complement of about forty staff, of which approximately half are professional psychologists. It is part of the headquarters of a very large public service organisation and provides a service for the entire industry. This includes a range of psychological services, but the bulk of the work relates to selection procedures. The unit has three sections. One is concerned with external selection and selection to higher-level management; another is concerned with internal selection, and the third is for training and special projects.

Most of the work is project-based and requested by clients. To simplify administration, a method of charging has been evolved which does not relate to specific projects. At the beginning of each year a budget is drawn up making broad predictions of the workload of the unit and its spread across the functions of the organisation. This is agreed at director level. In the event of specific projects developing during the course of the year which require expenditure, the particular clients may be asked to meet the extra costs.

Origins and history

The unit began when the organisation was formed as a result of a reorganisation by Government in the late 1960s. The first task was to evaluate and revise the recruitment procedures for management levels, which led to job analysis and other studies in the organisation. The first psychologists also spent some time identifying problems and building up their knowledge of the organisation. This also functioned, in the manager's words, as 'selling in a very covert, gentle way'. The unit gradually came to be known and requests for its services began to be made. Departments were not obliged to use the unit on recruitment issues except where there was a specific trade union agreement, but gradually more of them used the unit on their own recruitment problems and later on other issues of occupational psychology such as career appraisal, wastage, and so on. The unit grew in size as a result of these demands for work rather than from any desire for growth. As the manager explains:

> I would rather keep a small team, be assured of their quality and get good output from them. The build-up has been very strange; on every occasion I have said I don't want more staff. I have said, 'You may have a project you want doing, but I don't want to take on staff and find in a year's time when the project is complete that I don't need them.' But then they would go to the director level in their business and I would be told the work must be done and I must take on more staff.

The work philosophy

Over the years not only has the unit grown in size and in the variety of its work, but the philosophy of work acceptance and performance has also changed.

Initially, to demonstrate its usefulness, the unit tended to take on any projects offered. Some of them had serious, unforeseen, political implications. For example, management and unions were discussing flexitime and disagreeing what the effects would be. So the unit undertook an eighteen-month project to investigate the effects. After eleven months management and unions were in agreement about introducing flexitime, and the results of the study could have been embarrassing, whatever they were. The study was dropped with the work half complete.

Another aspect of the early work philosophy was to take the brief, work out an appropriate experimental way of tackling it, use the unit's professional staff to conduct the work and, when the work was complete, prepare a report for the sponsors. This method produced good research but met problems when it came to translating this into action. For example:

> We did a huge wastage survey of clerical staff. Anybody who resigned in a period of one year was interviewed and matched with another person who stayed and who had the same length of service, was of the same age, sex, grade, etc. Then we took the differences between those who went and those who stayed. But, in the middle, there was a slump and wastage disappeared overnight and everybody wondered what the fuss was about.

Gradually, the unit evolved a different way of working.

1. The criteria for accepting a project were more tightly defined and included the client contributing some resources. The manager explains:

> We talk of resources not just in terms of money for us but what people resources they would devote to it, because I was no longer prepared to take it away as a subcontractor, do the work and then bring it back. [They lose control and interest], so we test their willingness to devote their own resources to it; to give us access to their staff, to train them to do the work, to train them to interview people or administer and score tests etc.

The process of involving client resources extends to selection test construction. The unit gets the staff of the division which needs the new test to generate potential test items. The staff of the unit devise a preliminary test which the client's staff then administer to a sample defined by the unit, score the results and send them back to the unit, who use the data to refine the test. As a result the client's staff are involved throughout test construction, which can take up to three years, and the professional staff are able to spread their time across a number of projects.

2. The involvement of management and unions is sought from the beginning of the project and the programme is authorised in stages.

The organisation is strongly unionised and it is vital to have the co-operation of both management and unions throughout the project. This collaborative approach evolved after some early problems; now:

> We have had several very successful projects as a result, in which the union executives have gone back to their conference and said, 'This is the problem, this is how we are jointly approaching it and we want to continue with it.' If subsequently anybody gets awkward locally, the National Executive will want to know why.

Most projects are now set up with an *ad-hoc* working party which operates for the life of the project and then either disbands or carries the work through into implementation. The working party includes representatives of the unions, management and the unit. It is likely to sanction work a phase at a time.

3. Outputs from projects go to both sides and they carry the results through into action.

In the early studies there was much argument about the form taken by reports produced by the unit and they tended not to lead directly to action:

> We had to avoid the situation where management could say, 'We've got someone working on that problem' and hope we would not come back for two years and would then provide a nice fat report which no one could use. So we tried to keep it relevant and not to put in high-flown theories but to point out results, draw some implications in terms of what could be changed practicably and leave it to management. At one point we got pushed a bit hard to stop putting our interpretations into our reports. They wanted us to do the work, publish the tables and leave interpretation to them. For a time we did that, restricting interpretation to pointing out statistical differences in the data.

With the working-party structure there is a group ready to receive the results and convert them into action:

> There is so much commitment at that stage that it tends to go ahead and any attempts to put it into cold storage, or to slow it down fail because it has an inertia which carries it on. Most of the time both sides want to go ahead and our problem is keeping up with the promised timetables and delivering the goods at each meeting.

Staff recruitment and training

The unit recruits highly qualified staff. However, the manager finds that when they come from an academic setting, it takes some time to 'knock them into shape'. They tend, for example, to respond to requests in terms of the formal methods necessary to examine the problem thoroughly:

> If someone says, for example, that they have a selection problem you might conclude he needs a validity study which will take three years. But you might not be able to afford the luxury of an academic protocol which will set out all of the possible outcomes and design an experiment which will eliminate them bit by bit. I say what they need to do is to use their professional judgement. Over the years you build up a level of professional judgement and it should not be necessary to re-invent the wheel every time. So if one of my staff comes to me with an elaborate protocol I say, 'That is your experiment, now what is your professional judgement?' At first this can meet a lot of resistance. I say keep your professional skills for when they are needed. Never let them get rusty but at the same time if you use your professional judgement, you can cut the life of a project in half. If a general practitioner did things the way they teach undergraduates, he would never empty his surgery; he has to use his professional judgement.'

13 The work of the Commission for Economic and Social Change in Germany[1]

This is an account of an attempt to harness social research in a broad framework and on a large scale, to help policy-makers formulate a rational and humane strategy for managing technical change and its social implications.

Origins of the Commission

The Commission for Economic and Social Change was set up in 1971 by the then Chancellor, Herr Willy Brandt. Its mission was to produce a report on 'what economic, social and educational policy options are available for furthering technical and social change and for fashioning it in the interests of the population, within the framework of a market economy'.

In a speech launching the Commission, the Chancellor said:

> Our present and future are marked by permanent economic and social change. The development and use of new technologies, the rapid expansion of knowledge, the dynamics of our economy, are all components of continuous structural change which not only determines our broad economic and social development but whose consequences reach far into the lives of individuals.
>
> This presents both a challenge and an opportunity: the challenge to confront the situation and master it in the direction of social progress; and an opportunity to set about consciously shaping our common future ... Our citizens should not have to look with anxiety at technical, organisational and economic progress as a threat, but see in it a natural accompaniment and precondition of greater welfare.
>
> This requires far-sighted policies which mean to use scientific developments in a framework of social values and draw relevant conclusions from such developments early enough.

The Commission's existence also had some other antecedents. During the 1960s there had existed in the Federal Republic an institution called 'Concerted Action', consisting mainly of a meeting, several times a year, of

---

[1] The full version of this case study has been published (Klein, 1987). It was based on (a) documents (Kohn and Latzelsberger, 1977), (Bolte, 1978), (Bieneck, 1977) and (b) interviews with some members of the Commission and its scientific staff.

Employers' Federation and trade union representatives with the Economics Minister.

The metalworkers' union (IG Metall) had, at several of its congresses in the mid-1960s, criticised the then Government for short-sightedness and inaction about future problems which were likely to arise from technical change and its consequences. In the Coalition Government of 1966 one of the critics, Professor Karl Schiller, became Economics Minister. The trade unions then used the opportunity of the forum Concerted Action to get a specialised working party on automation established.

The Automation Group existed from 1968 to 1970 and initiated some forty-five research projects. After two years' work they had reached the conclusion that the base of research, about technical development, had been too narrow: technology had to be seen as one social phenomenon among many if it was to be properly understood and if a real grasp and control of future economic and social developments was to be obtained. The approach to research would therefore have to be much broader and more systemic, and a societal 'system study' was commissioned which should serve as the basis for a new programme.

Organisation and work of the Commission

The Government accepted the Automation Group's views. When the Commission for Economic and Social Change was created, it had a much broader remit. It was also substantially independent of Government. Apart from the obligation to produce a final report from which it was hoped to derive guidance for legislation, there were no 'strings' tying the Commission to Government departments or policies. Funds were made available to finance a secretariat of eight scientific staff with the necessary back-up, and to commission research.

The Commission consisted of 17 members, 11 of whom had been members of the Automation Group. Trade union and employers' organisations nominated 5 members each, and 7 academics were invited on a personal basis (2 sociologists, 2 economists, 1 industrial economist, 1 expert in the economics of education and 1 engineer). The emphasis on the economy as the basic frame of reference was strong. Some of the employers' and trade union representatives were economists by training, and even the two sociologists had come to sociology from economics. The balance of membership, in which the academics outnumbered – and could therefore outvote – members of either interest group signified, at least at that stage, the emphasis put on research and knowledge for the development of policy as outweighing – by a nicely judged small amount – the component of politically worked-out agreement.

The emphasis on knowledge as a basis for policy was also exemplified by the 'system study' inherited from the Automation Group. It set out forty-three themes or problem areas relevant to technical, social and economic change, and these were accepted as the basis for the Commission's work. They are shown in figure 9.

The members of the Commission met once a month, usually for a two-day session. They first went over the list of forty-three problem areas to try to arrive at some ordering in terms of priority. This was done by a system of voting.

There were then two main streams of activity: the Commission's scientific secretariat began to prepare a series of discussion and analysis papers about the various problems, and these were used as the basis of discussion during the Commission's monthly meetings. Discussion of the analysis papers revealed what were thought to be gaps in knowledge or information, and thus began the second main activity, the commissioning of research.

The research programme

Altogether, some 145 research projects were commissioned. Most of them eventually led to publication and, together with the 45 projects inherited from the Automation Group, they yielded 140 volumes of published research.[2]

Two features about the process of commissioning the research are worth noting: one is that the Commission did not wait for applications from researchers but actively went out into the field to find researchers for topics that it wanted tackled. On some topics it knew or took advice about which researchers to invite; on most topics it advertised the work it wanted done for open competition. In some instances the same project was commissioned from two different researchers, or a second opinion was sought, if a researcher was thought to be politically biassed but knowledgeable. There was considerable controversy about such items.

The second feature of this research programme is that it tended, on the whole, towards state-of-the-art reports, i.e. the collection, summarising and interpretation of existing knowledge rather than new, fundamental research. The Commission's remit did not give scope for programmes of new or basic research, and on most topics it was considered that an analysis of the existing state of knowledge was in itself very necessary. It therefore concentrated on assessing and evaluating existing and earlier research, which had frequently been neglected. It discovered in the process that research whose boundaries coincided with those of existing institutionalised political fields was much more likely to have been taken up and used than research on problems going across such boundaries.

---

[2] These are listed in Klein, 1987.

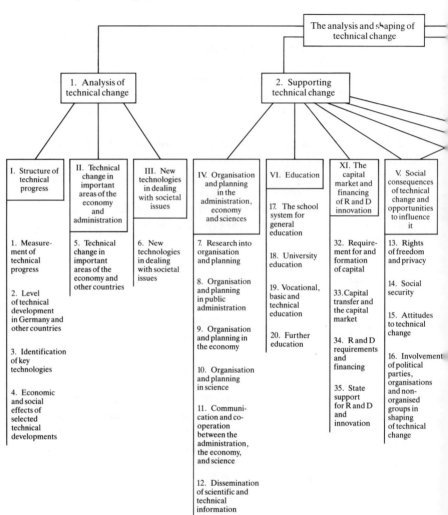

Figure 9   *System study on technical, social and economic change*

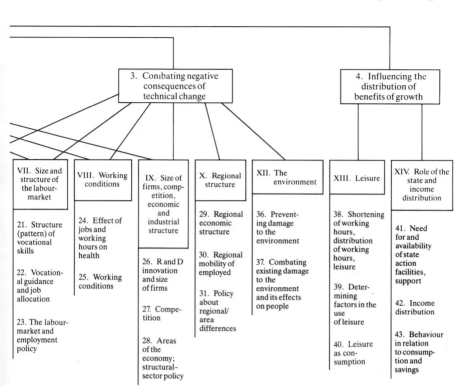

VII. Size and structure of the labour-market	VIII. Working conditions	IX. Size of firms, competition, economic and industrial structure	X. Regional structure	XII. The environment	XIII. Leisure	XIV. Role of the state and income distribution
21. Structure (pattern) of vocational skills	24. Effect of jobs and working hours on health		29. Regional economic structure	36. Preventing damage to the environment	38. Shortening of working hours, distribution of working hours, leisure	41. Need for and availability of state action facilities, support
22. Vocational guidance and job allocation	25. Working conditions	26. R and D innovation and size of firms	30. Regional mobility of employed	37. Combating existing damage to the environment and its effects on people	39. Determining factors in the use of leisure	42. Income distribution
23. The labour-market and employment policy		27. Competition	31. Policy about regional/area differences		40. Leisure as consumption	43. Behaviour in relation to consumption and savings
		28. Areas of the economy; structural-sector policy				

Preparation of the report

Once the research programme was under way, the Commission returned in a more concentrated way to the task of formulating its own views for its final report, and with this began its real problems.

The academics and members of the secretariat prepared 'theme papers' on the basis of the research material as it came in, while the social partners (i.e. the employers and trade unions) prepared 'position papers' on the same topics.

The first problem was who should draft the integrated text, combining both themes and positions. The social partners did not trust each other's representatives to do the drafting and were also unwilling to entrust it to the secretariat. Eventually the academics each took on some chapters, were allocated research assistants and obtained leave of one semester from their universities to do the work.

The first drafts were discussed in a laborious and painful two-week meeting, during which began the politicisation of the Commission's work. The drafts turned out to be very controversial – the academics had thought they were writing in a politically neutral way, but were accused of taking political positions, or of behaving like an interest group themselves, or challenged to reveal their political positions. In turn, the academics gained the impression that the employers were opposed to any proposals involving real change, while the trade unions were opposed to anything which implied criticism of current Government policy (many ministers and secretaries of state came from the trade union movement).

Controversy about various recommendations led to increasingly frequent threats by one or the other group to resign. The academics met as a group and promised each other that they would in any case finish writing a report and issue it with an explanation of events, even if the Commission should collapse. The announcement of this decision to the rest of the Commission unleashed a considerable storm because it was felt that the academics did not take the reality of political problems seriously and were themselves acting as an interest group; but it had the effect that threats of withdrawal grew less.

A second draft was prepared and was taken back into trade union and employers' organisations for very detailed discussion. The work during this phase was concentrated in working parties on different topics. Plenary sessions of the Commission had a smaller role and were mainly concerned with co-ordination.

In this way there gradually emerged clarity about the boundaries of consensus and disagreement. A system of recording minority opinions was agreed on, and it was this system which made completion of the report possible. Members of the Commission now see the mixture of consensus and majority and minority opinions as a very positive feature of the report.

The final report (Bundesminister für Arbeit und Sozialordnung, 1977) contains 83 minority opinions (out of 1,367 content paragraphs). It was not, however, possible to produce an agreed official short version. The trade unions and employers have each produced their own short version.

Thus to some extent the processes of research and recommendation had diverged: some of the outcome of the research was not yet available at the time opinion was being formed; in some phases there was simply too much research material coming in to be absorbed and integrated; and, of course, in some instances research itself became part of political controversy. It is said that, when some hitherto impeccably 'scientific' sources were investigated, the results were 'devastating'.

A change in emphasis and climate

The work of the Commission took five-and-a-half years. The report which emerged from all this work is in fact rather different from what the terms of reference and origins of the Commission might have led the reader to expect. It turns out to be strongly concerned with the furthering of technical change in the service of the economy and emphasises economic goals at least as much as social ones.

There are a number of reasons for this change in emphasis, and some differences of opinion about how and why it came about. One factor was the way in which, during the drafting, both trade union and employers' bodies began to take a stronger hand in influencing the work of their representatives on the Commission. The role of the academics changed, and the balance shifted considerably from scientific to political, or rather interest-group, influences. Another and most important factor was the fact that, while the Commission was carrying out its work, the economic climate changed and the oil crisis hit the industrialised nations; a third was undoubtably the fact that Chancellor Brandt resigned from office in 1974.

The Commission had begun its work during a time of full employment. The industrialised nations 'had just begun to permit themselves the luxury of talking about the quality of life' (Bieneck, 1977). Changes in the economic climate which followed the Arab oil embargo did not so much affect the research projects, which by that time were already under way, but had a profound effect on the thinking and work of the members of the Commission. Ideas coming from the trade union side met with increasingly self-confident resistance on the part of the employers, and the trade union members themselves began to concentrate more narrowly than had been intended on questions of job security.

The original aims, of presenting an essentially long-term strategy, of showing the interdependence between subject areas and in particular of treating economic considerations to some extent as means rather than ends, all suffered somewhat. But a good deal of the original perspective, particularly with regard to the long-term and interdependent requirement on policy-making, does remain in the report. The joint work, extending over several years and including academics, led to a broadening of perspective among members of the Commission which in turn influenced their home institutions.

Publication of the report

By the time the report was ready, Chancellor Brandt had resigned. His successor, Chancellor Helmut Schmidt, had a more pragmatic approach. Moreover, 1976 was an election year. Although the report was ready in June, it was decided to delay delivering it until after the election in October. After the election the Government was being formed, and then preparing its work programme, and appeared to have no time to receive the report. The date was repeatedly postponed until the Commission declared that it would hand the report over on 10 January 1977, if only to the porter!

At a press conference it was clear that many journalists were expressing opinions about the report without having read it. They criticised the fact that it contained minority views, whereas the Commission thought that the overall proportion of consensus was encouraging and the fact that its limits were defined very important and necessary. Press reports picked out sensational aspects of the report, i.e., areas of disagreement. It was very difficult to get attention for a distanced position.

The length and complexity of the report made it difficult to absorb, and it was a disadvantage that it had not been possible to produce a short version. Great disappointment has been expressed at the frivolity and superficiality of many comments, not only in the media but among politicians who, it is said, commented on the report without bothering to read it.

Here is one Commission member's view of the situation:

> During its work the committee enjoyed a high degree of autonomy. For a period of five years – a long time for a politician, who thinks in terms of election periods of four years – the committee could organise research and prepare its report ... For the scientist these seem to be ideal working conditions. But when the committee came to an end with the report, it seemed that the contact with government had been lost ... Unfortunately there had been major changes in government. There was still the same

coalition of Social-Democrats and Liberals, but there was a new Federal Chancellor, there were new ministers in charge of economic, social and labour affairs. The committee members had the impression that government behaves like somebody who gets something he has not ordered. The politicians who had initiated the committee's work were no longer in charge and their successors ... did not see what might be expected from the committee and what they should do with answers to questions they had not asked. (Hax, 1978)

Problems of implementation

Three important characteristics of the report are:

its delineation of the areas of consensus and disagreement;
its orientation towards long-term societal goals rather than the short-term ones dictated by the cycle of elections (for instance, ecology and the economic interdependence between generations – the burden on the middle generation of having to support the young and the old);
and, in particular, its emphasis on the interdependence between problems and subject areas (for instance, links between the education system and the structure of occupations; not just 'economic growth' but qualitative growth objectives aimed at evening out regional and sectoral imbalances, and so on.

However, such a systemic approach is difficult for individual ministries to work with. A strategic level of thinking takes place at high levels – in Germany the Chancellor's Office – but there strategy can only be specified in a very general sense and not in action-level detail.[3]

The Chancellor's Office distributed sections of the report to the different ministries, and thus emerged the main problem of use and implementation: whereas the main thrust of the Commission's work was systemic, dealing with issues and crossing the boundaries of the conventional subdivision of disciplines and subject areas, there were no institutions for taking action in such a holistic way. The ministries represent subject areas (economics, labour, research and technology, and so on) and are in turn organised internally according to subdivisions of these areas. It was a basic dilemma that the policy thinking was not matched by institutional change. It is also simply very difficult to relate strategic and comprehensive thinking to the pressures of everyday administration. Moreover, the more senior the

---

[3] Interestingly, the links between technical, economic and social factors were picked up as a theme by President Mitterand of France for the Economic Summit of 1981, to which the German Economics Minister took the translated summary of the Commission's report which we prepared at a time when we thought a volume of full case studies would be possible, and which we had submitted for clearance.

people, the less time they can make available 'and in the end it boils down to people'.

The report landed on the desks of civil servants, the general tenor of whose response is said to have been, 'It can't be done; we are doing it already; it costs too much.'

On the other hand, partial aspects did work their way through into administration. In the Ministry of Labour the report had considerable influence, for example, with respect to pensions policy. The great stress put on structural policy in relation to industrial sectors has influenced the way in which information and statistics are built up. Institutes of economics have orientated their statistical reporting more towards industrial sectors. There has also developed a more integrated way of reporting labour-market statistics, through the Federal Institute of Labour.

The greatest use is said to have been made by the Ministry of Research and Technology, which was young and whose staff were glad to be able to refer to 'sources'. One direct outcome was the institution of support for R and D staff costs of small and medium-size firms. Another has been the setting up of advisory centres on innovation for technology transfer.

The least positive response is said to have come from the Ministry of Economics, where the ideas of sectoral-structure policy came up against strong political opposition. Even there, however, more recent pronouncements seem to show the influence of these ideas, without explicit reference to them.

On the whole, those ministries which had been involved with the Commission took the report most seriously.

Other consequences of the Commission's work

Many people say that, although direct consequences are difficult to trace, the work of the Commission has had considerable indirect effect. The series of research publications has met with undisputed approval. Many of the reports have become standard works, and overall the research programme represents an unprecedented bringing together of the current state of knowledge.

It is also said to be very important that the various organisations, interest groups, committees, and so on, which concern themselves with these matters now have a common base of knowledge to draw on, and that this makes it much more likely that they can achieve results.

It must also be mentioned that the work of the Commission had a very strong influence on the officials who took part in it and who, after all, went back into public service.

It seems to be a characteristic of broad-based and systemic analyses that they have far-reaching indirect benefits, but that it is much more difficult to point to direct consequences. The experience of the Commission for Economic and Social Change exemplifies the difficulty of evaluation, and therefore also the degree to which this depends on personal optimism or pessimism. Here are two views of the same experience:

> With such comprehensive terms of reference, success lies in making the political actors more aware of the problems. One does not know what all the consequences have been, the important thing is that a process has been set in train.

On the other hand:

> There were so many good ideas, and so little has happened, and the next generation turns to something else.

Part III Discussion

14   A collaborative venture

In the first part of this book we discussed the issues involved in the utilisation of social science, as we saw them, before entering on the empirical investigation. In the second part we presented case studies in organisations and their analysis, as well as brief sketches of five practitioners and the story of an attempt at policy level. In this final part we want to see how the situation now looks, taking into the discussion all the empirical material, both the part which featured in the analysis and the part which did not, and our own further experience since beginning this work; and on occasion raising the discussion to a more general level. At the same time, we try to include some practical advice which should have relevance both for practitioners and for clients.

What it has been about

To begin the discussion, we need to reiterate the values and frame of reference which led us to undertake this work: it is important to make use of the social sciences, firstly, because it is important to relate the different value systems in society to each other and minimise their pursuit in a split way. The main form that this splitting has taken in industrialised societies is to pursue different values in different institutions: economic viability in industrial organisations, human well-being in health and welfare services, the pursuit of knowledge in academic institutions. While these may sensibly be seen as the primary tasks of such institutions, splitting means that they may come to be seen as the *only* tasks, and the neglect of other values come to appear justified. In a society which in fact values all three, this diminishes the people in these institutions, in all cases, and has many other dysfunctional effects. For example, it deprives industry of the contribution of many people who have not seen the opportunity for the expression of human values, and the intellectual interest, that industry in fact provides.

Secondly, it is also important to understand what one is doing, both individually and collectively. This means being aware of the relevance and impact of social processes and dynamics, and it means recognising where there may be a difference between espoused values and values in action. In the individual, self-deception or delusion is often a symptom of mental ill-health. While 'ill-health' may be too anthropomorphic a concept for the problems of an institution or a society, we cannot think of a better term for collective self-deception. On both these counts then, in the pursuit of synthesis and integration and the pursuit of reality, the social sciences have much to contribute. It is therefore also important to learn how to make this contribution.

We repeat this frame of reference, because the conclusions and guidance one looks for will be different according to one's aims. If our values were only or even primarily 'to change organisations', we would be looking for ways to achieve maximum change. If they were only or even primarily to improve the lot of one sub-set of the people in a system, without concern for the systemic implications and consequences, we would be political activists. As it is, we are looking for ways of integrating human and social considerations with the other things that are going on, and doing this in ways which do not themselves create more splitting.

Given the history of the split development of industrial society, and given the fact that its espoused values do, in fact, give overwhelming emphasis to the importance of people, their well-being and development, it is safe to assume that this brings with it a considerable need to give greater salience to the roles, tasks and experiences of people in their work, and a considerable need for change; but specific, discriminating changes, not a blanket commitment to anything that comes under the heading of 'change'. Preservation has a value as well as change; there is a need to discriminate between things that should be preserved and those that need to be changed. Also, a study may sometimes confirm that the costs of change outweigh the benefits – there is such a thing as the 'good-enough' organisation.

Some micro-level examples from the case studies illustrate what we mean. As a result of the activities that have been described:

there is an operator who has not been locked into a 20-second job cycle;
there is a production engineer who will never again see his job only in terms of the equipment to be installed, but also in terms of the roles that are being created;
a managing director understands the functioning of his company's marketing department better than he did;
the members of the marketing department have found a way of working together to understand its situation and environment, and developed and implement a form of organisation and a means of continuing review;
there are freightforwarders who understand the implications which information technology can have for jobs and who will know how to

play their part in any future technical developments to ensure that they get what they need;

staff in a motor-components factory have found ways of working on shared problems with people whom previously they saw as on an opposing side;

there are policies operating across a nationalised industry which provide a framework for supervisors to come within the management team;

supervisors in another large organisation have been helped to deal with the conflicts inherent in their roles, and their management to understand these;

there is a factory building, the shape and layout of which help the people working in it to identify with what they are doing;

there are thirty-two sub-managers in branch banking who have learned to work together on common problems and who enjoy this;

a generation of O and M staff in the bank retain an awareness that customers are whole entities, not separate transactions;

there are technical designers who understand the value of creating prototypes and pilots to help potential users communicate their reactions and requirements.

These are not grandiose, utopian developments. But we think that, multiplied, the impact of such improved matching between task and organisation, structural adjustments, changes in perception and growth in understanding would be very great indeed. They are, however, ways to improve situations to which no recognised, institutionalised path exists; the potential, after all, has existed for a long time. Some of them rely more on the input of substantive knowledge and some rely more on skilled management of the process of change. As far as we know, in none of them was the existence of conflict of interest denied (though there are some forms of 'applied behavioural science' which do imply such denial). Concern for reality implies clarifying and not fudging those situations where, if A gains something, B loses. A and B are not necessarily always the parties in traditional industrial relations, though they often are. In the motor components case (I) many months of work were necessary to bring the parties in conflict to a point where they could work together, in spite of their differences, on the critical problems facing their organisation. The dilemma showed most clearly in the food processing case (F), where the number of jobs to be created was a matter of legitmate dispute and it was therefore difficult to insert consideration of the design criteria and quality of the jobs. Institutions for handling conflict of interest existed, while institutions for handling quality-of-working-life issues did not. Both are necessary.

The case studies, the individual practitioners and the ÇESC

We recognise that the whole issue of the utilisation of social science is broader than the organisational level at which we entered it. There is much relevant literature, for example in the field of policy science, to which we have not related. The contribution we have hoped to make is one that is grounded in experience; the situations we have met are often microcosms of the broader issues. The Esso story, which may have appeared idiosyncratic at the time, turns out to have many parallels with other attempts at utilisation. The cases in organisations, in turn, have some striking parallels with the national strategy we had the opportunity to study.

Our study focussed mainly on attempts within organisations because that is where much of the life of an industrial society is played out, it is where our experience lies, and it is where we had most ready access to the experience of others. But the strategic issues are more general than that; many of the major issues are really the same whether the attempt is at national or organisational level. The German Government's CESC highlights many features common to the other cases and is especially significant for our purpose, not only because of its broad scope but because, in spite of its scale and resources, it was subject to many of the same problems as the smaller-scale cases.

The story of the CESC exemplifies much of what this book has been about. On the one hand, there was a visionary, strategic initiative aimed at integrating technical and economic with human and social goals. Within this broad aim, there was a wish to harness research for informed policy and action. There was painful experience and hard work in delineating and taking account of conflicts of interest. There was a strenuous effort to deal with splitting between topics and institutions, and arrive at some problem-centred strategies which would take account both of conflicts of interest and of the interdependence between subject areas. On the other hand, there were some major impediments to carrying this initiative through. The main issues faced by the CESC were as follows.

1. *The divergence between the paths of research and decision/action.* The CESC commissioned only state-of the-art reviews, not basic research, but even then its views had to be formulated before all the research material was available. This is mirrored in some of the other cases (it was the phasing problem in the confectionery case (E), Mrs A in her nationalised industry trade union discusses it) and it is particularly mirrored in national and even international research policies.

The issue of phasing has come up in many forms. When decision-makers become aware of a problem, the response is often to commission research. But research commissioned at that stage is unlikely to yield results when they are needed (there is a clear example of this in the experience of Mr E);

and by the time a similar problem arises again the research will have been forgotten, because so little in the social sciences seems to be cumulative. It may well be more useful to scan already-existing research for relevance, or ask those who have done it to review their experience for relevance or to synthesise existing knowledge. Such relevance is often lost because the circumstances in which the research was done appear superficially to have been different (perhaps a technology which is older but research around which may nevertheless have yielded general principles) or because it is simply easier for researchers to start again from scratch.

2. *Defining the boundary between 'detached' scientific contributions and sectional interests.* This issue features much in the social science literature, but does not appear to have caused many problems in the other case studies. This is probably because, on the smaller scale and practical level involved in these cases, it was more a matter of finding operational ways through the issue (which could quite often be done), rather than finding general theoretical answers to it (which cannot). The CESC itself found an operational way through with its system of voting on issues and recording minority views, and so delineating the limits of consensus. Expectations are so structured, however, that this was not recognised for the positive contribution forward that it was.

3. *Matching policy with institutional change.* In its scanning of earlier researches, the CESC found that research was most likely to have been taken up and used if its boundaries coincided with those of existing institutions. In turn, its own work ran up against the difficulty of a problem-centred report being handed over to discipline-based ministries. The issues arose in other cases: in banking (case B), an integrated study was commissioned by a committee which included both personnel and the management services functions, as well as the line department. But this committee disappeared before the study was complete, and the departments once again functioned separately. Where organisations intend to make serious efforts to work socio-technically, it could make sense to back up this work by merging the personnel and engineering or management services functions.

4. *Continuity of sponsorship.* People like initiating things, they find it much more difficult to be committed to something they inherit. There were examples of this issue in many cases. In addition, the story of the CESC highlights the key to the problem in that it points to the situation of the policy-maker who, in the end, is 'getting answers to questions he has not asked'. The implication is that programmes and projects need some protection from changes in key personnel where this is possible, if much waste and frustration are to be avoided. However, there is another factor.

5. *Change in the economic environment.* If a research phase is too insulated, as arguably the life-cycle of the CESC and the branch banking

study (case B) were, the environment may have changed significantly by the time it is over. This did not happen in the banking project, but it significantly affected the work of the CESC. In the food processing project (case F), too, which was going on soon after the work of the CESC, i.e. affected by the oil crisis of the 1970s, the changing economic environment made the social science contribution appear less crucial to the overall success of the cannery than it had at the beginning.

The result of the difficulty of integrating the research output with the policy discussions; the absence of institutions which might take ideas forward in a problem-centred way; the change in the economic context which enabled priorities to slide back to an older framework; and the loss of the sponsor who would 'hold' the original concept, meant that, while there were, on the one hand, valuable outcomes, probably more than can be traced, on the other hand, the people involved wondered whether these merited the time, energy and commitment that had been invested. This confirms us in our view that a shift towards understanding the dynamics of this difficult enterprise better, and thus making it easier, remains necessary and worthwhile.

The multiplicity of frameworks, and the differences in background and conditions, both within the social sciences and within client systems, mean that there cannot be a formula for a one best way. It is a matter of 'horses for courses', and clients generally have more choice than they are aware of. Because the 'resource' comes in many shapes and sizes, this does not mean that the undertaking is unscientific, but that each, whether it is an individual or team, or an institution, has a different mix. The brief sketches of five very different individual practitioners make this very clear.

These practitioners illustrate the issue of differentiation and integration within the social sciences: While Professor C refuses to be bound by the limits of a discipline and describes himself as 'de-disciplined', Mrs A and Mr E stay within their discipline of origin but relate it in a pragmatic way to the needs and possibilities of their organisations. Mr B uses mainly his knowledge of and relationship with his organisation and selects courses to attend, to add to his tool-kit, as and when he feels the need. Mr D, on the other hand, uses the fundamentals of his discipline to illuminate new situations that are different from that in which it was developed.

The case studies, too, demonstrate the issue of integration and differentiation. In some there was an attempt to work explicitly in an interdisciplinary way: in banking the team put together for the original study represented a contingency approach to organisation, clinical psychology to explore customer needs and relations with the bank in depth, social psychology to look at the relationships within the branch and between the branch and the customer, socio-technical approaches to look at work organisation, and computer ergonomics to look at the design and use of the computer system. Although people from these different frameworks and disciplines worked together in one team, 'knitting' their contributions into an integrated report was a very difficult task. In the electrical products case (C) there were also several disciplines deployed: production engineering, work pedagogy, ergonomics, industrial sociology and educational sociology. In this case they worked in separate institutions, pursuing separate paths. Integration was in this case found to be very nearly impossible; but the individual institutions themselves had considerable achievements.

The resource in question is not a homogeneous entity, and this also means that there cannot be an inclusive framework for analysis. While we felt a powerful obligation to attempt some systematic analysis, this could only pick out some of the elements. Isolating project activities for examination in this way does not, for example, capture the developmental quality of the relationship while a project is going on or for which the project may be merely a vehicle, or the testing out of boundaries which results in the evolution of a strategy, or the multiple roles taken by practitioners. The individual practitioners also give more of that particular kind of flavour.

A collaborative venture

Although there were indications of the views of clients in the case studies, it was not possible to explore the experience of the client systems as extensively as that of the social scientists. The descriptions have been mainly social science-centred and this is clearly a temporary selection of what constitutes the 'figure' and what constitutes the 'ground'. For purposes of the discussion it needs to be redressed, and this may be done by recalling the model that was first put forward in explanation of events in the Esso experience (Klein, 1976 chapter 11).

The utilisation of social science is not merely a question of bringing a resource system to bear on an action system, as in figure 10. Client systems have resources of their own already in place, and social science systems, both individuals and institutions, have needs (figure 11).

There is also a power relationship involved. The word 'collaboration' trips easily from the tongue, but it is a complex process in which power plays an important part. The power of clients derives from the fact that they are the principal actors and 'own' the situation. The power of social scientists derives from the fact that they are detached from the situation and not locked into it. Each has needs and may resent dependency on the other, or envy the other's power. This can lead to a cyclical process where those who experience powerlessness in one area avenge themselves by exercising power in the other. There were some indications of this in the case studies.

Client system   Social science

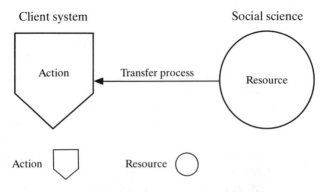

Figure 10   *Movement of resources: basic model*

Another aspect of the power relationship concerns territory. There are by now many examples of ideas which were developed and appropriate in one set of circumstances being marketed and exported as universal panaceas. In an age when physical conquest of territory is going out of fashion, conquest by consultancy has taken on many of its characteristics. There are institutes and consultancies on whose walls maps with red pins display the extent of their projects world-wide, and consequent areas of influence.

However, in a model highlighting the parity of and interplay between need and resource also lies the potential for resolving issues of power and territory, and therefore for a more creative rather than destructive collaboration. The utilisation of social science is not a simple exchange of a resource in return for pay. Success in utilisation depends on successfully regulating the relations between the needs and resources that are being brought together, on the one hand, and the resources that already exist in the action system and the needs which exist in the resource system, on the

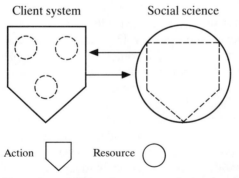

Figure 11   *Action and resource: content and context*

other; i.e. between the content of the joint undertaking and its context in both systems. Once this is recognised, real collaboration between equal partners becomes possible.

Having established the framework, we may now turn to our conclusions about what is involved in utilisation. The most significant lesson for us in reviewing all the material and our own experience is that the utilisation of social science requires four things:

(i)   *Vision*: in particular a sense that things are not immutable. Social science, if it is to be valuable, has to bring insights, perspectives and methods to bear on situations that bring with them the possibility of change and development.

(ii) *Competence*: or a range of skills, knowledge and understanding. Practice requires a repertoire of skills which have their own unique characteristics and are not simply, for example, research methods, on the one hand, or management consultancy, on the other.

(iii) *Infrastructure*: to fulfil its potential, social science practice needs enabling and supporting practical arrangements and resources.

(iv) *Institutionalisation*: valued outcomes and processes need to be embedded in the client system concerned.

These requirements are discussed in the next chapter. When things have gone less than well, it is because of some imbalance between them. We find that any one or two, or even three of them, by themselves, are not enough.

15 Elements of practice

We said that the four components of successful practice are appropriate vision, competence, infrastructure and institutionalisation.

On vision

Vision, in the social sciences, concerns system change, and hope. In the engagement between client systems and social science systems, clients generally have some vision of a desirable future before they ever approach the social scientists. It may be a future state that is different in level of understanding, or different in some tangible sense, or the mere hope that it may be so. Sometimes the main result of an intervention may be to effect a loosening up in the client system so that alternative futures may be envisaged, or that there may be a vision about a route as well as about a goal.

In all this, scale is a crucial factor. There used to be an advertisement for shaving cream, which showed three faces: one disappearing under lather, one with almost none, and one with the amount needed for shaving. The caption read, 'Not too little, not too much, but just right.' It applies to the visionary aspects of the social sciences.

Where there is 'too little', situations may not be seen as containing any potential for change or development, or the system being considered for change may be within very tight boundaries. These are some of the arguments that take place between ergonomists and other kinds of human or social scientists. An episode during the Esso work may be helpful in clarifying them.

There were, by chance, two teams of researchers working on projects for the company's marine department: a team of ergonomists, carrying out studies of human factors in ship design and contributing to the re-design of a ship's bridge; and a team consisting of an anthropologist and a social psychologist, studying problems of 'life and work at sea'. Both used systems terminology; both were concerned with relating human and technical aspects of the system to each other and, in the process, giving greater primacy to the human aspects; both were working on Esso's oil tankers, so that many technical and organisational factors were constant. Yet it was hard to see any connection between the things they did, which seemed to be completely different. This raised questions about the meaning of systems concepts.

When the teams were persuaded to meet in a seminar, the differences between them could be articulated along two dimensions: one concerned the different kinds of parameter – all of them within the definition 'human' – which they tackled: on the one hand, such things as human ability to judge distance, speed and acceleration and to see objects in the dark, on the other, such things as the concept of 'ship-mates' and controlling relationships in a confined space, and the ship as a 24-hour, total institution. The other dimension concerned how they defined the boundaries of the systems they looked at, i.e. what they considered to be 'the system', and subject to change, and what the environment, and given. The ergonomists took the organisation and its general policies, as well as the ship and its basic technology, as given. The other team took nothing as given except the continuing need to transport oil.

While this was in one perspective a difference in the definition of system boundaries, both in the sense of scale and in the sense of degrees of openness or closedness, it was debated in terms of values: the social scientists accused the ergonomists of accepting too much, i.e. of having too few values, while the ergonomists accused the social scientists of being so airy-fairy that nothing practical could in fact be done. (It is in this episode that the link between values and system boundaries, postulated in chapter 4, is grounded.)

'Too much' vision, in this sense of system boundaries, means that the whole world must change before anything at all may be done. Another form of 'too much' is to put the vision so far into the future that there can be no testing of its validity. No-one is in a position to contradict the pronouncements of futures-oriented 'visionaries' of this kind. In either case in fact, whether the grand design concerns the world system or the far-away future, its main characteristic is that it cannot be tested. So the first question to be confronted is, 'What system?'

The second question is, 'Whose system?' There is much need for care about powerful visions concerning systems in which one is not a stakeholder. Within organisations, too, the vision of one group may be the constraining environment of another. Reference has been made to the dynamic of transference ('What are they doing to you?') and how understanding it helps with finding a way through project situations. Equally, social scientists need to explore the converse, the counter-transference, and ask themselves, 'What am I trying to do to them (that I have not been able to do to my family/colleagues/political masters; or that derives from my own professional or technical culture)?'

It is not enough to say that one guards against the danger of using clients for one's own needs in this way by making sure that they become actively involved. It is not so much *whether* stakeholders in a client system are actively involved in a project but *how* they are involved, specifically whether they are involved in the role of objects or subjects, that provides clues about any counter-transference that may be at work. Some of the case studies involving management training appear to have been around a powerful vision of this kind, which eventually set up the inevitable reactions. A very strongly held vision can become a 'mission', which may then be thought to justify the use of power and even a disregard for damage that may be done in pursuit of the mission. Understanding the relationship between needs and resources that has been discussed should provide a way of arriving at a vision that is both sufficiently shared and free from this.

The case studies provide the opportunity to see in practice a variety of 'visions', both in scale and content. Sometimes such a vision is relatively bounded; such interventions are often successful in their own terms but the effects may be marginal, not extending in time or affecting much in the organisation. There is also the possibility that accepting such a narrow frame makes it possible to avoid addressing or calling into question wider issues.

The grander vision can avoid these dangers, but carries with it other dilemmas. The grand vision is very tempting for the client. When you are beset with problems, the prophet who offers hope, ultimate solutions, or panaceas can seem very attractive. The grand dream, however, often leads to disillusionment. Too often, it is either found to be a partial solution, unable to recognise many other realities in the situation, or the 'prophet' had neither the will not the wherewithal to turn the dream into operational practice.

Sometimes a client's vision is stronger than or different from that of the social scientist. Looking at these case studies, we see a range of ways in which social scientists and clients have negotiated their visions and collaborated to develop an appropriate vision around which work may take place. It may be that the generalised 'vision' of a piece of social science theory can be made specific to the client's situation. It may be that diagnostic studies provide findings that are the raw material which can then be used to build the vision. It may be that social scientists provide a process by which client staff engage with one another, with the problems, with the person of the social scientist or with concepts and findings.

In some of the organisations in the sample, activities of the kind described were fairly widely diffused, in some they were one-offs, and some have dissipated. Where they fell short of the vision, the vision was nevertheless necessary to make them happen. In all of them, the professionals involved and sometimes also their clients would have liked to see more, or more systematic, or more sustained or consistent outcomes. This then brings us to the other three components.

On professional competence: practice as a discipline

We began in chapter 4 to discuss the nature of social science as a practice profession. The examination of the fourteen cases and other examples of social scientists at work gives many additional insights into the nature of this practice, and provides the basis for a review of the skills and approaches of practice.

The professionals in our study showed much variety in their approaches to practice. However, there is also great commonality in the issues practitioners face and even in the ways in which they face them. Dealing with people, work and organisation in an attempt to support and help tends to trigger similar issues, whatever route takes you into the situation. It has been salutary, for example, to meet practitioners with an OD perspective who nonetheless (and perhaps with some feelings of not staying 'pure') deal with design and other structural issues. Similarly practitioners whose starting-point may be structural change have to deal with the dynamics of situations and take on facilitating roles that would fit a process-oriented OD approach. The ideology may say you never offer recommendations, but there are many examples where practitioners felt it was appropriate and valid to provide these inputs. Situations frequently pull one away from the 'pure' teaching of a discipline or methodology; it gets modified in collaborative action research. One of the most difficult issues a practitioner has to deal with is deciding when this becomes inappropriate collusion.

In this section we attempt to synthesise aspects of practice as a discipline by putting together what works which seems common to many or all of the case studies; what are the common roles that are played, what are the common methods employed, what are the common issues faced, and so on. By this means we hope to give a focus to what is distinctive about the emerging practice, what it has to offer and where development is still needed.

It may be useful to begin by summarising the ways in which there is broad agreement that social science practice involves unique characteristics. For example:

(i)   It is different from social science research. In research one investigates a particular topic, maybe tests a hypothesis, perhaps pursues a line of enquiry which fascinates one. In practice, while the methods of investigation need to be every bit as rigorous as those of research, the investigation has to be client-centred and problem-centred. It may involve problems one has not studied previously, it may need conceptual tools and models from a number of different areas and, in the investigation, it will be necessary to take heed of the action timetable within the organisation that the investigation is designed to serve. At the same time, it is valuable to help the client system acquire a hypothesis-testing way of working.

(ii) It is different from some other forms of practice. When the subject-matter is inanimate, a discipline that translates scientific findings directly into practice may be possible. Engineering practice has given us this model and there appears to be widespread expectation that a 'mature' social science practice would do the same. However, in social science practice the 'what' cannot be separated from the 'how'. On the one hand, structural change is not useful unless the people who inhabit the roles involved learn to understand it, own it, and equip themselves to work within it. The subject-matter is people who must internalise and work with findings and who, in the process, will develop their own versions and modifications. On the other hand, a process which develops individuals and groups is not necessarily valuable or lasting if it is abstracted from consideration of environment and task. For this intimate link between content and process, engineering practice has not provided the language.

These characteristics lead social scientists into adopting roles which are subtly different from the role models with which many professionals and clients are familiar, and this may itself be a cause of uncertainty and conflict. If the practitioner engages in an investigation that does not fit the model of 'research' it may be seen as low-quality research. If the practitioner engages in an action role but does not deliver the firm recommendations expected from the model of the 'consultant', the judgement may be that this is a poor consultant. To avoid these interpretations we need a statement of the specific character of these roles in social science practice against which a practitioner might more appropriately be judged.

In this section we make an attempt at such role definitions. We summarise these as *diagnostic roles* (including *evaluation*), where practitioner and clients are endeavouring to understand a situation, and *action and development roles*, where an attempt is made to engage with the client in work. The 'diagnosis/action' paradigm is a useful distinction, but it should not be assumed that all practice divides neatly into these phases. Some forms of intervention take place without explicit diagnosis. Also, as the cases show, episodes of intervention can contain within them many short problem-solving cycles which involve diagnosis, action and sometimes evaluation. The diagnostic activity is part of the action programme. The separation is therefore to demonstrate the nature of the function and role, the methods that support them and the issues that surround them, rather than to imply a neat sequential phase-structure to practice.

Whether in diagnosis or action, an important factor is whether the practitioner is a member of the organisation or comes from outside. The practitioner in motor components (case I) was able to do what he did by virtue of his detached and neutral role as an outsider, more than because of any specific professional background. In fact, he deliberately kept professional knowledge about payment systems out of the picture at first. But the inside/outside dimension is not so simple: there are insider-insiders, like Mr B, whose strength derived from familiarity with the business, its people and its politics; and outsider-insiders like Mr E, whose strength derived from his professional knowledge and frame of reference. In the latter case, the existence of a whole department helped to keep the professional culture going, albeit in a modified and adapted form. Where there is no such department, a network of professional colleagues becomes very important. A professional needs a reference group and needs to maintain contact with it.

Diagnostic roles

Diagnosis needs to be seen in the framework of development. This means that the institutions that will 'hold' the concern for its function in development should be in place before, during and after any explicit data-collection phase, and appropriate links agreed. Institutional aspects include: agreeing the brief, the methods of work and methods of follow-up, who is to be involved in steering groups, and so on.

Not all applied work includes an explicit diagnostic phase; where it does, the diagnostic activity has a number of functions apart from the manifest one of collecting and analysing data: it has a familiarisation function, enabling clients to test out the professionalism and way of working of the practitioners, and enabling the practitioners to get to understand the client situation; it has an education function, showing how familiar information may convey different meanings when presented systematically, or in a detached way, or processed through one or more different frames of reference. It also has a development function: the feedback and working through phase may take on the characteristics of a system that facilitates transition, in the course of which issues, conflicts, differences in perception, begin to come to the surface and be worked on.

It follows that diagnostic studies, even those which most resemble research, require some action skills. If there is a written report, practitioners need to frame it in language which is comprehensible to the readers, in categories which are relevant to the problems they experience, and with a minimum of methodological ifs and buts. They may also, minimally, need to advise on how the report may be handled. They may need to present in meetings the essentials of what comes out of the study and to be able to handle the reactions which not only the study, but their own role and behaviour, provoke. An action role means having to decide between options about how to proceed constantly, on one's feet. The only tool for doing that is one's self, and what one has genuinely internalised; formal models are fig-leaves and likely to be recognised as such.

Engaging in an explicit diagnostic exercise involves a range of agreements with the people concerned, and these have to be negotiated. Considerations include the following.

1. *The rights of those who give information.* Contributing to an investigation has to be voluntary and should be on the understanding that confidentiality will be protected in reporting findings. In circumstances where this is not possible, for example where the population being studied is very small and everybody knows the individuals, what is reported must be cleared with the individuals. For many, good practice includes checking with individuals what has been learned through them, in order to confirm the findings and also to offer some benefit in return. It is an important part of the professional role of the practitioner to establish this kind of 'contract' with the people taking part and to maintain it whatever the subsequent pressures to reveal sources. Practitioners who are junior in status to those exerting the pressure may find this difficult. It is important, therefore, that the support of senior levels or the back-home institution is somehow visible. There are, in fact, many ways in which it makes an important difference whether a practitioner is seen as working solo or as part of a team or institution.

2. *The process of reporting information.* Ideally the maintenance of a non-partisan position should be supported by reporting findings to all parties concerned. There may be reasons why this cannot be fully achieved but the practice of getting findings that originate from a particular source back to that source can and should be sustained. The process of reporting findings may include the formal preparation of a report but this by itself is not enough. Engaging client staff with new perspectives on their situation involves working through with them the nature of the findings and their implications, if the diagnosis is to act as a vehicle for sharing knowledge and as a bridge to action.

3. *The role of the client in data gathering for diagnosis.* The process of internalising the findings within the client organisation is greatly helped if client staff are themselves involved in the data gathering and analysis. Such a collaborative venture also institutionalises the research methods and reduces dependence on the practitioner. In the transport case (A) this was accomplished by assigning two members of staff to work with the social scientist. In the oil marketing case (H), the marketing staff undertook the diagnosis themselves in a process designed by the social scientist.

However, there are two restrictions on this general principle. Firstly, many client roles are incompatible with diagnostic ones. Anyone in a power relationship with those taking part in a study, such as most obviously line managers with their own departments, cannot suddenly take on the role of detached data-gatherer: they cannot 'forget' the data when they get back to their previous roles, and they cannot forget who supplied it (if indeed it was supplied in such a situation). Client staff who take on this role must be in a position to carry all its attributes.

The second restriction is that, if the organisation is to gain from the theoretical perspectives the social scientist can bring to bear, there must be a point at which the social scientist plays a role in interpreting the findings. If there is no direct engagement, the organisation may get the benefit of the process or method but not the frame of reference.

There are many options with regard to project strategy, and each has its benefits and costs. The benefit of the involvement of members of the client system has to be traded off against the value of a detached input. This is one of many instances of strategies needing to be chosen in knowledge of their consequences.

4. *Scale and duration.* In research methodologies the size and nature of the sample is crucial to the extent to which findings can be generalised, hypotheses tested statistically, and so on. This often demands large samples and studies of long duration and may not be appropriate in a diagnostic study. In this kind of study the practitioner often uses his or her knowledge, as well as intuition based on experience, to make the best use of limited time and resources. It is better to offer possibilities for later testing than to devote time to validation and miss the time-scale when action would have been possible, or the opportunity to share insights with client staff.

Adapting in ways like this to the circumstances of action does not mean that one abandons or denies a previously learned set of standards or values. It means that they get overlaid with another set and that the trade-offs are understood.

Action and development roles

The action and development roles taken by practitioners also have a number of functions simultaneously:

(i)   They are a vehicle through which knowledge informs action.
(ii) They involve collaborative action with clients so that the decisions belong to the client.
(iii) They facilitate development opportunities for individuals and groups.
(iv) They act as receptacles or containers for the anxieties evoked by change.

(v) They create a safe space within which the organisation may review its situation and decide on next steps.

(vi) Valued knowledge and methods should become institutionalised so that the withdrawal of the resource leaves a more competent client system.

One perennial dilemma for the social scientist practitioner has been that direct application of (i) in the form of knowledge inputs and recommendations precludes some of the more developmental functions, while methods that emphasise learning from experience often leave no room for the contribution of substantive knowledge.

It may be useful to discuss the types of contribution that may be made under two headings: process design and direct intervention. Practitioners may be involved in designing a process by which the client can move towards action, and will then be involved in this; or they may be involved directly without such a vehicle.

1. *Action process design*

The design of an action process has elements of designing a learning experience and elements of designing a process or institution in which planning decisions, technical design decisions, and so on, are taken. It was a common feature of those projects where the practitioner was helping the client work on a particular problem. Although the practitioners did not recommend specific solutions to the problem, they recommended a process by which a solution could be found and implemented. In doing so, they created the necessary space for the work that had to be done. This process might involve a temporary institution with temporary roles for members of client staff (and for the practitioner), goals to be achieved, activities to be pursued and methods to support the activities.

The temporary structure may be a working party, committee, conference, negotiating system or some other organisational form to which people either belong in addition to their normal role responsibilities, or to which they are seconded temporarily from their normal roles. (In that case, re-entry may become an issue.) Depending on the background, membership is drawn from the client organisation to include those with a stake in the outcome, who have to live with the consequences, and those who have relevant knowledge and expertise to contribute (which may include the practitioner). The design of such a structure – who is part of it, how selected, what roles they are asked to adopt, the way in which they interact with the rest of the organisation – is vital to success. There were many such temporary structures in the cases, with different design characteristics: the job design committee and steering group in food processing (case F), or the CSC and computer users' committee in freightforwarding (case G). In the motor components case (I), the practitioner's diagnosis led him to conclude that relations between groups of staff were so poor that they would not be able to work together in any temporary structure. He therefore created a structure in which groups at first worked separately. When common problems had been identified and exchanged, joint problem-solving groups became possible.

Temporary systems, such as training courses, negotiations, working parties, will have the function of facilitating transition if they create an environment where options can be explored in safety without later repercussions, where people can experiment with roles and behaviours beyond their habitual ones and where issues can be worked on which the normal working culture may not encourage to surface. The temporary system then takes on the quality of transition in the Winnicott sense of permitting exploring and testing out, in order to move on. Thus not all temporary systems facilitate transition; for them to do so some conditions have to be met.

In such a system there may be a phase in which diagnostic studies are undertaken and the group receives and works on the findings as a means of developing shared perspectives on the topic under consideration. There will probably be a phase of searching for solutions and testing them against goal criteria before a specific plan is agreed, developed and implemented. The process may involve separate exercises for particular training purposes but the problem-solving activities themselves have the simultaneous objective of developing team functioning on reflective and planning activities. This is where the temporary system takes on the function of facilitating transition. Techniques and exercises will not facilitate transition if they only present the issues intellectually and do not enable the work to be done that deals with the anxieties involved and develops the necessary inner resources.

The characteristics of such temporary systems obviously vary greatly. If they are training courses, they have to provide opportunities for people to test out new approaches in an environment where they can take risks without punishment. Negotiating systems generally put some limits to conflict by involving a high degree of structure. People may then co-operate in operating the structure where they cannot co-operate on substance. Progress may be made by moving between the two.

When the task involved concerns design, there is a particular set of such methods by which people can be supported as they create and evaluate alternative futures. In such cases it proved particularly useful to create a physical representation of the future as when a factory layout was created out of Lego bricks in the confectionery factory (case E). Sometimes a working prototype can be tested or given a trial implementation as in freightforwarding (case G) when a trial system was introduced into a branch as a 'vehicle for learning'. When a concrete manifestation of the future scenario is not possible, it seems important to create at least a paper representation which is sufficiently objective and 'out there' to be the focus for debate and analysis. Such structures may be as simple as cardboard-box prototypes of workstations and control rooms or as sophisticated as computer-based working simulations. What they must be is sufficiently flexible to permit alternatives to be demonstrated and sufficiently real for informed members of client staff to be able to imagine the consequences of such alternatives. They must also incorporate the human and social, or 'soft systems', aspects in a realistic way, i.e. in a way that is not merely the result of wishful thinking. They may then simply support a freewheeling discussion of consequences, or support an experimental programme which shows the various outcomes.

2. Action and development

Practitioners may provide a number of kinds of direct contribution. The first will be their frame of reference. Whatever they are doing, or even if they are not 'doing' anything, they will convey by their own behaviour, implicitly as well as explicitly, the frame of reference within which they are operating. Depending on their background, this may be about the strategic interdependence between an organisation's environment, its primary task, its values and culture and the technical and other arrangements to meet that primary task; or it may be about the interdependence between technical and social aspects at the level of the primary work group; or about the interdependence between task and process in the life of a group; or about the links between the inner and outer worlds of people occupying organisational roles; or any number of others. Whatever it is, this framework will inform any diagnosis they may undertake, the design of any transitional system they suggest, and the issues to which they direct attention; it is in any case likely to add a perspective which is different from the ones already in use.

The practitioner who holds such a framework, for example one concerning the interplay between organisation and environment, is in a position to convey it. Once clients have internalised it themselves, they apply it to their own data and come up with syntheses that would not have occurred to the social scientist. This is very different from refusing to make any contribution for dogmatic reasons.

A second contribution is to bring in relevant empirical research findings. Sometimes empirical research will have a direct relevance to the situation being considered, more often it is likely to need re-interpreting and translating. This is the process of 'internalising and translating into use' which was discussed in chapter 3. In this way the use of empirical research enables the contribution to be a proactive one. Much research in the social sciences has been concerned with *post-hoc* analyses of things that have gone wrong. This may be turned into predictions of how to set things up so that they are less likely to go wrong, or at least so that their consequences are faced knowingly: 'If you set it up in this way there are likely to be consequences of that kind – is that what you really intend?'

A third kind of contribution is process facilitation, supporting individual and group development. In the case studies, this involved supporting specific developmental needs, for example management style, language needs, team building, and so on. It may also be of general character, for instance when groups, teams or individuals explore their own dynamics. It is a process which often follows the same structure as that described above in relation to 'transitional systems': suspend normal business, reflect, consider and evaluate alternatives, examine goals and values, and so on.

Within the process orientation there are also roles that permit knowledge transfer. This may, but need not, lead to drawing consequences in the form of recommendations. As a group deals with the 'transitional' process there are spaces and times when an input may be appropriate. When future possibilities are being considered there may be room for teaching to enlarge the number of options that can be considered, for example, by referring to job design or socio-technical systems theory, or bringing in relevant experience. When options are being evaluated there may be opportunities to include findings from research studies that inform the evaluation. The practitioner will need to have the capacity to adapt to the learning style of a particular professional group.

Evaluation is indeed a fourth kind of contribution. When trials or experiments are undertaken, one of the roles often adopted is evaluator of the outcomes, a role that can be extended after a change has been introduced. In the knowledge-into-use framework, evaluation of policies or experiments by detached outsiders may be carried out systematically, and there is a large literature on evaluation research. In the framework of dynamics, the cycle of evaluation and consideration of next steps is much shorter. It becomes more a matter of reviewing and considering next steps on a continuing basis, with management committees or other relevant bodies.

Once a transition has been accomplished it may be appropriate for the practitioner to withdraw. The objective at this stage is to institutionalise the learning. Sometimes this means that the process of creating a 'transitional system' itself has been learned and is used in other circumstances. It may be embodied within the management procedures of the organisation or in the way it undertakes change. Commonly, training events are taken over by the institution and offered as part of the development process provided for staff.

Issues associated with the action/development roles

There are a number of themes which emerge from consideration of the action and development role, and which are relevant to the further development of practice.

The first of these concerns staying in role. The role that we have elaborated is not easy to describe and does not relate easily to other role models that may be familiar to client staff. It is therefore important that practitioners are able to signal clearly the nature of the role so that expectations are realistic and are fulfilled. There is also a heavy responsibility on the practitioner to stay in role at all times.

Clients may invest a great deal and take on big risks when they commit themselves to social scientists. They are likely to test out how safe they are in having taken these risks, i.e. whether the professionals both know what they are doing and will not exploit clients or abuse their own position. Attempts to trip the professional out of role may be quite unconscious testing of this kind. They may seem to offer rewards which on the surface appear very reasonable and appealing, such as a special relationship or access to information which could not be obtained otherwise. But there is always a price to pay: things which go wrong can very often be traced back to a consultant having fallen out of role. In a seminar for young researcher/consultants, the members of the group were asked to think back to an occasion when they had found clients inexplicably angry, i.e. angry in a way they could not understand. When some of them had located such an occasion, they were asked to think back to what had been going on before that particular episode. It turned out that some form of falling out of role had generally been involved.

One defence in the face of this risk, for the consultant, has been to draw very formal, distancing boundaries round the role, and that has sometimes been the strategy undertaken. It is a viable strategy but it brings with it a greater likelihood of fantasies being projected onto the consultant, and this in turn has consequences. Such distancing is not essential, it is perfectly possible to be informal and stay in role. Staying in role is, however, a total commitment, without any let-up. As a non-partisan resource the practitioner cannot, for example, while having a drink at the bar, appear to join in the general denouncement of absent colleagues. In a role that supports the development of others by not providing specific recommendations, it may be dangerous to announce views on related issues. Staying in role includes reacting in role to things that happen or are said, rather than merely reacting to them. It also means being able to cope with expectations, assumptions, hopes and fears that may be projected onto the practitioner, including when these are unrealistic. (It is useful to explore what earlier experience of social scientists a client may have had, since this may well have influenced such expectations.) It becomes clear that, to be able to maintain their capacity to stay in role, practitioners themselves need a professional support system.

Establishing and sustaining a role may also be affected by stereotypes associated with age and gender. Relatively young social scientists, no matter how competent, may have difficulty gaining acceptance among senior and probably older members of the client organisation, and it has sometimes been necessary to 'match hierarchies': to field an older and senior social scientist (whose involvement may not have been functionally necessary) at a time when senior client staff were directly involved. Gender by itself needs to be recognised as having an influence. In some organisations, accepting that a young woman may have knowledge and skill that an older man does not have can be problematic for the client staff. Establishing and holding a professional role under these circumstances can tax the poise of even the most mature practitioner.

A second theme concerns the management of resources. One of the dilemmas that confronts the successful practitioner is how to manage one's own resources. The practitioner task is not a closed one, and once it is seen as valuable and important, tends to expand in many directions. The initial group of people with whom one works may engage progressively more attention as they grapple with difficult issues. It may become obvious that there are others working on parallel activities who also need attention. There will always be a reason to extend one's own understanding by deepening and widening the diagnostic or exploratory efforts. As is seen in the next section, there is also a continuing need to monitor and work on the structures that support the practice within the organisation. If the fruits of the work are to be disseminated and institutionalised, work will be required away from the main focus of practice. Given limited time and resources, these conflicting demands make it difficult to establish priorities, and many of the problems encountered in the cases appear to arise because practitioners have chosen some avenues and neglected others. The strongest temptation appears to be to continue working closely with those who demonstrate that they need you. Individual or group development may then continue, but at the risk that the organisation becomes a progressively more inhospitable place for those individuals or groups. There is also a temptation of becoming over-invested in some kinds of innovation or experiment because they are interesting or because one does not see the institutional constraints.

A third issue concerns managing the withdrawal. The objective of withdrawing, so that the client with the new capability that has been developed can further extend it, is shared by many practitioners. It is also one of the most difficult to manage. In one of the cases a client explained frankly that he was so afraid that his own dependency needs might turn out to be uncontrollable, that he would rather not risk getting involved at all to the extent needed. One way in which clients in the case studies managed this process was by creating a 'ghost' consultant in the absence of the real one ('What would he say under these circumstances?'); another was by relating to the consultant indirectly, via the supervision of a student. Another common problem is when the client begins to feel able to manage the process and wants to act independently but the practitioner does not feel the situation has made sufficient progress for this to be effective. At the same time, the practitioners also need to manage their own dependency on the client: practitioners depend on clients for a sense of being needed, for a sense of contributing to worthwhile activities, for continuing learning, and indeed for income. Maintaining these issues as matters of professional judgement, when they obviously also affect the contractual position and funding of the practitioner, is obviously difficult. It is yet another reason why practitioners need a professional support system.

A related issue is when and in what form client staff take over these roles or functions. To institutionalise the learning, many of the functions should remain present within the organisation. Some of them can sensibly be taken on by people operating within their normal roles; group members can suspend business to review progress, individuals can build in time for reflection, in-house trainers may be able to take on skills training, and so on. Some of the activities, however, require the full practitioner role, i.e. the ability to be independent, impartial, maintain confidences, and so on, and this may not be possible for people in normal organisational roles and positions. It may indicate a need to institutionalise the practitioner role within the organisation. Other aspects of the contribution that may be lost are firstly, 'stranger value', and secondly, the knowledge-into-use element that depends upon the social science training of the practitioner. This may also be achieved by recruiting, by sending staff for appropriate training, or by establishing links with research organisations.

Action research

We have dissected these roles and functions, in order to be able to spell out some of their attributes. Together, they form the pattern of activities which is generally called action research. There are many forms of action research, but they have in common three elements. Action research aims:

to make a contribution to problem-solving or development;
to make a contribution to knowledge;

to involve the people in the system in active roles rather than the passive ones of only being the subjects of research.

Where there are differences between different kinds of action research, they are likely to be differences in the proportion of these three elements involved. One characteristic of action research is that the situation is changing while the work is going on. This can trouble academics. The difference between action research and consultancy is that consultancy may not have an explicit research objective as well as a problem-solving one; and some forms of consultancy do not involve the participation of the members of the system in active roles. It is also the case that in-house practitioners, while generating important knowledge, may not have the time or opportunity to publish it. We have at various times discussed the splitting that has occurred between the world of research and the world of practice and which has resulted in research not feeding into practice. It is at least as regrettable that academic research and teaching have not been informed by the experience of practice.

Action research can and should be totally rigorous. There are likely to be 'working hypotheses' that are jointly explored and may be jointly modified as the work proceeds. As regards methods, it is not a matter of intervening in an *ad-hoc* and uncontrolled way, 'letting it all hang out', but of selecting and agreeing strategies (a) in a way that fits the problem, and (b) in knowledge of their consequences; generally documenting them; and staying in role.

Even if, for example, the agreed strategy is only to provide a feedback report, there will still be different consequences according to whether this is done in writing or verbally; with or without the opportunity for discussion and revision; with all interested parties together or different parties separately; reporting only what has been found; including analysis and comment; including inputs from other research and experience. All of these have different implications, and rigour in action research means selecting and agreeing the strategy with some understanding of the likely consequences.

Implications for the development of practice skills and competence

The processes described above are difficult and demanding. They demand knowledge, maturity and professionalism from those in practitioner roles and from those in client roles who engage and support them. There are implications for the development of people in all of these roles; indeed there is a need for 'matching competencies' as well as hierarchies.

1. *The professional development of practitioners.* The description above

requires practitioners, firstly, to be knowledgeable about theories, methods and empirical findings of social science if they wish to operate as 'general practitioners' rather than specialists in a particular area, and, secondly, to be skilful in managing the processes involved in practice. The first capability could and should be developed in social science teaching. The difficulty is to avoid transmitting the value that research and research methods are good and practice is less than good. Ideally the teaching should convey what is characteristic and worthwhile about practice, to prepare would-be practitioners so that they hold realistic expectations about the rewards and frustrations of practice. They need to recognise, for example, that it is difficult to undertake doctoral studies in practice because the conflicts between the academic research-centred thesis and the client-centred practice may jeopardise both pursuits.

Most disciplines teach their particular research methods, at least at postgraduate level. It may be possible at the same time to begin the process of developing the skills necessary to manage the dynamics of change and getting knowledge-into-use. It is possible, for example, to undertake supervised diagnostic studies and to develop some of the diagnostic methods. It is difficult, however, to see how the full repertoire of skills can be developed except in a kind of apprenticeship with a mature professional. The development of these skills is so dependent on experience and the evaluation of the experience, that real engagement with practice is essential. Such experience is not easy to organise. Since the process often calls for client staffs to put themselves at risk by questioning their values, purposes and behaviour, they would not wish to be in the hands of someone learning the trade and, as we all do, learning from mistakes. It may be that there is a route to the gradual building of these capabilities that also maintains the integrity of the professional service. It would begin with data gathering and diagnosis, develop into support roles in the design of action processes and lead ultimately to direct support for the learning and support of others.

2. *The development of in-house practitioners.* Some very able practitioners have developed from in-house roles where they have had managerial or technical responsibilities. It is important not to preclude this kind of development by establishing a closed profession in which membership depends on formal academic routes to qualification. The strength of in-house development is that the perceptive individual may develop a deep intuitive understanding of organisational dynamics and behaviour from experience in organisational roles. This is the weakness of the academic route, which provides only limited exposure to the realities of organisational life. By contrast, the weakness of the in-house route is that student practitioners come late to the formal acquisition of knowledge and the skills of supporting change and development processes. There has been a tendency for in-house practitioners to attend experiential courses to

acquire the skills for managing processes. This leaves them unable, for example, to contribute the knowledge-into-use element of practice and serves to reinforce the divide between contributions about content and structure, on the one hand, and process, on the other. One possibility of bridging this gap could be the formal teaching of diagnosis.

3. *The management of competition.* One situation for which no amount of professional training prepares the practitioner is how to cope with competition. When an organisation throws several consultants at the same problem, this may be a way of avoiding commitment to any of them or to the change effort involved; or it may reflect conflicts and competition within the organisation itself. The best response would be for the professionals, together, to confront the issue with the client and explore its meaning. But the anxieties of the competitive situation may make this impossible. To throw competing solutions at a problem, leaving their proponents to fight it out, may appear to be in some sense 'fair'. If it is intended as a rational strategy for finding the 'best' solution, some evaluative mechanism needs to be put in place, to which the practitioners can relate. Otherwise the competitive situation will absorb much of the available energy and resources.

4. *Teaching clients about social science practice.* Much of what social scientists do in organisations has an educational function. The aim, after all, is for members of organisations to be aware and take account of the human and social aspects of systems as a normal part of what is going on. There is also, however, a specific need for clients to know what they are taking on if they engage with social science practitioners in a more explicit way, so that realistic expectations are promulgated in the client community. If the expectation is direct transfer of knowledge into usable practice via direct recommendations, there will be disappointment. If the expectation is that social scientists will use the opportunity to conduct academic research, the engagement may not even begin. If the belief is that the social scientist will quickly wash away the frustrations and dysfunctions of existing organisational life, there will be disillusionment. The cases show many ways in which social science practice has been valuable. This section has shown the nature of the practice that leads to successful outcomes. It has its own distinctive character and requires distinctive competencies. It is this value and this distinctive character that needs to be conveyed to prospective clients.

Structured methodologies

Clearly, the skills that have been discussed are complex ones. This has had two consequences. The first is the development of structured and 'packaged' methods, which aim to take some of the complexity out of practice, and systematise and prescribe how to go about it.

In many instances there is a discernible trend from open-ended, grounded diagnosis and action formulation to a more prescriptive and formalised approach to the same problem. It seems natural that, having invested heavily in a learning and development activity in the first place, the organisation should then want to disseminate and institutionalise the outcomes and not repeat what may have been a laborious and expensive process. As a result of a project, therefore, the results may be encoded in a set of standards for others to follow. The standard may refer to the outcomes to be achieved or to the process by which the outcomes are to be achieved. Codifying knowledge so that others may use it without having to go back to first principles has been a basis for the development of civilisation and it is not unexpected to find it occurring here. If it embeds useful findings and practices from social science in the structure and functioning of the client organisation, it has obviously served its purpose.

But there are dangers. A standard and even a process can be applied automatically and the person applying it may learn nothing. This may result in inappropriate application. It also does not further one of the principal objectives of practice, that of development and learning. The challenge is to produce forms of institutionalisation which provide appropriate opportunities for development, guard against inflexible and inappropriate application, but do not require everybody to rediscover the wheel.

In recent years we have both been involved in major programmes of R and D of information technology, the Alvey Programme of Advanced Information Technology Research in the United Kingdom and the European Strategy Programme of Research in Information Technology (ESPRIT) programme of the Commission of the European Communities. A technical feature of these programmes is attempts to encode research findings into products, software tools and methodologies, and so on. This model of 'research into practice' may be appropriate to computer science, but there is an expectation that it also applies to social science. It is exciting that these programmes recognise the importance of human and organisational issues in the development and application of information technology, and it is a major challenge for social scientists to respond without being drawn into an inappropriate model of practice. At present the social science community is accused by many technologists of 'not getting its act together' and of expecting technologists to wait while fundamental research is undertaken on the implications of new technologies. What the technologists want are 'user models' and 'enterprise models' which automatically embody human and organisational issues so that designers do not need degrees in social science, and systems can be designed without elaborate organisational research. The challenge for the social scientist is to respond with methods and tools which encourage exploring and learning strategies in technologists and users. The outcome should not be a product that can be applied without understanding, but a process that leads to the development of appropriate understanding.

The second consequence of the complexity of the skills involved is that practitioners (including ourselves) have been preoccupied with the need to explore the nature of these skills and develop them, and have tended to neglect the other two essential elements of successful practice, namely infrastructure and institutionalisation. These are discussed in the next two sections.

Infrastructure

As a general concern infrastructure, we believe, has been missing so far in discussions of the subject of practice. The importance of this aspect is not that our pet concerns are otherwise not as successful as they might be, or that the world has to be kind to social scientists, but the waste that is involved when genuine attempts, jointly initiated, turn out not to fulfil the hope and promise that launched them. This may be the place to point out that there is a distinction between the system of entry and the system of continuing work or intervention. It is at the stage when the shift from entry to intervention is taking place that matters of infrastructure begin to be important.

The topic divides into two aspects:

(i)   The supporting infrastructure that will help sustain the work.
(ii) Strategic issues involved in the management of social science practice.

There may be appropriate vision and skill, but the undertaking will not realise its full potential unless attention is also paid to these aspects.

Infrastructure support

It would seem to make sense, if an organisation is going to go to the trouble and expense of engaging with social science professionals, that both parties should pay some attention to the necessary infrastructure. It may be just because this is so obvious that it has tended to be neglected, or it may appear too mundane a concern in the euphoria surrounding a new venture. At any rate, those of the case studies in which care was taken of it, whether through policy or by accident, tended to be those where success was more demonstrable.

We can distinguish six aspects of supporting infrastructure:

1. *Funding structures.* Funding structures not only have practical consequences but are also at the same time an important part of the dynamics. The main – if somewhat obvious – issue is that the funding structure

should be appropriate to the needs of the work. No-one's funding these days is totally secure, but some funding bases have a longer time perspective than others, and this will affect the kind of work undertaken.

An in-house practitioner does not have to worry about day-to-day funding, but may need to negotiate on an annual basis the scale of what is being done. If client departments fund the projects they engage with, this is an indication of commitment. On the other hand, one can be too purist about this when, in the early stages of an activity, other aspects are in the forefront of people's minds, and some central support may be valuable. In the first model there is more chance of client departments really owning and taking responsibility for the work, in the second there is more chance of adventurous, untested activities being tried.

Funding is also not a problem for the social scientist in the day-to-day sense where the funding base is the state, either because the work is being done from an already-funded university department, or from a funded programme such as the Humanisation of Life at Work programme in Germany or the Alvey programme in the United Kingdom. The client, one might say, is paying indirectly through the tax system, but it creates a problem for the relationship and raises the question of who, in fact, is the client. In such cases, there have always been conflicts about the freedom of academics versus their responsibility for useful outcomes, and whether the quality of the academic output that has been bought at the cost of usefulness has been high enough to warrant the sacrifice. If practice itself came to be regarded as an intellectually respectable discipline, that would go a long way towards solving this perennial problem.

When researchers are publicly funded, a long-term grant may require manpower estimates to be firm at the beginning, allowing no flexibility for later changes in circumstance. Academics whose source of income does not arise directly from the work done may lack a sense of commitment to getting usable results, and client systems will in general be much more committed to use work for which they are paying. On the other hand, consultants whose only source of income is project work may be tempted to use projects to generate more projects by encouraging dependency. As before, the concept of 'not too little, not too much' applies: the work needs to be protected from the immediate financial worries of those who are doing it, but not too much so. We still believe that a model of dual funding, where public funds pay for the research component and clients for the action component of work, would be valuable: the costs of work to client organisations would be reduced, in return for opportunities of making valuable knowledge available to the research community.

Where assignments are funded more directly by a client organisation, an open-ended per diem arrangement, i.e., charging explicitly for every day's work, is suitable for occasional consulting, but was not helpful in the project work of the confectionery case (E), as the consultant did not feel able to propose visits and activities. Budgets estimated for whole projects or phases leave greater flexibility. In any case, the size of the budget will of course profoundly affect the mode of intervention.

It is generally thought better if clients rather than sponsors pay for the work (we take sponsors to be those who bring social scientists in, while clients are those for whom they actually work). Where sponsors and clients are not the same, the funding structure becomes a function of the relationship between them. In-house, there was one situation (oil marketing, case H) where the client departments were charged for the practitioner's work, and one (Mr B) where they were not. Both worked well, which indicates that the sponsor departments had good relationships with the client departments. A 'seeding' arrangement, where the first exploratory part of work is funded centrally but clients take on the cost of taking it further, is a useful model and has been cited as used by a Government department (see p. 19).

2. *Continuity of key people in post.* Obviously, one cannot expect other systems, such as career development systems or the election of trade union officials, or indeed political elections in the wider system, to be accommodated to project activities (of whatever kind, not only those involving social science). Nevertheless, the evidence by now is overwhelming, and the instances too numerous to list, that enormous waste of resources, including the resources of skill and enthusiasm, results from these discontinuities. Knowing this should therefore at least influence the timing of the beginning of projects, as well as strategies concerning timing when projects are being designed. In addition, the terms of reference of project committees, steering groups, the members of joint teams, and so on, should include paying explicit attention to the issue of individual or collective handover where that becomes unavoidable.

Social scientists who have not learned this lesson the hard way, as we have, need to know that they will need to spend at least as much effort, if not more, with those who enter a project activity part-way through as they did with those who started it off. Client organisations need to recognise the demands this makes on the social scientists' resources. It needs to be allowed for in money and time budgets. Sometimes, if the project activity is taken seriously, one might even suggest considering some adjustments in the timing of other systems.

3. *Links with the organisational environment.* The links between a project activity and its organisational environment need to be considered, in two senses: firstly, social science activities have often been undertaken in a framework of 'demonstration project'. If such a project is successful, and its participants enthusiastic, this is at least as likely to put others off as it is to encourage emulation; demonstration projects tend to become encapsulated.

Secondly, most worthwhile project activities are likely to have systemic implications. These need to be considered, strategies for dealing with them designed, and linkages built in, from the outset. Social scientists often point to the broader systems implications of what they observe. In many of the cases, systemic links between different levels are clear from the accounts. Some of the issues encountered could only be dealt with at higher systems levels. The problem about working at the higher systems levels, however, is that one might never get among the nuts and bolts. In freightforwarding (case G), the practitioners thought this a reason to discontinue the work. The problem about working among the nuts and bolts is the lack of connection with the higher systems levels. That is why, very soon after an activity begins to look as if it is taking root, an institutional framework which links it with the wider system is needed.

4. *Institutional change.* The three items above were concerned with infrastructure support to on-going work. But there is also a need to consider from an early stage the infrastructure, in the form of transitional systems, that will be needed to support institutional change as the work comes to fruition. One of the most significant findings, when the CESC reviewed the state of existing economic and social research, was that those researches were most likely to have been taken up and used whose boundaries aligned with existing institutions. Similarly, one of the difficulties in the way of using the CESC's own work was that it was problem-centred and cut across the boundaries of discipline-based ministries.

5. *Institutions for review.* Both at the level of individual projects, and at the level of the total social science activity, there is a need for a locus where progress can be reviewed, difficulties worked on, next steps discussed, strategic objectives held in review. Such a 'locus' may be a single senior individual, as in the transport case (A); more often it is likely to be some kind of steering committee, with appropriate representation. If the internal dynamics of an organisation make that impossible, there may be a need for parallel bodies.

Some practitioners encourage institutions such as steering committees to evolve as and when it seems appropriate in the course of the work. Others insist on a pattern of institutions to be agreed, if not put in place, at the beginning, even using them as a kind of trademark. The danger of the latter strategy is that it may seem to be artificial and dogmatic; the danger of the former is that it may not be explicit enough or taken seriously enough.

6. *Structures of authority and power.* Linked to the previous point, it is important to identify the power structures in the client system, so that there is some understanding of where the critical decisions are going to be made. Discussions about participation and consultation are generally about involving those at junior levels in the system in decision-making.

But it can also happen that key individuals at senior levels have not been involved, or not soon enough. Mechanisms for steering and review need to include the stakeholders in the undertaking and need to be linked appropriately into the power and authority structure.

Strategic issues

We have been discussing project work in terms of a supporting infrastructure and links with the project's environment. But there is a serious question about whether a 'project' is in any case the best mode for engaging with social science, or whether project activities, if they occur at all, should be less strongly defined and be seen more clearly as stages on a path of continuing development. We said earlier that a consultant may have the function of containing (in both senses of the word) the anxieties evoked by change processes. This may also be true of entities called 'projects'. Indeed, it may be a reason why there have by now been so many projects and so little matching change in basic assumptions. There is a need for strategic thinking both on the part of clients and the social scientists they engage with.

Possible strategies will depend on the extent to which a 'project' is in phase with the surrounding culture. In the development of new plant or systems there are many things going on simultaneously. If one of these is an attempt to develop ways of working that are more participative, there will nevertheless be decisions needed in the other streams before these methods are learned, practised and part of the culture. Where the culture is already participative, it will more easily be extended to include technical matters. At the level of organisations, a project may have the function of mutual exploration and testing out, but a number of organisations by now have got beyond this. This shows in the way in which strategy featured in the reflections of some of the individual practitioners in chapter 12. The three who were working in-house all discussed strategies designed to develop a practice, in the sense of a medical or legal practice, which would bring something new while remaining congruent with the values and culture of the organisation. For the two with professional qualifications in parts of the social science spectrum, the 'something new' was the knowledge and methods of their disciplines, adapted so as to be need-oriented. For the one who was 'home-grown', the something new was the sanctioned role of process facilitation, cutting across normal departments and hierarchies. In all three cases it seemed likely that values and culture might, in turn, eventually be affected.

For client systems, strategic questions arise about whether to engage with social science sporadically, as and when a need is felt, or systematically, and what parts of the social science spectrum to engage with. It is clear from the case material that the application of social science to practical affairs can come in many forms and the forms it takes can be influenced by many different factors: political context and goals, the desire to disseminate the benefits of one's experience, different skills, experience and training, and so on. The range of inputs and of types of skill, knowledge and approach is very great and, as we have seen, practitioners have different mixes of them. There is also the question to what extent to rely on external professionals or grow the skills and knowledge in-house; whether to develop and deepen relationships with known and trusted professionals, or 'play the field'.

Institutionalisation

The final question concerns institutionalisation: what should be put in place by the client system to enable the system to retain what it has gained and continue with its learning and development?

To institutionalise something is to build it in. Once the excitement of doing something new simmers down, the less exciting, but possibly more important, task of making it go on happening has to be confronted. Only individuals learn. For institutions and societies, although the term 'learning' is frequently used, it is only a metaphor. Institutional 'learning' depends on whether it is possible for individual learning to pass from one to another.

In societies, the constant overtaking of generations, and the dynamics between generations, means that much learning is lost. Those learned things which are institutionalised in laws or artefacts have the greatest chance of surviving. Thus in the legal, or engineering or medical professions, with much institutionalisation, one generation builds on the achievements of the last.

In the field we have been considering there is much less institutionalisation. What there is takes different forms. When something is formulated as a standard, that is a form of institutionalisation. Where it is integrated into technology, such as computer dialogues that provide genuine options, or counters on a machine that provide feedback, that is a more powerful form. In some situations, the remedy becomes costly or even impossible if the value is not thus structurally embedded. An example is pacing: if people doing a job are inappropriately paced by the equipment they work with (being coerced by it into a pace which is too fast, too slow or, most importantly, too inflexible and out of their control), this is one of the most powerful sources of frustration and discontent and, at the same time, one of the most difficult to undo.

On the other hand, there are other values whose whole point will be lost if they are structurally enforced. One cannot force people by dictat to learn, to explore, to work through differences. Something in the data suggests that people for a time are playing with new concepts. Some developments are less of measurable institutional change, and more of conceptual growth. Such efforts require enabling institutions rather than structural ones, and the enabling institutions then need to be provided with the means of making use of them.

To give an example of an enabling institution: the European Parliament has passed a resolution saying that applicants for grants under the various technology development programmes of the European Commission should be required to state, as part of their grant applications, what effect they expect the developments they propose to have on 'employment, the nature of the work, skills, health and safety at work and older workers for whom retraining is no longer possible'. It would not be expected that applicants get such predictions right, nor are they required to pay specific kinds of attention to these factors. But they are required to think about them seriously and this, in turn, may have a knock-on effect on the education of technologists. (To date, this resolution has not been implemented.) The problem for the design of work organisation is not merely that technical and social aspects of technology have become split off, but that the splitting is itself deeply institutionalised, in education systems, research funding, professional organisations, and so on.

The general idea of institutionalisation may be illustrated by a rather simplistic example. Society has made a policy decision, crystallised in law, to restrict driving to one side of the road. This apparently simple decision is supported by a surprising number and range of institutions: the assumption that it must happen is built into the design of vehicles. It is built into the training of drivers, as well as into their legitimation (licensing). It is built into the formulation of codes and standards (the Highway Code, standards about the width and layout of roads, and so on). Then there is the continual reinforcement of seeing that others do it and, finally, sanctions (punishment) if it does not happen. These institutions, in turn, are supported by funds, training establishments, staffing and monitoring (traffic police).

Together, these institutions are very powerful, and they have been in force for a long time. In addition, a breach of the policy is generally clearly visible and unambiguous. As a result of all that, the policy is mostly carried out: drivers are not in the position of having continually to decide on which side to drive.

Clearly, many of these institutions are of the mandatory kind whic. is not appropriate to our topic. But some have more of an enablii ; character and, when one considers their whole range and mutual reinf   >ment, it is little wonder that the project activities which have featured in ι. is study, relying as they did mainly on small teams or even single professional practitioners engaged with the topic for a limited time, tended to lose force as they moved out from the small-scale, bounded area.

The issue is about balancing development and institutionalisation. We pointed in chapter 5 to a tendency in Germany to institutionalise early, i.e. to try to capture 'proven findings' in legislation and standards, while the UK tendency has been to avoid institutionalising altogether, i.e. to treat each development in a unique way. If the German cases in the sample do not appear to bear this out – all but one of them are OD activities – this is precisely because the German research team became fascinated by this type of work, which was new to them, and tended to select it. Conversely, we looked with some envy at the systematic attempts to build knowledge into structure and institutions which we saw, and selected, in 'the German scene'. We said that it would be good to get a little nearer to having the best of both worlds. Well, the research does now point to such a possibility.

1. Start in a developmental, exploratory, learning way; don't begin by formulating regulations or structured packages, or there will be little learning, and eventually a reaction by those who feel they have been manipulated. When the processes of entry shift into the beginning of a system of engagement, start taking care of elements of infrastructure. Then, when a project or other form of work appears to be gathering momentum, build in a review activity for selecting those aspects which should become institutionalised, and begin to build those institutions; later than would have been the case in the 'German model', and earlier than would have been the case in the 'UK (or Anglo-Saxon?) model'.

This is the phase that was mainly left out in the UK case studies. One of the weakest aspects of current practice appears to be the tendency to achieve some of the necessary elements of institutionalisation but not others. There may, for example, be a training scheme which develops individuals but no change in control structures so they are unable to use their new capabilities. A policy to operate enriched job structures may not be supported by changed career paths, and so on. Attention to the various elements that have to come together to sustain a change is what matters.

2. Institutionalise reviewing and evaluation and 'hypothesis-testing'. But beware of continuing the rituals and procedures associated with such processes as if they were the essential core.

3. Institutionalise 'permission' for roles, relationships and dynamics to be a normal part of the agenda. This is sometimes taken to mean merely that people should express their feelings: 'I feel angry' is not a contribution. But 'I feel impossibly squeezed between the demands of department X and those of department Y; I think they are loading their difficulties onto me' is a valuable contribution and a potential growth point.

4. Include institutions, i.e., transitional systems, for handling the outcomes of possible research loops.

5. In the design of transitional systems:

avoid splitting by involving all stakeholders;
provide the data/experience that will facilitate internalisation ('knowledge-into-use');
provide the 'space' for reality-testing;
provide the 'space' for personal and group review and development;
relate to the infrastructure that sanctions and supports the activity;
provide the basis for subsequent institutionalisation/wider dissemi-nation (the 'vehicle' may be a large part of what is institutionalised).

In projects for specific purposes the project purpose, for instance a design process, may itself be a transitional process for which systems have been set up. In that case, the task is to see what extra characteristics they need to have or what additional systems need to be put in place.

6. Slant the institution-building towards processes rather than content, so that the institutions that are created are enabling ones that will ensure continuing learning, rather than ones which merely require conformity.

7. However, express in structured ways the values that are declared in policy: in budgets (time as well as money budgets), in the criteria on which members of the organisation are assessed (for example, where job satisfac-tion is an expressed value, job design and work organisation should feature in the training of management, and department managers should be assessed on the job satisfaction of their staff), in the factors that have to be included for consideration in technical and organisational project proposals and in the training of those who shape organisational life, like systems designers, production engineers and accountants.

It will be seen that there is a limit to what can be done in this direction through projects or even strategies within organisations. The splitting is deeply embedded in the institutions from which succeeding generations of professionals emerge. Projects in organisations are therefore not enough.

We have no sense of omnipotence on behalf of the social sciences and are very conscious of the criticisms that may be – and have been – levelled at the professional worlds both of academic social science and of OD. But much has also happened that has been valued in client systems, and that has contributed to the aim that we have expressed, of synthesising and integrating different value systems. It is a vital part of the task to try to secure the institutionalising of the good things that have happened. This set of perspectives and approaches needs to become integrated as a normal part of what goes on. It helps people to gain understanding of their own operational settings and thus, in turn, equips institutions to relate in a strategic and integrated way to their environments.

References

Bennis, W. G., Benne, K. D., Chin, R. and Corey, K. E. (1975) *The Planning of Change* (3rd edition). New York, Holt, Reinhart & Winston.

Bieneck, H.-J. (1977) Ein deutsches Experiment: die Kommission für wirtschaftlichen und sozialen Wandel (unpublished). Bundesministerium für Arbeit und Sozialordnung. Göttingen.

Bion, W. R. (1948) Experiences in groups. *Human Relations*, vol. 1, pp. 314–20.

Blackler, R. and Williams, R. (1971) People's motivations at work. In *Psychology at Work*, ed. P. B. Warr. Harmondsworth, Penguin, pp. 283–303.

Blake, R. R. and Mouton, J. S. (1964) *The Managerial Grid*. Houston, Tex., Gulf Publishing.

Bolte, K. M. (1978) Die Arbeit der Kommission für wirtschaftlichen und sozialen Wandel. *Hamburger Jahrbuch für Wirtschafts- und Gesellschaftspolitik*, no. 23.

Buchanan, D. A. and Boddy, D. (1983) *Organisations in the Computer Age*. London, Gower.

Bundesministerium für Forschung und Technologie. (1974) *Forschung zur Humanisierung des Arbeitslebens*. Bonn.

Bundesminister für Arbeit und Sozialordnung. (1977) *Wirtschaftlicher und sozialer Wandel in der Bundesrepublik Deutschland, Gutachten der Kommission für wirtschaftlichen und socialen Wandel*. Göttingen.

Burns, T. and Stalker, G. M. (1961) *The Management of Innovation*. London, Tavistock Publications.

Butera, F. (1975) Contributions to the analysis of structural variables affecting emerging patterns of the job design: the Olivetti case. In *The Quality of Working Life*, New York, Free Press. Eds. A. B. Cherns and L. E. Davis.

Cherns, A. B. and Clark, P. A. (1972) *An Investigation to Study the Application and Utilisation of Social Science Research*, SSRC Report no. HR86. London, HMSO.

Department of Scientific and Industrial Research. (1957–67) Problems of Progress in Industry Series. London, HMSO:

No.   1. Department of Social Science, University of Liverpool. *Men, Steel and Technical Change*.

2. Stewart, R. *Managers for Tomorrow*.

3. Woodward, J. *Management and Technology*.

4. Calder, N. *What They Read and Why: The use of Technical Literature in the Electrical and Electronics Industries*.

5. Croome, H. *Human problems of Innovation: Based on a Study of some Scottish Firms by T. Burns and G. M. Stalker*.

6. Clay, H. M. *The Older Worker and his Job.*
7. Welford, A. T. *Ergonomics of Automation.*
8. Crossman, E. R. F. W. *Automation and Skill*
9. Social Science Department, the London School of Economics and Political Science. *Woman, Wife and Worker.*
10. Lupton, T. *Money for Effort.*
11. *Human Sciences Aid to Industry.*
12. Thurley, K. E. and Hamblin, A. C. *The Supervisor and his Job.*
13. Kay, H., Annett, J. and Sime, M. E. *Teaching Machines and Their use in Industry.*
14. Belbin, E. *Training the Adult Worker.*
15. Clay, H. M. *How Research Can Help Training.*
16. Seaborne, A. E. M. and Thomas, L. F. *Subjective Standards in Industrial Inspection.*

Eason, K. D. (1988) *Information Technology and Organisational Change.* London, Taylor and Francis.

Fricke, E., Fricke, W., Schönwalder, M. and Steigler, B. (1979) *Beteiligung und Qualifikation.* Bonn, Forschungsinstitut der Friedrich-Ebert-Stiftung.

Hax, H. (1978) An enquiry on economic and social development. European Coordination Centre for Research and Documentation on Social Sciences. Round Table Conference on Social Sciences and Policy Making, Bucharest.

Herbst, P. G. (1976) *Alternatives to Hierarchies.* Leiden, Martinus Nijhoff.

Jaques, E. (1951) *The Changing Culture of a Factory.* London, Tavistock Publications.

King S. D. M. (1960) *Vocational Training in View of Technical Change.* Parish, European Productivity Agency.

Klein, L. (1964). *Multiproducts Ltd: A Case Study in the Social Effects of Rationalised Production.* London, HMSO.

(1976) *A Social Scientist in Industry.* London, Gower Press.

(1980a) *The Role of the Anaesthetist: An Exploratory Study.* Association of Anaesthetists of Great Britain and Ireland.

(1980b) What the social sciences have to offer and some of the issues involved in making use of them. In *Organisation Development in Europe*, ed. K. Trebesch, vol. 1A: *Concepts*, Bern, Stuttgart, Haupt.

(1987) The work of the Commission for Economic and Social Change in Germany. In *Social Science Research and Government*, ed. M. Bulmer. Cambridge University Press.

Klein, L. and Newman, W. (1988) *A Strategy for Intergrating Human–Computer Interface Considerations into Alvey-2 Application Projects. 1. Action Version for the Reader in a Hurry. 2. Working Papers.* London, Department of Trade and Industry.

Kohn, H. and Latzelsberger, F. (1977) Steuerungsprobleme in Wirtschaft und Gesellschaft: zum Gutachten der Kommission für wirtschaftlichen und sozialen Wandel. In *Aus Politik und Zeitgeschichte*, Beilage zur Wochenseitung das Parlament, vol. 18, no. 77.

Kunstek, R. (1986) *Das Konzept der Lernstatt im Industriebetrieb.* Verlag Rene F. Wilfer.

Likert, R. (1961) *New Patterns of Management*. New York, London, McGraw-Hill.

Lupton, T. (1961) *On the Shop Floor*. London, Oxford University Press.

McLean, A. et al. (1979) Implications of interventions in organisations (unpublished). Final Report to the CAPITB Research Sub-Committee, Centre for the Study of Organisational Change and Development, University of Bath.

Minister of Labour and National Service. (1952) *Human Relations in Industry*. Conference, 18–20 March, London, HMSO.

National Institute of Industrial Psychology. (1951) *The Foreman: A Study of Supervision in British Industry*. London, Staples Press.

(1952) *Joint Consultation in British Industry*. London, Staples Press.

Patterson, T. T. (1955) *Morale in War and Work*. London, Max Parrish.

Ravetz, R. R. (1971) *Scientific Knowledge and its Social Problems*. Oxford, Clarendon Press.

Roethlisberger, F. J. and Dickson, W. J. (1939) *Management And The Worker*. Cambridge, Mass., Harvard University Press.

Rosenbrock, H. H. (1979) The redirection of technology. IFAC Symposium on criteria for selecting appropriate technologies under different cultural, technical and social conditions. 21–23 May, Bari, Italy.

(1983) Developing a technology which provides satisfactory work. *IFAC Newsletter*, October, no. 5.

Rothschild, Lord. (1982) *An Enquiry into the Social Science Research Council*. Cmnd 8554, May. London, HMSO.

Scott, W. H. (1952) *Industrial Leadership and Joint Consultation*. Liverpool University Press.

Stansfield, R. G. (1981) Occupational research and sociology, In *Science and Public Policy*, vol. 8, no. 4.

Task Force on the Practice of Psychology in Industry. (1971) Effective practice of psychology in industry. *American Psychologist*, vol. 26, no. 11 (November).

Trist, E. L. and Bamforth, K. W. (1951) Some social and psychological consquences of the longwall method of coal-getting. *Human Relations Journal*, no. 4, pp. 3–38. London, The Tavistock Institute of Human Relations.

Trist, E. L., Higgin, G. W., Murray, H. and Pollock, A. B. (1963) *Organizational Choice: Capabilities of Groups at the Coal Face Under Changing Technologies*. London, Tavistock Publications.

Vall, M. van de, Bolas, C. and Kang, Tai S. (1976) Applied social research in industrial organisations: an evaluation of functions, theory and methods. *Journal of Applied Behavioural Science*, vol 12, no. 2, pp. 158–77.

Wall, T. D., Kemp, N. J., Jackson, P. R., and Clegg, C. W. (1986) Outcomes of autonomous workgroups: a long-term field experiment. *Academy of Management Journal*, vol. 29, no. 2, pp. 280–304.

Winnicott, D. W. (1971) *Playing and Reality*. London, Tavistock Publications.

Woodward, J. (1965) *Industrial Organization: Theory and Practice*. London, Oxford University Press.

(ed.) (1970) *Industrial Organization: Behaviour and Control*. Oxford University Press.

Index

A, Mrs (ergonomist in trade union research department), 190–2, 222, 224
academic social science/academics, 8, 37, 248, 255; links with industry, 51–2, 69; see also external consultants; research
action, dynamics of, 7, 13–20, 21; in case studies, analysed, 157–72 passim; see also action research; clients; implementation phase; role of social scientist
action process design, 236–8
action research, 14–16, 38, 39–40, 52, 55, 242–3; boundary between consultancy and, 15, 45, 195–6, 243
Advisory Council for Scientific Policy, 47
Alvey Programme of Advanced Information Technology Research, 51, 246, 248
anaesthetists' role problems, study of, 9, 25–32
analysis workshops, 137, 149, 166
Anglo-German Foundation for the Study of Industrial Society, 2
anthropologist (working on Esso project), 228–9
attitude surveys, 15, 62–4, 125–6, 158
Automation Group (German trade union working party), 206, 207, 210
awareness: improvement in client, 183–4, 185, 187; self, by social scientist, 18

B, Mr (internal OD adviser), 192–4, 224, 233, 249
banking, improvement of customer services (case B), 37, 56, 61, 69–70; content of process of social science utilisation, 158–60; factors facilitating and impeding use of social science, 173, 174, 175, 183, 185, 186, 223–4; objectives and outcomes, 58, 87, 88, 89, 170
behavioural change: and development for management, cases concerning (cases L–N), 57, 141–56, 167–72 passim, 180–2; and problem solving (cases H–J), 57, 117–40, 165–7, 168–72 passim, 178–80

behavioural science, 8, 10, 23, 50; seminars, 136; unit, 124–5
Blake, R. R., 151
booklet, recommendations, 128–9, 167
bounded projects, 178–9, 182 (fig.), 185–6; see also diffusion of social science learning
Brandt, Chancellor Willy, 205, 211, 212
Burns, T., 49

C, Professor (organisation theorist), 194–6, 224
canning plant, design of, see food processing company
case studies, 1–3, 45–6, 224–5; classification of, 55–7; evaluation methods, 57–60; see also behavioural change; organisational structure and policies; technical systems development
Centre for the Utilisation of Social Science Research (CUSSR), 49
change processes, 13–14, 50–1, 59–60, 184–5, 220; social science practitioner's role in helping clients deal with, 148–9, 235–6, 251; system study on technical, social and economic change, 205–15
Chemical and Allied Products Industry Training Board study (1979), 50–1
Cherns, Professor A. B., 49
clients: involvement in design process, 114–16, 164, 165, 166, 184–5; learning of social science skills (see also internalising-and-converting-into-use), 41–2, 89, 245; relations with social scientists, see social science practitioners; role in action programme, 88–9, 169, 171, 184; role in investigative and diagnostic processes, 158–60, 165, 166, 170, 184, 234–5; see also staff, client
cognitive methods, 136, 144, 149
collaboration, between clients and social scientists, 225–7
commercial consultants, 1, 45, 51, 124

Commission for Economic and Social Change (CESC), 46, 53, 55, 205–15, 222–4, 250
Committee of Social Studies (Heyworth Committee), 48–9
Committee on Industrial Productivity (UK), 47
competence, professional (of social science practitioners), 227, 231–47
computer steering committee (CSC), 108, 110, 111, 163, 237
computer technology, 90, 224–5, 252; computer-based working simulations, 171, 238; human implications, 73, 106–14, 161–4 *passim*, 176–8 *passim*
confectionery firm, design of new factory (case E), 57, 90–7, 222; content and process of social science utilisation, 161–2, 170, 171, 172, 237; factors supporting and hindering use of social science, 176, 177, 178, 249; objectives and outcomes, 114, 115, 116
confidentiality, 35, 46, 234
consultancy, social science: attitudes of social science community towards, 33–4; boundary between research and (*see also* 'splitting'), 15, 195, 243; historical development 48–55 *passim*; payment methods, 37, 69, 97; *see also* commercial consultants; practice profession, social science as
contact groups, 152, 154
contractual issues, 175–6
control systems, 10, 24
counselling sessions, 148, 149, 153 (fig.)
creativity seminars, 148, 152, 153 (fig.)
customer service working party, bank, 70–1, 74

D, Mr (psychoanalytically oriented consultant to organisations), 197–201, 224
data gathering and analysis, 158–9, 234–5; *see also* diagnostic process
data processing manager (of freightforwarding company), 108–14 *passim*
data processing typists, team seminar with, 154
demonstration projects, 249
Department of Employment Work Research Unit (UK), 51
Department of Scientific and Industrial Research (UK), 48
design process: client's participation in, 114–16, 164, 165, 166, 184–5; social science practitioner's contribution to,

90–5 *passim*, 114, 115, 161–72 *passim*; temporary structures, 237–8; *see also* job design
diagnostic process, 21–2, 25–32, 33, 174, 245; functions of 233; involvement of clients in, 158–60, 165, 166, 170, 184, 234–5; role of social scientist, 62–3, 69–70, 168, 170, 232, 233–5; *see also* exploratory studies
diffusion of social science learning from 'bounded' origin, 166–7, 180, 183, 185–8 *passim*
distribution company, management training programme (case L), 57, 141–8; content and process of social science utilisation, 167, 168, 172; factors facilitating and impeding use of social science, 180–2 *passim*; objectives and outcomes, 155, 156
Dortmund Sozialakademie, research studies, 52
drawings, explanatory, 145, 163

E, Mr (manager of psychological services unit), 201–4, 222, 224, 233
Economic and Social Science Council (UK), 51
economic environment, effect on social science contribution, 223–4
educational aspects of social science practice, 40–2, 245
electrical products company, work structuring programme (case C), 56, 61, 79–85; content and process of social science utilisation, 157, 160, 169, 170, 225; factors supporting and hindering social science contribution, 173, 174–5, 186; objectives and outcomes, 87–9 *passim*
engineering institute, contribution to humanisation programme (Germany), 55, 80, 82
engineering science model of social science practice, 35–7, 232
ergonomics, 70, 86–7, 107, 157, 191, 225
ergonomics institute, contribution to humanisation programme (Germany), 55, 80
ergonomists, in social science practice, 190–2, 228–9
'erosion' of social science concepts by clients, 75, 178; *see also* fragmentation
Esso Petroleum project, ix, 22–3, 49, 222, 225, 228–9
ethics, 14–15, 35, 234
European Community, 246, 253

European Strategy Programme of Research in Information Technology (ESPRIT), 246

evaluation: methodological issues, 57–60, 182, 186; of social science interventions, 113–14, 139–40, 146–7, 159, 194, 254; social scientists' role as evaluation researchers, 81, 83–4, 160, 232, 239; studies, 162, 163, 168

exploratory studies, 25–32, 69–74, 91–5, 107–8, 158–60, 234–5, 254; familiarisation function, 21, 162, 233; *see also* analysis workshops; attitude surveys; needs analysis

external consultants, 61, 90, 132, 181, 233; based in academic institutions, 45, 62, 69, 71, 79, 106–7; based in independent research institute, 69, 97; *see also* commercial consultants

factories, social science contribution to design of, *see* confectionery firm; food processing company

familiarisation/mutual education phase, 21, 98, 107, 162, 175, 233

'family-training-seminars', 136

flexitime study, 202

food processing company, development of new factory (case F), 17, 57, 90, 97–106, 221; content and process of social science utilisation, 161, 162, 163, 164, 170, 171, 236–7; factors supporting and impeding social science contribution, 176, 177, 178, 185, 224; objectives and outcomes, 114–16 *passim*

foreign workers in German motor industry, *see* motor industry, development of 'learning shops'

fragmentation of social science concepts, 89; *see also* 'erosion'

freightforwarding, design of computerised system (case G), 57, 90, 106–13, 250; content and process of social science utilisation, 161, 162, 163, 164, 171, 237–8; factors facilitating and hindering social science contribution, 176–7, 178, 185; objectives and outcomes, 114, 115, 116

Friedrich-Ebert-Stiftung humanisation project, 39

funding structures, 2, 37, 247–9; central/departmental, 154, 179, 181, 194, 201–2, 249; dual (public/private), 37, 248; effects on social science projects, 95, 97, 175–6, 186; per diem arrangement, 95, 248–9; 'seeding' arrangement, 19, 249; state, 39, 80, 175–6, 248

'gate-keeper' problem, 42

Germany, 147; case studies in (*see also* distribution company; electrical products company; motor industry, development of 'learning shops'; motor industry, programme of organisational and personal development for supervisors; news technology industry; precision engineering industry; rubber industry), 2–3, 45, 56–7, 254; historical development of social science utilisation, 46, 52–5; social science legislation, 36, 53; *see also* Commission for Economic and Social Change; governmental policy; Humanisation of Life at Work programme

'ghost' consultant, creation of, 41, 100, 159, 242

Glacier Metal Company, 48

goals, *see* objectives

Golding, W., *Lord of the Flies*, 200

governmental policy on social science research and application: in United Kingdom, 46–52 *passim*; in West Germany, 39, 52–5, 205–15; *see also* funding structures

group(s): autonomous work groups, 93, 95–6, 98, 178; dynamics, 18–19, 23, 40, 141, 148, 149, 150, 155; sessions, 126–8; social scientists' work with groups in organisations, 19, 117–40, 165–7, 172, 178–80

guest workers, *see* motor industry, development of 'learning shops'

Hawthorne experiments, 9, 23

Health of Munition Worker's Committee, 47

Herzberg, F., 7

Heyworth, Lord, Social Studies Committee, 48–9

hierarchies, 19; removal of, 142–3, 144, 168, 181

hierarchy-of-needs concept, 7

historical development of social science use: in United Kingdom, 46–52; in West Germany, 46, 52–5

Human Factors Panel (Schuster Panel), 47, 48

human relations, 23–5, 40–1, 70, 167, 178–9; situational factors, 23–4; training activities, 25, 50, 153, 156, 171, 181, 196; workshops, 117, 137

Human Relations Movement, 152

Humanisation of Life at Work programme, 39, 55, 79–80, 83, 84, 186, 248; origin and aims, 53–4
hypothesis testing, 231, 232, 254

implementation phase, 81, 83, 87, 129–31, 132–4, 149–50, 160, 166; *see also* action, dynamics of
in-house units/internal practitioners, 1, 45, 78, 141, 148–9, 190–4, 201–4, 243; advantages and disadvantages of, 123, 165, 233, 244–5, 248; funding, 154, 179, 181, 194, 201–2, 248, 249
Industrial Health Research Board (UK), 47
industrial relations, 95, 124, 128, 131, 136, 173, 178–9, 221; as factor in social science projects, 97–106 *passim*, 125, 138; *see also* trade unions
industrial sociology, 55, 70, 81, 90, 225
industry: contacts with academic institutions, 51–2, 69; industrial process, *see* manufacturing process
infrastructure support for social science practice, 186–7, 191–2, 227, 247–51, 254
institutionalisation (of valued outcomes and processes), 12, 89, 116, 185, 227, 239–40, 242, 252–5
integration, issue of, 224–5
interdisciplinary approaches, 55, 71, 80–4 *passim*, 194, 224–5
internalising-and-converting-into-use (social science concepts and methodologies), 9–10, 36, 79, 98, 157, 184, 185; consequences for social scientists, 59, 88; process of, 59, 100, 123, 164, 172, 186, 238–9; role of social scientist, 41–2, 159, 160, 255
interpersonal relations, *see* human relations
interview programmes, 158, 166

Jaques, Elliott, 35
job: analysis, 93, 94, 103–4, 107, 112, 162, 164, 202; enlargement, 81, 86; enrichment, 10, 86, 88, 98, 193; rotation, 86; satisfaction, 90, 91, 163, 255; *see also* job design
job design, 10, 19, 157, 255; committees, 103–4, 161, 163, 236; and industrial relations, 97–106; role of social scientist in projects, 40, 90–5 *passim*, 96, 114, 115, 163, 169; *see also* work organisation

Klein, L., 2, 49, 50
knowledge-into-use framework, 7–13, 21,

36, 239; applied to case study analysis, 157, 161, 164, 167, 168–72
Kunstek, Rolf, 2

language skills of foreign workers, improvement of, 117, 131, 132, 139
leadership training, 152, 153 (fig.); for managers, 141, 148–51, 167, 195; for supervisors, 117, 136–8, 165
'learning shop' model, 131–4, 154, 166, 179; difficulties of transferring to a different location, 133–4, 140, 167, 180
legislation, social science, 36, 53
Liverpool University joint consultation research project, 47
Lupton, T., 49

management: attitudes to social science practice and practitioners, 82, 83, 128, 130, 133, 150, 203; consultancies, 51, 124; development and training, 57, 136–8, 139, 141–56, 167–8, 184, 230; planning groups, 127; relations with workers' representatives, 68–9, 85–7, 97–106 *passim*, 124–31 *passim*, 173, 178–9; research, 48, 50–1; style, 23–4, 168, 239
Management by Objectives (MbO), 151, 192, 193
Managerial Grid concept, 151, 152, 153, 193
manufacturing process, 91–3, 98, 101
marketing roles, redefinition of, *see* oil industry
Maslow, A. H., 7
medical/clinical model for social science practitioners, 34–5
metalworkers' union, German (IG Metall), 206
microfiche, problems of introducing, 191
Mitterrand, François, 213n.
models, used to help clients understand design proposals, 93, 163, 171, 237
moderators (in departmental seminars), 145, 146, 148, 149
motivation: seminars, 148, 149, 153; theory, 7, 193
motor components factory, payment systems as factor in modifying organisation structure (case I), 57, 117, 124–31, 221, 237; content and process of social science utilisation, 165, 166, 167, 169, 170, 172; factors supporting and impeding social science contribution, 178, 179, 180, 233; objectives and outcomes, 138, 140
motor industry, development of 'learning shops' for guest workers (case J), 46, 57,

117, 131–4; content and process of social science utilisation, 165, 170, 172; factors facilitating and impeding social science contribution, 178, 179, 180, 183; objectives and outcomes, 138–40 *passim*

motor industry, programme of organisational and personal development for supervisors (case K), 57, 117, 134–8; content and process of social science utilisation, 165, 166, 170, 172; factors supporting and hindering social science contribution, 178, 179, 180; objectives and outcomes, 139, 140

Mouton, J. S., 151

multinational companies, 2, 85, 97, 117–18, 148

National Economic Development Office (NEDO), 19–20

National Institute of Industrial Psychology (NIIP), 47

needs analysis, 153, 168, 170, 181

negotiation: systems, 236, 237; training, 148, 157

Netherlands, applied social research projects, 12

news technology industry, management training and Organisation Development (case M), 57, 141, 148–51, 155, 181; content and process of social science utilisation, 167, 172

North-Rhein-Westphalia, social research programme, 52

objectives/goals: bounded, 178–9; congruity of, 58, 178, 183, 230; and outcomes, 58, 87–9, 114–16, 138–40, 155–6

oil industry, redefinition of marketing roles (case H), 57, 58, 117–23, 249; content and process of social science utilisation, 165, 166, 167, 170, 172, 234; factors supporting and impeding social science contribution, 178, 179–80, 183; objectives and outcomes, 138, 140

organisation and methods department, bank, 74–6, 87

Organisation Development (OD), 42, 53, 91, 95, 114, 255; internal OD specialists, 118, 142, 167, 168, 179, 192–4; programmes, 85–7, 117–23, 136–8, 141–56, 170, 180–2; 'splitting' between research community and OD community, 14, 33, 51; theory and practice, 13–14, 50–1

Organisation Development for Advanced Practitioners course (Columbia, USA), 192

organisational base, for social science activity, 187–9

organisational environment, links between social science project and, 249–50

organisational structure and policies, programmes leading to changes in, 56–7, 61–89, 124–31, 157–60, 169, 173–6

organisations: psychoanalytical concepts applied to, 197–201; research programmes, 48, 49, 194–6; theories of, 10, 21–5, 38–9, 157; *see also* organisational structure and policies

outcomes of social science projects, 84–5, 87–9, 95–7, 114–16, 121–3, 138–40, 155–6; client's assessment of, 67–8; evaluation of, 58–60; factors contributing to successful, 173–89, 228–55; social scientists' reactions to, 68–9, 89, 106, 113–14, 115–16, 140

'packages', social science, 11–12, 41, 50, 245–6; 'off the shelf' programmes, 157, 160

Parsons, Talcott, 13n.

payment: negotiations, 83, 87; systems as factor in modifying organisation structure, 124–31, 169; *see also* funding structures

personal development, 22; techniques, 152–3, 168, 181

personnel: development, 86, 87; directors, 69–70, 90, 97, 130

Personnel Development Department (PDD) in distribution company, 142–8

phasing problems, 37, 91–2, 204, 222–3

pilot systems, 63, 110, 111–12, 113, 115, 116, 164

policy-change cases, *see* organisational structure and policies

political aspects of social science practice, 38–40, 52

power relationships, 225–6, 250–1

practice profession, social science as, 2, 33–42; components of successful practice, 228–55

precision engineering industry, work structuring in (case D), 57, 61, 85–7, 88, 89, 160; factors supporting and hindering social science utilisation, 173, 174, 175, 176

problem solving, training in, 137, 148, 149, 151

process, 8, 169; facilitation, 14, 239

production process, 134–5; need for social

production process *cont.*
scientists to understand, 91–3, 98, 101;
see also work organisation
'professionalism' of social science, *see*
practice profession, social science as
Programme for Information and
Communication Technologies (UK), 51
progress bulletins, 128
project initiation, factors governing: in
behavioural change/ development for
management cases, 142, 148–9, 151,
180–1; in behavioural
change/problem-solving cases, 117–18,
124, 131, 136, 178–9; in organisational
structure and policy cases, 62, 69–70,
79–80, 85–6, 173–4; in technical
systems development cases, 90–1, 97–8,
106–7, 176–7; *see also* sponsorship
prototypes, working, 237–8; *see also*
models; pilot systems
psychoanalytical concepts, 16–20, 34–5,
48; applied to organisations, 197–201
psychology/psychologists: educational, 55,
81; humanistic, 141, 149; industrial, 41,
42, 55, 81; occupational, 70, 107, 202;
psychological services unit, 201–4;
social, 81, 224, 228–9

'quality circles', 138
Quality of Working Life movement, 19

Rationalisierungskuratorium der Wirtschaft
(RKW), 52
Ravetz, R. R., 7n., 13n.
reports, 13, 14–15, 64–6, 72–4, 102–3,
159, 204, 233–4
research, social science: 'accompanying
research' project, 79, 80; applied social
research projects, 12; engineering science
model of research-into-application, 35–7;
funding, 37, 39, 80, 248; gulf between
academic and applied, 11, 12–14, 21,
33–4, 49, 243; historical development,
46–55 *passim*; interventionist aspects of
empirical, 14–16; political aspects, 38;
'research loop', 37, 74; usability of
findings, 9–12, 21, 162–3, 222–3, 224,
238–9; validity and replicability of
findings, 7–9; *see also* academic social
science
research institutes, independent, 1, 69, 97,
190
resources, social science, 11, 224, 225–6;
management of, 241
review mechanisms, 250, 251, 254
role of social scientist, 58, 81–4, 130, 157,
170, 171; action and development, 34,

171, 184, 232, 233–4, 235–43;
educational, 40–2, 245; effect of age and
gender stereotyping, 241; evaluation, 81,
83–4, 160, 232, 239; facilitator, 127,
129, 160, 165, 166, 167; importance of
staying in role, 240–1;
investigative/diagnostic, 62–3, 69–70,
168, 170, 232, 233–5;
outsider/detached, 15, 38, 68–9, 151,
233; process design, 90–5 *passim*, 114,
115, 161–72 *passim*; profession role
models, 34–42; separation of client's role
and, 88
roles, 88, 254; role-play methods, 145,
150, 162, 171; *see also* anaesthetists'
role problems; clients; oil industry,
redefinition of marketing roles; role of
social scientist
Rost-Schaude, Edith, 2
rubber industry, change of topic and
method in OD programme (case N), 57,
141, 151–5, 156, 181; content and
process of social science utilisation, 167,
168, 170, 172

sales training, 151, 152, 155
Schiller, Professor Karl, 206
Schmidt, Chancellor Helmut, 212
Schuster, Sir George, 47, 48
Science and Engineering Research Council
(UK), 51
Second World War, impact on social
science research, 47
'seeding' contracts, 19, 249
selection procedures, 22, 201, 203;
training, 148, 150
seminars, 153 (fig.), 163; departmental,
143, 144–6; leadership, 148, 149–50;
management, 109, 110, 136, 137–8,
151, 152–4
sensitivity training, 136, 148
simulations, 150, 171, 238
social science concepts and methods,
transfer of, to clients, 41, 42; *see also*
institutionalisation;
internalising-and-converting-into-use;
'packages'
social science practice, *see* practice
profession, social science as
social science practitioners, 33–4;
development and training, 16–17,
243–4; experiences of individual
practitioners, 190–204; need for
professional support system, 16, 191–2,
233, 241, 242; qualities and skills
required by, 1, 11, 228–55; relations
with clients (*see also* familiarisation),

16–20, 67–9, 82, 96, 99–101, 113, 176–7, 225–7; *see also* external consultants; in-house units; interdisciplinary approaches; management; outcomes of social science projects; role of social scientist; trade unions

social science research, *see* research

Social Science Research Council, 37, 49

sociological institute, contribution to humanisation programme, 55, 80

sociology, *see* industrial sociology

socio-technical theory, 8, 47, 157; application of, 112, 114, 161–4, 224

'splitting', 18, 161, 164, 219–20, 222, 255; between research and practice, 14, 17, 33, 37, 243, 253; historical evolution, 51

sponsorship of social science programme, 187 (fig.), 224, 249; continuity of, 183, 188–9, 223; *see also* project initiation staff, client: continuity vital to social science intervention, 179–80, 186, 187 (fig.), 223, 249; numbers involved in social science programme, *see* bounded projects

Stalker, G. M., 49

Stansfield, R. G., 47

steering committees, 250

strategic issues involved in management of social science practice, 247, 251–2

strikes, 124, 127–8, 134

structural factors, 10, 24–5; *see also* organisational structure

studies, initial, *see* exploratory studies

success or failure of social science intervention, factors contributing to, 173–89, 228–55

supervisors: organisational and personal development programmes for, 117, 134–8, 137–9, 148, 150, 154; role and motivation in transport industry, 61–9

surveys, *see* attitude surveys; exploratory studies

systems concepts, 228–9; relationship between value stance of social scientist and system boundaries, 38–9, 40, 229

systems design processes, *see* technical systems development

task analysis, 93, 94, 103–4, 107, 112, 162, 164, 202

Task Force on the Practice of Psychology in Industry (1971), ix

task-oriented training, 144

Tavistock Institute of Human Relations, 34, 47–8, 49

teamwork development, 118, 122, 130, 148, 149, 167, 239

Technical Change Centre, 51

technical systems development, cases in, 57, 90–116, 161–4, 176–8, 188, 190–2; *see also* confectionery firm; food processing company; freightforwarding

technology, 25, 79; social science contribution to managing change in (*see also* technical systems development), 134–5, 190–2, 205–15

telecommunications equipment manufacturer, *see* news technology industry

temporary structures, *see* transitional systems

territory, issue of (in power relationships), 226

Theme-Centred Interaction (TCI), 136, 143, 145, 147, 153–4, 155

time/timing, issues of, 24, 177–8; *see also* phasing problems

trade unions, 142, 170, 202; involvement in social science projects, 54, 82, 110, 124–8 *passim*, 179, 203; relations with social science practitioners, 54, 68–9, 82, 99, 102, 177; *see also* industrial relations; works council

training, 22, 50, 85, 104–5, 165; activities, as 'transitional systems', 171, 237, 239–40, 254; departments, industrial, programmes run by, 148–56; role of social scientists, 40–2, 80, 165, 183–4; *see also* management

Transactional Analysis, 136, 152–3, 155

transfer: of social science learning from place of origin to new location/client population, 167, 180, 183, 185–6, 188; *see also* social science concepts and methods, transfer of

transference and counter-transference, concepts of, 17–18, 20, 197–8, 229

'transitional object', concept of, 199–200

transitional systems, 21, 163–4, 166–7, 239, 250, 254–5; organisational structures, 163, 171, 236–7; physical manifestations of the future, 163, 171–2, 237–8

transport industry, role of supervisors (case A), 56, 61–9; content and process of social science utilisation, 158–9, 160, 169, 171, 234, 250; factors facilitating and hindering social science contribution, 173, 174, 175; objectives and outcomes, 87, 88, 89

United Kingdom, 254; case studies in (*see*

United Kingdom *cont.*
    also banking; confectionery firm; food
    processing company; freightforwarding;
    motor components factory; oil industry;
    transport industry), 2–3, 45–6, 56–7;
    historic development of social science
    utilisation, 46–52
United States, OD tradition, 13, 50

Vall, M. van de, 12
values, x–xii, 255; of social scientist, link
    between system boundaries and, 38–9,
    40, 229
vision, in the social sciences, 176, 228–31

wastage survey, 203
weighing machine manufacturer, work
    structuring project by, *see* precision
    engineering industry
Winnicott, D. W., 199, 201, 237
withdrawal of social scientist from project,
    problems of, 241–2
Woodward, J. 49

Work and Technology programme
    (Germany), 54
work groups, autonomous, 93, 95–6, 98,
    178
work organisation/structures, 54, 78,
    107–8, 147, 166, 255; changes in, 10,
    40, 79–87; impact of computerisation,
    107–8, 112; *see also* job design;
    organisational structure
Work Organisation Research Centre, 51
Work Research Unit, Department of
    Employment, 51
working hours, 87
working parties, 171, 203–4, 236, 237
works councils, 53–4; attitude to social
    science activities, 142, 150;
    collaboration with management in work
    structuring programme, 85–7, 173
workshops, 137, 148, 149, 163, 166

Y, Mr (OD practitioner in distribution
    company), 142, 143, 148